"This is fascinating, thorough and, sadly, often deeply disturbing reading. Fatah knows and writes the truth and has managed to convey its complexities and nuances in a highly readable and compelling manner. Should become an essential work for anybody interested in the contemporary political and religious situation." – Michael Coren

"Tarek Fatah boldly goes where few committed Muslims have the courage to follow. Delivered in crisp, accessible prose, *The Jew Is Not My Enemy* is a compelling blend of investigative journalism and scholarly interrogation of the religious texts, historical events and ideological currents propelling virulent Judeophobia in the Islamosphere. In this thoughtful blueprint for Islamic reform, Mr Fatah, a personal role model for his vision, offers hope to those stranded 'on the lonely path towards peace among the Israelite and the Ishmaelite.'" – Barbara Kay, columnist, *National Post*

"As a Muslim member of the Danish parliament, I am aware of the role of Islamism in whipping up anti-Semitism and hatred towards Europe and the West. Tarek Fatah has run the gauntlet of hate and come out victorious as he does a brilliant exposé of the myths that sustain Jew hatred in the Muslim World. This book is a must-read for any Jew and Muslim who wishes to honour the memory of Averroes and Maimonides."
– Naser Khader, Member of Parliament (Folketinget), Denmark

THE
JEW
IS
NOT
MY
ENEMY

TAREK FATAH

UNVEILING THE MYTHS THAT FUEL MUSLIM ANTI-SEMITISM

 McClelland & Stewart

Library and Archives Canada Cataloguing in Publication

Fatah, Tarek, 1949-
The Jew is not my enemy : unveiling the myths that
fuel Muslim anti-Semitism / Tarek Fatah.

Issued also in electronic format.
ISBN 978-0-7710-4783-1

1. Islam – Relations – Judaism. 2. Judaism – Relations – Islam. 3. Jews in the Koran. 4. Jews in the Hadith. 5. Antisemitism – Islamic countries. 6. Antisemitism in literature. 7. Muslims – Attitudes. I. Title.

BP173.J8F37 2010   297.2'82   C2010-902282-3

Library of Congress Control Number: 2010934188

Typeset in Dante
Printed and bound in Canada

ANCIENT FOREST
FRIENDLY

This book is printed on acid-free paper that is 100% recycled, ancient-forest friendly (100% post-consumer waste).

McClelland & Stewart Ltd.
75 Sherbourne Street
Toronto, Ontario
M5A 2P9
www.mcclelland.com

1 2 3 4 5   14 13 12 11 10

For Noor Inayat Khan
better known as Nora Baker (1914–1944)
George Cross, MBE, Croix de Guerre with Gold Star

The forgotten Muslim Indian Princess who died as Agent Madeline
in the Dachau Concentration Camp at the hands of
a Nazi execution squad.

Morality is doing what is right,
regardless of what we are told;
Religious dogma is doing what we are told,
no matter what is right.

—Elka Ruth Enola

CONTENTS

Foreword by Bob Rae   xi

Preface   xiv

CHAPTER ONE "O Allah, Completely Destroy and Shatter the Jews"   1

CHAPTER TWO Bird Flu and Other Jewish Conspiracies   18

CHAPTER THREE Allah, Hitler, and the Mufti   38

CHAPTER FOUR Is Israel Fuelling Anti-Semitism?   78

CHAPTER FIVE Is the Quran Anti-Semitic?   103

CHAPTER SIX The Jews of Banu Qurayza   130

CHAPTER SEVEN Muhammad Comes to the City of Jews   148

CHAPTER EIGHT Towards a New Jerusalem   174

Epilogue   202

Notes   209
Bibliography   217
Index   231

FOREWORD

by Bob Rae

Just after the end of the Second World War, an English scholar and cleric, James Parkes, wrote a succinct little book on anti-Semitism called *An Enemy of the People*. With the discovery of the Nazi death camps came an ever wider recognition of the end game of two thousand years of Jew-hatred: Hitler's plan to eliminate the Jewish people from the face of the earth.

Many scholars since that time have documented the Holocaust and traced its origins in Christian theology, medieval torture and expulsions, Tsarist pogroms, and racial theories given new life by bowdlerizing Darwin. We now understand that what seemed a catastrophic illness in Hitler's Germany and occupied Europe is in fact a chronic disease that has erupted in quite disastrous ways from time to time. Any idle exploration of the Internet, any scratching of the underbelly of politics today, would remind us that the eruptions of this terrible chronic condition continue.

Tarek Fatah opens our eyes to a world with which we are less familiar, but whose importance is critical for the times in which we live. Never one to pull his punches, he wades into debates about Islamic theology and politics and reminds us of the ugliness of Jew-hatred within parts of the Muslim tradition. It is, he argues, both alarmingly widespread and a deep offence to Islam's humanistic traditions.

No doubt the book will arouse debate and controversy. To those of us who have known Tarek for a long time, that comes as no surprise. But it is a debate that needs to happen, because if Jefferson was right when he said that democracy is an infectious idea, so too is hatred. And no hatred has been more widespread and pernicious than hatred of the Jews.

What Tarek Fatah's critics will miss is that he speaks as a Muslim who refuses to allow his religion to become an exercise in propaganda. He points out the moments in human history when enlightened Muslim leaders welcomed Jews in their midst and encouraged scholars to understand the depth of what is common to great religious traditions. The golden age of Maimonides in "al Andalus" can come again.

There are passages in the Torah, the Bible, and the Quran that speak of death to infidels and the necessary slaughter of others for the survival of people chosen by God. Those who seek theological support for the narrowest of hatreds can, and have, found it in sacred texts.

But what Tarek Fatah points out is how toxic this has become in today's world, and that a demonization of the Jews, and Israel, is a particular feature of extremism that needs to be exposed.

The book combines history, theology, and politics. It shows that far from being anti-Semitic in its early years, Islam stressed its common heritage with the people of The Book, and that it is a return to this deeper understanding that could be a basis for hope.

No doubt Fatah's exposure of the futility of singling out Israel for all the troubles in the Middle East will earn him much predictable criticism, but readers should also recognize that Israeli settlement policy also comes in for criticism as he points out that a two-state policy requires a viable Palestine. He is nobody's patsy and calls it as he sees it. It is his independence of spirit and his willingness to engage in debate and discussion that have always marked his life. He criticizes freely and accepts the rules of the arena in return.

This book should be read and debated widely. Osama bin Laden is not alone, and his popularity on the streets of Khartoum and Baghdad has to be understood. Nor should anyone believe that a resolution of the conflict in the Middle East between Israel and its neighbours, as necessary and desirable as that is, will put these issues to rest. Life is more complicated than that.

Tarek Fatah is now coming into his own. He has written a book of weight and substance, and attention must be paid to what he says. Let us also realize what he is not saying. He is not saying that "Islam is anti-Semitic." He is not saying "The war between Islam and the West is inevitable." He worries rightly about Islamophobia and tells his readers that Islam is a great religion to which attention and respect must be paid. He is also saying that through a curious twist of politics and ideology too much hatred is now working its way into some preaching, and the wider world needs to understand the nature of this threat.

As he rightly points out, the victims of this pernicious theology are not just Jews: they are all those who take issue with extremism. What is happening is a battle for the soul of Islam, and all of us have a critical stake in the outcome.

PREFACE

The words were as pungent as could be, the message seething with unmistakable hate. Jews, he said, were "diseased and filthy." Salman Hossain's article, published in March 2010 on the website Filthy Jewish Terrorists, did not end there. Hossain went on to describe Jews as "the scum of the earth," labelling them "psychotic" and "mass murderers."[1] Elsewhere, Hossain called for "a genocide" that "should be perpetrated against the Jewish populations of North America and Europe."[2]

Had Salman Hossain been spouting his anti-Semitism from an Al-Shabab hideout in Somalia or an al Qaeda cave in Yemen, one could have simply shrugged off the hatred as just another clichéd rant from a frustrated jihadi. However, Hossain's hatred had originated in one of Canada's leading educational institutions – Toronto's York University, where he was a student. It was not as if he came from a dispossessed Palestinian family or had lost his loved ones in an Israeli attack. No, this young man's roots were in Bangladesh, where the only genocide ever committed on his people was by fellow Muslim Pakistanis, in 1971. Yet this Bangladeshi Canadian reserved his odious hatred for the Jew, not the Pakistani army that had massacred a million of his parents' generation. The only Pakistani he did vent his wrath at was me, calling me a traitor. My crime? Despite my solidarity with the Palestinian cause, I denounce anti-Semitism and refuse to hate either Israel or the Jewish people.

Salman Hossain is not an isolated case of a Western Muslim youth imbued with anti-Semitism. Websites and social-networking forums such as Facebook are littered with posts by young Muslims in Canada, the United States, and Europe who openly espouse hatred for Jews. Take, for example, the British Muslim who posted a comment on my Facebook page, saying, "Muslims who drink [alcohol] are Jews in reality." This single sentence spoke volumes about how the word *Jew* is used as a slur by so many Muslims. This man's comment came during a vigorous debate on Facebook in December 2009, when a well-known British Islamist, Inayat Bunglawala, slammed the group British Muslims for Secular Democracy because their head, the author, columnist, and BBC commentator Yasmin Alibhai-Brown, was a connoisseur of fine wines. It was not sufficient to attack her as an apostate who had committed the ultimate sin of developing a taste for Turkey Flat Shiraz; the added slur of her being a "Jew" was needed to complete the insult.

Today, a growing number of Islamists and Muslim intelligentsia accept that the Jews control the world, and that everyone, from David Cameron to Barack Obama, from Stephen Harper to Nicholas Sarkozy, dances to the tune of the Jew.

When one of the towering political leaders of the Muslim world joins in the talk of Jewish conspiracies, it is time to be concerned – not for the sake of Jews, but for Muslims. Tun Mahathir bin Mohamad, the former prime minister of Malaysia, stands, for all his faults, like a giant among the Muslim world's ragtag army of pompous, overdressed, self-conscious, self-righteous, ego-ridden leaders. A product of a democracy and the leader of a multiracial and multireligious society, Mahathir led Malaysia for twenty-two years, from 1981 to 2003, and is credited not only with engineering Malaysia's rapid modernization but with rescuing the country from the 1997 Asian economic crisis.

The son of an Indian father and a Malay mother, Mahathir is widely respected and admired in the Muslim world. I have met him twice, once in 2005, when he was still prime minister, and again in 2009, in his office on the eighty-second floor in the Petronas Towers of Kuala Lumpur. I have known him as one of the wiser elder statesmen of the Muslim world. This is why I was shocked when I read his remarks at a 2010 conference in Indonesia. In his speech, Mahathir voiced his disappointment that Barack Obama had not yet ended the war in Afghanistan, and suggested that it was the Jewish lobby in the United States that was behind the president's decision not to pursue peace. He said, "There are forces in the United States which prevent the president from doing some things. One of the forces is the Jewish lobby." That was bad enough, but it was what he said next that made me shudder. Jews, he said, "had always been a problem in European countries. They had to be confined to ghettoes and periodically massacred. But still they remained, they thrived and they held whole governments to ransom . . . Even after their massacre by the Nazis of Germany, they survived to continue to be a source of even greater problems for the world."[3]

Beyond the young Salman Hossain of Toronto and the former prime minister of Malaysia, there are over one billion Muslims worldwide, and they are constantly being told by clerics about the essential deviousness of the Jew and the global conspiracies he weaves. Adding to this paranoia is the global Muslim community's false sense of victimhood, which is leaving a deep scar on our consciousness. As the rest of the world makes rapid advances in technology, culture, arts, literature, and social development, the Muslim world seems frozen in time, obsessed with the past, and outpaced by such developing nations as Brazil, India, South Africa, and China. The Muslim community – better known as the ummah – is left paralyzed in the quagmire of stagnation. In the absence of any rational explanation for this malaise, all we can do is indulge in blame, self-pity, or hate.

And at the top of the Muslim blame game is the continued occupation of the Palestinian territories. Irrespective of who is responsible for the sorry state of the Palestinians, after thirty-five years of occupation, the cause of Palestine is still invoked around the Muslim world, both to distract the community from its own needs and to blame all our short-comings on some fictitious Jewish conspiracy. By refusing to recognize not just the legality of the state of Israel but also the right of Jews to have a state of their own in the Holy Land, the Arab leadership has failed the Palestinian people time after time.

For me, a discussion about Muslim-Jewish relations or the Arab-Israeli dispute becomes a non-starter the moment the right of Israel to exist as a Jewish state is challenged. Having said that, I firmly believe Israel, in continuing its occupation of the West Bank, is in serious violation of international law. I am against this occupation not because I am Muslim, but because I am against the occupation of any people by a foreign country. Whether it is Morocco's continued occupation of Western Sahara, Sudan's occupation of Darfur, Indonesia's now ended occupation of East Timor, or the refusal by four Muslim countries – Turkey, Iraq, Syria, and Iran – to permit the Kurdish people a state of their own, for me, they all merit equal attention. For the Muslims of the world, the 1925 invasion of the Kingdom of Hejaz by the Sultanate of Nejd and the continued occupation of the holy cities of Mecca and Medina by the Saudi royal family should be our primary reason for anger. But it is not. In fact, you would be hard pressed to find any scholar or sheikh who would dare mention this sad part of contemporary Islamic history.

I am neither Arab nor Jew. I am an Indian born in Pakistan whose Hindu ancestors in the Punjab converted to Islam in the nineteenth century. My heritage was deeply interwoven with that of the Sikh religion and Hinduism's ancient wisdom. The Islam of Punjab had no room for hate. The three faith communities were woven together by a common culture, cuisine, and clothing, and by a humour that could defuse the most intense altercation. Yet in 1947 – Muslims, Hindus, and Sikhs

– we managed to break a thousand-year-old relationship in a frenzy of bloodletting that killed a million people in a matter of six short months. How then could I, a child of a maniacal religious massacre, afford to hate the "other"?

As I write in this book's closing chapter, my birthplace had no tradition of anti-Semitism in the late 1940s and '50s. Yet, in a visit to Pakistan in 2006, I was taken aback by the ubiquitous hostility towards the Jewish people. I was told incessantly that the Jews "controlled" the United States and that throughout history the Jews have connived to become the puppet masters of the rest of the human race. My host and his friends were among the wealthy and well-educated elites of the land. The home where Muslim marginalization was being discussed boasted half a dozen cars in the driveway, a retinue of servants, and a front lawn that was larger than several backyards put together. Yet they talked as if they were plotting the Bolshevik uprising in Petrograd.

"Why are all cab drivers in Chicago Muslim, why not Jewish?" one friend asked. I pointed out that the net wealth of American Muslims is almost equal to that of American Jews, but it failed to have any influence on the assembled group. I was accused of being brainwashed by the Jews, of being on their payroll. I laughed off what in the Islamic world is the ultimate insult to a Muslim – an allegation of being a Jewish lackey. I asked my friends if they were aware that Jews had come to the United States as poor immigrants escaping persecution in Europe in the nineteenth century, yet were able to assimilate and, through hard work, make incredible contributions to American life. I urged them to consider the fact that even though Jews make up just 2 per cent of the U.S. population, they form 21 per cent of the Ivy League student body. I pointed out that this 2 per cent of the American population accounts for 38 per cent of *Business Week*'s list of leading philanthropists, 51 per cent of the Pulitzer Prize winners for non-fiction, and 37 per cent of Academy Award–winning directors. But they saw in the same statistics the evidence of their conspiracy theories: "That just proves the Jews control the U.S.A." I was speechless. Instead of recognizing the Jewish community's hard work and its focus on education, innovation, and entrepreneurship, my friends attributed Jewish success to the fact that they controlled all the avenues to power.

That was the moment I decided I had to write, to right the wrong. I mulled over the subject for more than a year, talked to a few Islamic scholars, met a couple of rabbis, and read well over a hundred texts of history and theology, but in the end decided to give up. "You will end up antagonizing both the Jews as well as the Arabs," my wife counselled. "This is not your fight, and no good will come of it." I reluctantly hung up my gloves.

Then, in November 2008, came the terrorist attacks on Mumbai, in which Pakistani jihadis murdered hundreds, among them a rabbi, his pregnant wife, and other members of a local Jewish community centre. I was horrified. Why would a group of Punjabi villagers seek out a Jewish centre in a densely populated part of Mumbai to massacre Jews? It is unlikely they could ever have met a Jew, let alone have a grievance with him, yet they had been brainwashed by their Islamist handlers to the extent that they were willing to die to kill a few Jews. What had the Jews done to Pakistan? As I watched the television coverage of the flames rising over Mumbai, I resolved to challenge this hate before it consumes all of us in an Armageddon foretold in medieval literature, but one that will occur in the shadows of nuclear mushroom clouds.

This book is an attempt to answer the question, why do Muslims hate Jews? What is the source of this hatred, and how can we end this cancer before it consumes us Muslims?

In my fight against Muslim anti-Semitism, I am not alone. Muslim voices around the world are making brave attempts in the face of intimidation and slander to fight the rise of jihadi Islamism. My friend and Danish member of Parliament Naser Khedar, the son of

Palestinian parents, has spoken eloquently against Islamic extremism, despite several death threats. British Muslims for Secular Democracy, the American Islamic Forum for Democracy, the Muslim Canadian Congress, German M.P. Elkin Deligöz, American-Egyptian columnist Mona Eltahawy, Sweden's Burundi-born minister of integration Nyamko Sabuni, Algerian-born French cabinet minister Fadela Amara, and the Moroccan-born mayor of Rotterdam, Ahmed Aboutaleb, are just some of the prominent Muslims standing up against hate.

Another of them is Cem Özdemir, the head of the German Green Party. Of Turkish ancestry, he is the first Muslim to head a major political party anywhere in Europe or North America. In February 2009, Özdemir told the German newspaper *Frankfurter Rundschau* that he was worried by the rise of Muslim anti-Semitism in Germany, and asked Berlin to take anti-Semitic tendencies among its Muslim population seriously. "We must unfortunately acknowledge that there are anti-Semitic mindsets not only in the right-wing or among the so-called left-wing anti-imperialists, but also in the Muslim community – particularly among male Arabic, Turkish and Kurdish youths," he said. He urged other Muslim-German leaders to draw clear lines and to stress that anyone who displays anti-Semitic sentiments would not be allowed to represent the community. Özdemir was responding to a study by the German Interior Ministry that found that almost 16 per cent of Muslim students surveyed agreed with the statement "People of Jewish faith are arrogant and greedy for money."[4]

For Jew-haters like Osama bin Laden and Mahmoud Ahmadinejad, the question of Palestine is merely an excuse, not the reason. The Islamist hatred of the Jew has little do with the state of Israel or a supposed love for Palestine. If tomorrow Ahmadinejad was able to fulfill his threat to wipe Israel from the face of the earth, hatred of the Jew would continue unabated. The only way to end it is to challenge with courage the fundamental myths that sustain Judeophobia.

To help understand this phenomenon of hatred, consider this speech by Egyptian cleric Muhammad Hussein Yaqub that aired on Al-Rahma TV on January 17, 2009:

> If the Jews left Palestine to us, would we start loving them? Of course not. We will never love them. Absolutely not. . . . They are enemies not because they occupied Palestine. *They would have been enemies even if they did not occupy a thing* [emphasis mine]. . . . You must believe that we will fight, defeat, and anni-hilate them, until not a single Jew remains on the face of the Earth. It is not me who says so. The Prophet said: "Judgment Day will not come until you fight the Jews and kill them. The Jews will hide behind stones and trees, and the stones and tree will call: O Muslim, O servant of Allah, there is a Jew behind me, come and kill him. . . . As for you Jews – the curse of Allah upon you. The curse of Allah upon you, whose ancestors were apes and pigs. You Jews have sown hatred in our hearts, and we have bequeathed it to our children and grandchildren. You will not survive as long as a single one of us remains."

There is no denying that Islamic texts contain language that depicts Jews in unfavourable terms. But much of what inspires Muslims to hate Jews comes from man-made texts known as the Hadith literature, the supposed sayings of Prophet Muhammad recorded two hundred years after his death and passed off as divine truths. (I will address these in more detail in chapter 5.) Sheikh Yaqub is just one of countless cler-ics schooled by Saudi universities or Saudi-funded madrassahs in the Hadith literature. The clerics study Islamic history not as history per se, but as theology.

By any rational standard, Muslims and Jews should have been, and could be, partners. Their faiths are very similar; the Jewish Torah, customs, rituals, and diet found their way into Islam to the extent that one Muslim has described Islam as "the Jewish faith planted on Arab pagan culture." That may be an exaggeration, but the fact remains that far more unites the two people than divides them. We pray to the same God; Muslims honour Abraham, Moses, David, and Solomon as our prophets; and we are free to marry among the Jews. There were times when Muslims and Jews even prayed together around the stone covered today by the Dome on the Rock.

Prof. Moshe Sharon of Jerusalem's Hebrew University writes about an early Jewish Midrash – a commentary on Hebrew scripture – known as Nistarot Rabbi Shimon Bar Yohai, which hailed Muslims as the initiators of Israel's redemption and the Muslim caliph Abd al-Malik, who built the Dome on the Rock, as the builder of the House of the Lord. Sharon quotes one tradition that says, "The Jews used to light the lamps of Bayt al-Maqdis." "Bayt al-Maqdis," he writes, "is the exact Arabic rendering of the Hebrew Beit Hamikdash, and is reminiscent of the lighting of the Menorah in the Temple." Other Islamic traditions mention Temple customs practised by Jews in the Dome, such as the use of incense and oil lamps, and prayer services conducted by *wuld Harun*, Arabic for "the sons of Aaron."[5]

Where we Muslims differ from Jews is also significant. Jews consider themselves a specific monotheistic people, with roots going back to Abraham, his son Isaac, and the ancient Holy Land, whereas Muslims, while adhering to the same tradition of strict monotheism, define themselves not in geographic or ethnic terms, but rather as a community that transcends ethnicity and race, at least in principle. This makes it possible for anyone to embrace Islam, be they from China or Brazil. The Muslim is tied not to land, but rather to God and Muhammad's message. The Jew, on the other hand, defines his identity with a return to Jerusalem and Eretz Israel as his eternal homeland.

Over the centuries, the incessant Hadith-inspired attacks on the very nature (fitra) of the Jew have left Muslims indoctrinated to the belief that a Jew cannot be trusted to be straightforward or truthful. If this racist doctrine slowly corrupted the attitudes of generations of Muslims, the Israel-Palestine dispute was the catalyst that lent this hate respectability and credence. The myths and legends of seventh-century Arabia have been dusted off and rejuvenated to make Jew-hatred the norm, not the exception.

I begin this book by describing the events that led to the slaughter in Mumbai, and in chapters 2 and 3, I write about the effect of fascist and European anti-Semitic literature on twentieth-century Arab Islamists, long before the creation of the state of Israel, and describe how this cancer has destroyed us Muslims rather than our supposed enemy.

Whereas anti-Semitism in Europe has its roots in Christian mythologies that depicted the Jews as a dark and demonic force, responsible for the murder of the Son of God, Judeophobia in the Arab world stems from a completely different legend. Modern-day Muslims hold anti-Jewish prejudices not because their Prophet Muhammad was a victim of the Jews, but because he vanquished them in a decisive battle in Medina. And so I will challenge the primary legend of Islamic history that has made the killing of Jews literally an act of Sunnah, the practice of the Prophet. Chapter 6 will dwell on the Battle of the Trench and the legend of the slaughter of the Jews of Banu Qurayza by Prophet Muhammad. This collective punishment of prisoners of war has seeped deep into the Muslim psyche and is the cornerstone of the Muslim attitude towards Jews. In challenging this widely held view that Prophet Muhammad slaughtered nine hundred Jews in cold blood, I am conscious that I am exposing a myth that has defined Muslim thinking for centuries. The radical ayatollahs of Iran, the sheikhs of Saudi Arabia, and self-styled reformist academics such as Tariq Ramadan praise this massacre in glowing terms.

In chapter 7, I will demonstrate why, in the absence of physical and textual evidence, there is reason to reject this legend outright instead of celebrating it as an act of bravado by Prophet Muhammad.

Let me begin my jihad against Muslim anti-Semitism with a verse from the Quran that should define Muslim attitudes towards members of other faiths, but is often ignored by Islamists:

> *Surely those who believe,*
> *And those who are Jews,*
> *And the Christians and the Sabians,*
> *Whoever believes in God and the Last Day,*
> *And does good, they have their reward with their Lord,*
> *And there is no fear for them,*
> *Nor shall they Grieve.*

(QURAN 2:62)

CHAPTER ONE

"O Allah, Completely Destroy and Shatter the Jews"

"When you kill one [Jew] . . . it is worth more than killing fifty people." The voice of the Pakistani commander crackles over the cellphone as he urges on two jihadis who have taken over the ultra-Orthodox Chabad House in Mumbai on the evening of November 26, 2008. Already, a rabbi, his pregnant wife, and two house guests have been shot dead, while two Jewish women are being held hostage in this suicide mission.

In conversations recorded by Indian intelligence, the Pakistan-based handlers warn the jihadi terrorists not to contemplate surrender under any circumstances. "Getting arrested alive is not an option. Remember . . . For your mission to end successfully, you must be killed. The virgins are waiting for you in paradise." Exhorting the jihadis to spread terror, the handlers tell them, "Create so much havoc that the enemy should fear us till the end of times."

A day earlier, ten Pakistani terrorists had landed on the beach at Mumbai, the city that symbolized everything repugnant to these Islamists – modernity, secularism, and joy. All through their teens they had watched Bollywood movies on pirated DVDs, which tantalized them with dancing damsels and titillating tunes, weakening their faith, challenging their manhood, and corrupting their morals. Now, it was time to get even.

Splitting into five pairs, they each have a specific target. One pair, however, has a special assignment. The group leader takes aside the two gunmen, Babar Imran and Nasir, and reminds them of the significance of their mission. They are to target and kill Jews. He stresses to the two jihadis that their task is the most important one. Even if all the other attacks fail, the Chabad House operation to kill Jews must succeed. Attacking the Jewish community centre that also serves as an ultra-Orthodox synagogue, he reminds them, will send a message to Jews around the world.

In the days to come, these ten Islamic terrorists would turn Mumbai into a living hell before nine of them would "ascend" to heaven and the tenth would beg a judge to hang him, so he too could join his fellow "martyrs." Their handlers have promised them seventy-two virgins each, more beautiful and sensual than anything Bollywood could create in its hundred-year sinful history.

Before they could land in Mumbai, however, there was the little matter of their hostage, Amar Singh Solanki, captain of the Indian fishing trawler the jihadis had captured three days earlier. All four of Solanki's crew had been killed, while Captain Solanki was forced at gunpoint to navigate the 550-mile voyage to Mumbai.

As the trawler bobbed in the waters off the coast, Ismail Khan, the leader of the jihadi group, called his handlers in Pakistan for directions. "What do we do with the hostage?" he asked. On hearing that the four other Indian fishermen had been killed and their bodies dumped into the Indian Ocean, the handler exclaimed: "You ate those four goats?" Ismail then asks, "Can I eat the fifth one?" Yes, came the answer.

Ismail ordered two of his men, Shoaib and Babar Imran, to blindfold the "goat" and take him down to the trawler's engine room. Having served his purpose, the Hindu father of three was forced to lie down on the floor. With Ismail and Babar holding on to him, Shoaib slit the helpless Indian's throat, just as he had slaughtered many a goat back in his village. What better way to launch holy war on a city than to make a human sacrifice to the gods.

This would be the first of many deaths in the orgy of killing that consumed the next forty-eight hours, before Shoaib and his co-jihadis were shot dead by Indian security forces, fulfilling the Pakistani men's wish for martyrdom.

The honour of slaughtering the first infidel has gone to Shoaib, but Babar Imran is not disappointed that he has been overlooked. Solanki was, after all, just another run-of-the-mill infidel, a Hindu. Babar is excited that he and another mate, Nasir, have been specially selected to carry out the task that would earn them the most prized kills, the mother of all infidels – the Jews.

In the 2,500 years since Jews have called the Indian subcontinent their home, they have never faced anti-Semitism. The Bani Israelis, as Indian Jews refer to themselves, are believed to have arrived in India when their ancestors were shipwrecked off the Konkan coast in 175 BC. Even when the persecution of Jews was widespread in Europe, India was different. From the Muslim Mughal emperors of Delhi to the ordinary Muslim villagers living in towns along the Ganges and the Indus, there is no recorded animosity towards the "Yahudi," a term of respect. All of this was about to change.

Around 8:20 p.m., the men dock their inflatable dinghy at a fishermen's slum next to Mumbai's Cuffe Parade neighbourhood. The area is home to some of India's most prominent citizens, among them the controversial artist M.F. Husain and the billionaire Ambani family. On any other night the neighbourhood near the docks would be teeming with people, but tonight, most of the cricket-crazy residents of the city are glued to their TV sets watching the satellite feed of the India vs. England match being played in London.

A local resident, Ajay Mistry, is one of the first to witness the Pakistanis land on Indian soil. He remembers the ten as dressed smartly in navy blue and black; with their heavy backpacks they look almost like college kids. A teenager steps out of his house and asks them who they are. Just students, they say, coming back from a boat ride. The Pakistanis are polite with the men, but when a woman approaches them, their demeanour changes.

Anita Rajendra Udaayar, another neighbourhood resident, has been watching the young men with their oversized backpacks. It is an unusual sight for her, even though she is accustomed to tourists taking boat rides. When she asks them what they are doing, one of them scornfully tells her to mind her own business. No woman has ever questioned them – how dare an infidel raise her voice!

This is the last time some of them will see each other – that is, until they meet in their hoped-for paradise. To make sure there is no mistaking their Islamic identities at the gates of heaven, all of them have adopted Arabic *noms de guerre,* some meaningless but nonetheless comforting to these villagers from the Punjab. Thus Babar Imran is Abu Akash, and Nasir is known as Abu Umer.

Before the jihadis split into pairs, their leader, Ismail Khan, briefs them for the last time. Eight of the men are assigned the task of spreading terror and killing Indians without distinction, be they Hindu, Sikh, Christian, or Muslim. The job assigned to Babar and Nasir, however, is very specific: to kill Jews, and as many as possible. They must not fail, he reminds the two. He emphasizes that the other targets – hotels, a café, a train station – are merely intended to amplify the effect of the attack on Chabad House, the Jewish community centre.

The two make their way to the crowded residential neighbourhood of Mumbai's Colaba district. Tucked inside an area that is home to a large Muslim population, the five-storey Nariman House is a meeting place and refuge for the city's tiny Jewish population and Israeli backpackers. It is one of several hundred Chabad Houses operated around the world by the Orthodox Chabad-Lubavitch movement. The Mumbai Chabad House is run by the twenty-nine-year-old American Rabbi Gavriel Holtzberg and his twenty-eight-year-old Israeli wife, Rivka. Since 2006, thousands of Jews have visited and stayed at the centre and have had no problems with their Muslim neighbours.

Although their colleagues have already begun their killing spree, lobbing grenades and randomly firing their AK-47s into the nearby Leopold Café, Babar and Nasir take their time locating Nariman House. Once there, they know it should be a cakewalk. Despite its tight connections with Israel, the Chabad House is a soft target – much easier to hit than, say, the tightly guarded Israeli diplomatic mission or the offices of El Al, Israel's national airline.

By ten that night, scores of people have already died across the city. It is time for Babar and Nasir to strike. To divert attention away from their mission, they throw a hand grenade at a nearby gas station. On hearing the explosion, Rabbi Holtzberg calls the police.

Startled by the blast, Vicky Patel, who owns a sweet shop nearby, is surprised to see the two Pakistanis head straight for Nariman House: "A common man would have had difficulty in finding the place, but these people knew every lane as if they had studied the entire place." Later, when the siege was over, Patel would help to recover the bodies of the hostages.

While neighbours come out of their homes and businesses to watch the fire at the gas station, Babar and Nasir force their way into Nariman House, where they are confronted by Rabbi Holtzberg and his wife.

An eyewitness would later say that she heard Rivka defy the two gunmen: "Shoot me . . . shoot me," she yelled. Without hesitation the jihadi pulled the trigger and Rivka fell to the floor in the hail of bullets. Then the witness heard Rabbi Holtzberg also confront the two. "Shoot me," he said before more shots rang out.

Babar and Nasir kill two more Jews before taking fifty-year-old Norma Rabinovitch and sixty-two-year-old Yoheved Orpaz hostage. Leaving the four bodies behind, they force the two women to the upper floors. The gunmen do not know that the nearly two-year-old son of the Holtzbergs is in bed on another floor while his nanny, Sandra Samuels, is hiding in a closet. TV coverage would later show the boy wandering among the dead before the nanny grabs him and escapes from the siege.

After securing the Jewish centre, the two terrorists establish contact with their handlers in Pakistan over their cellphones equipped with Indian SIM cards. They are unaware that by now Indian Intelligence is monitoring all cellular phone calls and recording all conversations.

On hearing about the killing of the rabbi, his wife, and two other Jews, the Pakistani handler congratulates the terrorists and reminds them that killing a Jew is far more significant than killing any other non-Muslim: "You should understand that when you kill one person where you are, it is worth more than your colleagues killing fifty people elsewhere."

By now the entire neighbourhood is alive with people watching the action from their balconies and the street. The handlers are anxious to see more casualties. They are watching the incident unfold live on TV, but nothing from Nariman House. One calls again: "Do you see any movement to your left and right?" Babar informs him about the growing crowd. "There are lot of people watching from their balconies both on our left and right," he says. The handler confers with his superiors. He is overheard asking, "There are regular civilians on the street. What should we do?"

He tells Babar to fire into the crowd. "Shoot anyone you see," he orders. Babar immediately fires, hitting several people, many of them Muslims.

The handler justifies this random shooting of civilians by assuring the terrorists, "The enemy must fear us. When this is over, there will be much more fear of us in the world, forever."

The terrorists' strategy is working. The world watches in horror as out-of-control fires engulf the picturesque Taj Hotel, and Israelis wake up to hear about Jews being targeted in India. Shortly after the takeover of Nariman House, Israel's defence minister, Ehud Barak, offers the Indian government assistance in dealing with the attacks.

As dawn breaks, the Pakistani handlers learn that one of the terrorists, Kasab, has been captured after a shootout with police. Their orders had been clear: "Getting arrested alive is not an option . . . For your mission to end successfully, you must be killed."

Now the handlers play the hostage-exchange card. They ask Norma Rabinovitch, one of the two hostages, to call the Israeli consulate in Mumbai and ask them to put pressure on the Indian government to work for her release.

In a breaking voice, Norma tells the Pakistanis she has already made contact with the Israelis: "I was talking to the consulate just a few seconds ago and they have said to leave the line free. They are calling the prime minister and the army from the embassy in India."

The Pakistani handler patronizes Norma Rabinovitch: "Don't worry, ma'am, just sit back and relax, and don't worry, and just wait for them to contact. Okay?" As Rabinovitch sobs, the Pakistani chuckles: "And save your energy for good days. If they contact right now, maybe you're gonna celebrate your Sabbath with your family."

He then issues instructions to the terrorists: "The Indian authorities will call you on this number and ask you what you want. Just say, 'Release our guy and his weapons in our hands within half an hour.' You must not disclose to them that you have only two hostages. You must say that you will release all the hostages. Tell them, only then will you negotiate with them."

7

As the two jihadis and their Pakistani handler await the call from the Indians, Babar Imran uses the dead rabbi's phone to call up a local TV station and vent his anger at Israel. He pretends he is Indian and sprinkles his Urdu with a few words of Hindi, but his accent fools no one.

INDIA TV: Hello, Imran, where are you?

BABAR: We are here . . . You call their [Israeli] Army Staff to visit Kashmir . . . why is it so? . . . Who are they to come to Kashmir? . . . This is a matter between us and Hindus . . . the Hindu government . . . Why does that Israel come here . . . ?

INDIA TV: Imran, you claim that you are in Nariman [Chabad] House. How many of your friends are there in Nariman House?

BABAR: We know how to live . . . how to snatch our rights . . .

INDIA TV: Imran, are you able to listen to what I am saying?

BABAR: Yes, I can hear you.

INDIA TV: Just reply to my question . . . How many of you . . . are there in Nariman House?

BABAR: I have five persons with me.

INDIA TV: And when did you come to Mumbai?

BABAR: We have come here for our work . . . we waited . . . everything is before you . . . We are tired of facing tortures and injustice, we are forced to do this . . . The situation is in front of you . . . I am merely repeating history to you, but . . . I don't understand why you people talk like this.

After hanging up, Babar waits for the call from the Indian government. But neither the Indians nor the Israelis have taken the bait.

It is now 10 p.m., twenty-four hours after the takeover of Chabad House. Finally the phone rings, but it is his handlers from Pakistan calling. Babar informs them that the Indians have not called. What should he do, he asks.

The handler confers with his superiors sitting in the Pakistan office: "Do you want them to hold on to the hostages or kill them?" A voice in the background says, "Kill them." The handler gets back on the line with clear instructions to Babar: "Listen to me. Save yourself the hassle and get rid of them [the hostages]. Kill them. You could come under fire at any time now and they may be left behind . . . Kill them now."

Babar hesitates. He tells his handler, "Yes, but I do not see any movement from the police. It is all quiet over here."

HANDLER: No, do not wait any longer. Kill the hostages. You never know when you might come under attack and with what intensity or which direction and at that time, you will not have the time to kill the hostages.

BABAR: OK.

HANDLER: And when you shoot, make sure the bullets do not ricochet from the walls and hit you . . . Come on, do it now . . . I'll stay on the line.

[A long pause.]

HANDLER: Come on, do it, do it . . . I am listening.

BABAR: What? Should I shoot them?

HANDLER: Make them sit up, turn their faces away, and then shoot them in the back of the head. Do it, do it. I am waiting.

BABAR: The problem is that I just asked Umer [Nasir] to get some sleep. He has not been feeling too well. I am hoping he gets some sleep and then we will do the job.

HANDLER: OK. I will wait for half an hour and call you back. Will you do it then? OK? I will phone you back.

One hour later Babar and Nasir have still not executed the two women hostages, and the handler starts to lose patience.

BABAR: Please do not get angry. I had to change some settings.

HANDLER: Has the job been done or not?

BABAR: We will do it right now. I was just waiting for you to call so you could listen.

HANDLER: OK, then do it in the name of Allah.

[There is a pause before the shots are fired.]

BABAR: Hello?

HANDLER: Was that just one?

BABAR: No, both of them killed, yaklakht [at once].

Nine hours after the two women hostages are shot dead, Indian commandos land on the roof of Nariman House and the final battle begins. In his last phone call, Babar asks his handler in Pakistan to pray for him so that he can attain martyrdom. He says he has been hit in the arm and leg. Amidst the din of rapid gunfire, the phone goes dead.

The only Jew to escape the slaughter is Moshe, who turned two the day after his father and mother were killed.

If the Pakistani terrorists had hoped to disrupt Muslim-Jewish relations in India, the reaction of the leaders of the two communities reflects their failure.

Ezra Moses, head of a congregation that is home to many Indian Jews, told the Indian magazine *Tehelka,* "It has never happened on Indian shores that a Jew is attacked." Another prominent member of the community, Solomon Sopher, said the high school he manages was founded as a Jewish school but now enrolled mostly Muslims. "Jews have been more close to Muslims in India than to people of any other faith," and this, he said, is what made the attack by Muslims on Nariman [Chabad] House all the more disturbing.

"People who committed this heinous crime cannot be called

Muslim," Hanif Nalkhande, a spokesperson for the Bada Kabrastan graveyard, told *The Times* of London, explaining why Mumbai Muslims were not permitting the terrorists a Muslim burial. Another prominent Indian Muslim leader, columnist M.J. Akbar, agreed: "Indian Muslims are proud of being both Indian and Muslim, and the Mumbai terrorism was a war against both India and Islam. . . . Since the . . . terrorists were neither Indian nor true Muslims, they had no right to an Islamic burial in an Indian Muslim cemetery."

A year after the attack, the bodies of the nine terrorists lay unclaimed in an Indian morgue, as no Indian Muslim cemetery would agree to bury them. The leadership of India's Muslim community referred to the dead men as "murderers," not "martyrs." (Finally, in April 2010, after the Pakistani government refused to accept the bodies, the terrorists were buried in secret unmarked graves by the Maharashtra state government, in what it said was a "dignified" manner.)

While Indian Muslims were vocal in their denunciation of the jihadis, right-wing Pakistani Islamists claimed that the attack on Mumbai was the work of Israel. Surprisingly – or perhaps not – a large section of Pakistan's intelligentsia has bought into this conspiracy theory. Self-styled Pakistani security expert Zaid Hamid, interviewed on TV while the attack was unfolding, accused "Western Zionists and Hindu Zionists" of planning the operation. (Hamid, who claims he once fought for the cia-backed mujahedeen in Afghanistan during the 1980s, is the founder of the Pakistani think tank BrassTacks and is believed to have close links to the Pakistani intelligence service, the isi.) Hamid said, "The Indians have themselves always wanted to orchestrate a 9/11, to create the same drama in which they could include Americans and Israelis. We have no doubt this [attack on Mumbai] was a joint plan by Israelis, Americans, and Indians – in other words, this was a joint plan by Western Zionists and Hindu Zionists; in it Israelis are directly involved, there is involvement of Mossad."

He further argued that the now iconic image of Kasab with an AK-47 entering the Mumbai railway station indicated that he was a Hindu, not a Muslim. In the picture, Kasab is wearing an orange wristband. "If you look at the images, the terrorist shown firing . . . with a machine gun in his hand, he has tied in his hand a saffron band of Hindu Zionists. Muslims do not wear this type of band – their faces are like Hindus', the language in which they are speaking, this language no Pakistani uses."

In May 2010, Kasab was sentenced to death by a Mumbai court on the charge of waging war against India, and the world would discover that this jihadi operation involved Muslim Pakistanis living in Canada and the United States.

The previous October, U.S. authorities arrested two Muslims – Tahawwur Hussain Rana, a forty-eight-year-old Pakistani-Canadian immigration consultant, and his accomplice David Headley, forty-nine (whose real name was Dawood Sayed Gilani) – on charges that included providing reconnaissance to the Pakistani jihadis who attacked Mumbai. In March, Headley pleaded guilty and agreed to testify against his Pakistani-Canadian co-conspirator.

—

In late November 2008, as the ten Pakistani jihadis were killing Jews in Mumbai, on the other side of the world, three African-American converts to Islam and a Haitian Muslim were plotting to blow up New York synagogues.

The four men – James Cromitie, forty-four; David Williams, twenty-eight; Onta Williams, thirty-two; and Laguerre Payen, twenty-seven – had been on the FBI's radar since June, when an undercover agent ran into them at the Masjid Al-Ikhlas mosque in Newburgh, New York, and found them, in the words of prosecutors, "eager to bring death to Jews."

All four had criminal records; they had entered the prison system as Baptists or Catholics but came out as Muslims, converted in jail by Islamic chaplains. Somewhere inside the New York correctional system, the men, who had had little interaction with Jews, came to hate them.

The FBI states that at an October meeting at a house in Newburgh, the four men discussed Cromitie's desire to strike a synagogue in the Bronx and military aircraft at the Air National Guard base in Newburgh. Cromitie, aka Abdul Rahman, bragged that blowing up the synagogues would be a "piece of cake." "I hate those motherf – ers, those f – ing Jewish bastards . . . I would like to get a synagogue," Cromitie told a police informant.[1]

After months of planning and acquiring explosives and a Stinger surface-to-air missile, the four men and the informant each declared their willingness to perform jihad. On May 6, they drove to Stamford, Connecticut, to take delivery of the bombs and the Stinger missile. Long before they arrived, though, the FBI had disabled both the Stinger and the explosives. After testing one of the detonators for the bombs, they drove the weapons to Newburgh, locked them in a storage container, and celebrated, shouting, *"Allahu akbar!"*

Two weeks later, on May 20, they drove to the Bronx with the bombs. At around 9 p.m., after planting the bombs in cars outside the Riverdale Temple, a Reform synagogue, and the nearby Riverdale Jewish Centre, an Orthodox synagogue, they were about to head to the National Guard base, planning to shoot down military aircraft with their missile while simultaneously detonating the bombs with a cellphone. But just after they had planted the last of the dud bombs, police swooped in and arrested them.

This was by no means the first attempt by radical Islamists to attack Jewish centres in the United States.

March 1977: Hanafi Muslims seized three buildings in Washington, D.C., including the headquarters of B'nai B'rith, and held hostages for thirty-nine hours, resulting in one death and one severe injury.

February 1993: Ramzi Yusuf, the mastermind of the bombing of the World Trade Center in New York City, which claimed seven lives and injured more than a thousand people, declared the towers not a civilian target, but a military one, by virtue of the fact that it might house a "Zionist official."

June 1993: "Boom! Broken windows. Jews in the street" is how one of the plotters described the carnage that would ensue from a planned "day of terror" with simultaneous bombings of the United Nations complex, the Lincoln and Holland tunnels, and other New York landmarks.

March 1994: Rashid Baz opened fire on a van carrying Orthodox Jewish boys across the Brooklyn Bridge, killing one sixteen-year-old.

July 1997: Ali Hasan Abu Kamal shot seven tourists atop the Empire State Building, killing one and seriously wounding another. In his suicide note, he accused the United States of using Israel as "an instrument" against the Palestinians.

July 1997: Ghazi Ibrahim Abu Maizar nearly succeeded in detonating a pipe bomb in the New York City subway system.

July 2002: Hesham Mohamed Ali Hadayet attacked the El Al counter at Los Angeles International Airport, killing two.

September 2005: Jam'iyyat Ul-Islam Is-Saheeh's plot against two Los Angeles–area synagogues was disrupted because of a dropped mobile phone.

July 2006: Naveed Haq assaulted the Jewish Federation of Greater Seattle, murdering one and injuring five.

Neither the Mumbai terrorists nor the Haitian and African Americans were Arab or had been affected by the Israel-Palestine dispute. Chances are they had little or even no interaction with Jews in their day-to-day lives. So what motivated them to harbour so much hate in their hearts that they would give their lives for a chance to massacre Jews? Could it be that the religious education they received in the New

York prison system or in the madrassahs of Pakistan turned them into vessels brimming with hateful bigotry?

The seeds of such hate are planted in the minds of Muslims at an early age. The first time we attend Friday prayers at our neighbourhood mosques, as boys accompanying our fathers (most Muslim women never attend Friday congregations), the sermon we hear ends with the clarion call, "O Allah, defeat the kuffar" – Jews and other non-Muslims. We grow up having this prayer drilled into us week after week, though in time most of us ignore it as nothing more than the rhetoric of the screaming cleric. Nevertheless, this repeated prayer does leave a lingering suspicion about the Jew that stays with most Muslims for our entire lives, even if we never meet one.

Not only has the prayer asking God to defeat the Jews and Christians become a regular feature at most Friday congregations, it has gone unchallenged. In Muslim countries, no one seems to find it at all objectionable, while in the West there is a fear of upsetting Muslim clerics and community leaders. Many Westerners feel this hate is protected under provisions for minority religious rights. Some imams in the West have become so emboldened by the cowardice of the multiculturalists that they have placed their call for the defeat of Jews and Christians on their websites, ensuring that the large majority of Muslims who do not regularly attend mosque will not miss the message.

At a Toronto mosque in October 2009, a cleric ended one Friday sermon with this prayer: "O Allah, give victory to Muslims and Islam . . . O Allah, give defeat to the kuffar and mushrikeen" – non-believers. "Allah, destroy them from within themselves, and do not allow them to raise their heads in destroying Islam." When asked to explain his use of the pulpit to spread such hate, Imam Said Rageah, who was schooled in Saudi Arabia, told the *National Post* that he did not intend to insult non-Muslims. Moreover, he said, his use of the word *destroy* did not mean he wanted to destroy anyone, "but rather to confound or weaken those that would infringe on their [Muslim] rights."[2]

He did not deny that the word *kuffar* meant non-Muslims, including Jews, but Islamists across Canada came to his aid, claiming that the word was not at all a label for Jews or other non-Muslims. This despite the fact that scholar after scholar in all of Islamic history and to the present day, in the Middle East as well as North America, has referred to Jews and other non-Muslims as the kuffar.

Among them is Sheikh Muhammad al-Shinqati, director of the Islamic Center of South Plains, in Lubbock, Texas, and a resident scholar on the Islam Online website that gives fatwas on various issues raised by Muslims from around the world. In 2005, Sheikh al-Shinqati was asked on that forum whether Muslims are "allowed to call a Christian person kafir? Who is, exactly, a kafir?" He answered: "Christians and Jews are kuffar because they rejected the Prophethood of Muhammad." The good sheikh added: "Kafir is now a derogatory term, and that is why I would encourage Muslims to use the term 'non-Muslims' when referring to people of different faiths."[3]

The good news is that some clerics have begun to question the inclusion in Friday prayers of this call to defeat Jews. Senior Saudi cleric Sheikh Salman al-Awdah, director of the website Islam Today, has said that Muslims should avoid prayers that call for the destruction of non-Muslims. "Praying for the ruin and the destruction of all infidels is not permitted because it goes against God's law to call upon them . . . to take the righteous path."[4]

If an imam in Canada, with all its laws restricting hate speech, fears no consequences of his anti-Semitic prayer, imagine what is happening in the Arab world and Pakistan, where Muslims form the overwhelming majority of the population, and where asking Allah to "crush the Jews" has been the norm, not the exception, for centuries.

On March 9, 2009, a young Arab boy appeared on Egypt's Al-Rahma

Television. This is what he had to say under the watchful eyes of his Islamic teacher:

> O Allah, completely destroy and shatter the Jews. O Allah, torment them with a disease that has no cure or remedy. Send a thunderbolt down upon them from Heaven. O Allah, torment them with every kind of torment. O Allah, send upon them flocks of swallows that will pelt them with stones of baked clay, and turn them into straw that has been eaten. O Allah, turn their women into widows – just like Muslim women were widowed. Allah, turn their children into orphans – just like Muslim children were orphaned. O Allah, bless the efforts of the mujahedeen. O Allah, bring victory upon us soon. Amen.

Such a prayer may shock the non-Muslim listener, but to Muslims around the globe, such prayers and injunctions, if not always so explicit, are perfectly common. But although the clerics and imams of today may be the instruments of such fanatic hate, we need to look elsewhere for the roots of this rancour.

CHAPTER TWO

Bird Flu and Other Jewish Conspiracies

In Karachi on a warm spring day in 2006, as I walked through the city's posh Clifton district, a banner hung across a street caught my eye. It read, "Bird Flu is a Jewish conspiracy."

I was dumbstruck. At first I thought that perhaps this was some dark Pakistani humour I had failed to appreciate returning to my birthplace after a gap of seventeen years. However, when I asked around, I found that this view was widespread: Israel, I was told, was to blame for the bird flu because it wanted to destroy the poultry industry of Indonesia, a Muslim nation. When I found a similar banner adorning the entrance of a grocery store, I asked the owner to explain to me the link between Jews and bird flu. He handed me a copy of *The Protocols of the Elders of Zion*. "Here, take this book gratis – but read it," he commanded. With an air of supreme confidence he explained that it was not just the bird flu that the "Yahoodis" had used to attack an Islamic country. The tsunami of December 2004 too was a result of a joint effort by the United States and Israel to drown and destroy Muslim nations. I was flabbergasted, and had to be pulled away by a buddy who had the foresight to see the consequences of what might happen if I started arguing with the store owner.

The city and country I had first left in 1978 had changed dramatically. Karachi was both wealthier and poorer. Opulence was reflected in its buildings and SUVs, but its intellectual and artistic heritage had been bankrupted.

While the city's religious working-class neighbourhoods teemed with people eager to move to the West to embrace the American dream, its upper-class secular elites peppered their talk with anti-imperialist rhetoric and an infatuation with Islamism. Among them were families who, after having secured U.S. or Canadian passports, had come back to Islamdom to enjoy privileges they missed in the West.

At a gathering one evening, whisky-drinking admirers of Osama bin Laden lectured me about the five thousand Jews that never reported to work at the Twin Towers on 9/11, while their peroxide-blond wives looked on lovingly through blue contact lenses, rearranging coffee-table books on ice hockey, and the strains of Shania Twain – appropriately singing, "You don't impress me much" – wafted from their children's bedroom. The city that had once launched popular uprisings, going back to the great Royal Indian Navy mutiny of 1946; that had toppled military dictatorships; that had been home to Pakistan's best and brightest writers, dancers, singers, architects, and atheists; and that once had a healthy Jewish population and synagogues was now a hotbed of Jew-hatred and pseudo anti-Americanism that defied the most elementary logic. Almost every anti-American millionaire who had not yet acquired a Western passport would spout his share of hatred towards the United States – and then moments later ask me how he could send his son to the States so he could secure a green card and then sponsor the rest of the family.

The hatred of Jews was not restricted to the Karachi Press Club or the charity balls held by the Pakistani upper crust. It was aired on television talk shows as well. At quaint tea parties hosted by blue-eyed, blond begum-sahibs in the clubs that have become the hub of the proletariat-mimicking Islamist bourgeoisie of Pakistan, expressing hatred of the Jew, it seemed, is the easiest way to establish one's intellectual credentials.

Later I leafed through my copy of *The Protocols of the Elders of Zion*. *The Protocols* is a collection of articles concocted in 1895 by the Russian Czar's secret police in order to depict the growing strength of Marxists as a Jewish conspiracy. It was first published in Russia in the early 1900s, and claimed to expose a plan by the Jewish people to achieve global domination. It was published again after the 1905 Russian Revolution, when the ruling monarchy, stung by the mass uprising, used it to blame the Jews for instigating the workers' strikes, peasant uprisings, and military mutinies. The monarchy had also invoked *The Protocols* when it blamed the Jews for Russia's defeat at the hands of Japan in 1904. By the time the Czar was overthrown in the Bolshevik Revolution of 1917, anti-communist Russian exiles made *The Protocols* an instrument for blaming Jews for that upheaval, too. They depicted the Bolsheviks as overwhelmingly Jewish and allegedly executing the plan embodied in *The Protocols*.

In the 1920s, the London *Times* exposed *The Protocols* as a forgery. The newspaper revealed that much of the material was plagiarized from earlier works of political satire having nothing to do with Jews.

Today, the primary consumer of this forgery is the Muslim world, where *The Protocols* is cited as an authentic document validating the widespread belief that Jews control the world. Over time, *The Protocols* has been used to blame the Jews for both the horrors of communism and the excesses of capitalism, though this irony appears to have escaped the attention of its readers.

Pick up a newspaper in any part of the Arab world and you're likely to see Hitler's swastika superimposed on the Israeli flag. Such anti-Semitic imagery was once unheard of, but today caricatures of Jews – with fangs and exaggerated hook noses, for example – are common. Arab intellectuals and political leaders often insist that such images reflect a dislike for Israelis and Zionism, yes, but not necessarily of Jews and Judaism. However, a look at school textbooks shows otherwise. In one government-approved textbook for Jordanian high school students, Jews are described as innately deceitful and corrupt. "Up to the present," it states, "they are the masters of usury and leaders of sexual exhibitionism and prostitution."[1] It is not uncommon to hear Islamist televangelists and Saudi clerics in their sermons refer to Jews as descendants of apes and monkeys.

In Pakistan too, textbooks continue to depict Jews in a bad light. Conservative officials regularly block attempts by the government to delete anti-Jewish material from textbooks. In one instance, the textbook board agreed, under pressure from the World Bank and other funding agencies, to remove a section from ninth- and tenth-grade textbooks that urged pupils to "fight against those who believe not in Allah" and that asked for "Allah's curse" on Jews and Christians. However, after removing the offensive text from books for grades nine and ten, board officials sneaked it into the books for grades eleven and twelve.[2]

There is also evidence that Muslims are picking up anti-Semitism that is rooted in Christian dogma, which for centuries had little traction in the Muslim world. When Pope John Paul II visited Damascus in 2001, President Bashar al-Assad greeted him with a speech in which he suggested it was Jews who had killed Jesus. When Assad's crude attempt to curry favour with the pope drew no response, his minister of religious affairs, Muhammad Ziyadah, went a step further. In a separate speech made before the pontiff, Ziyadah said: "We must be fully aware of what the enemies of God and malicious Zionism conspire to commit against Christianity and Islam."

There is some truth to the claim that Judeophobia among Muslims is partly a consequence of the creation of the state of Israel and its continued occupation of the West Bank. However, there is clear evidence that contemporary anti-Semitism predates Israel and Zionism by decades, and that it seeped into the Arab world from Europe as part and parcel of nineteenth-century colonization.

Few Jewish scholars would deny that notwithstanding the dhimmi, or second-class, status of Jews under all caliphates, life for Jews under Islam in the Arab world and North Africa was far better than in Christian Europe. At a time when Maimonides, the pre-eminent medieval Jewish philosopher and one of the greatest Torah scholars of the Middle Ages, served Saladin as his physician in twelfth-century Cairo, such a relationship would have been impossible to imagine in the domain of the Catholic pope or the Orthodox patriarch. Imagine Maimonides gracing the court of Louis VII of France.

For centuries, a virulent form of anti-Semitism afflicted Europe. That disease has now, unfortunately, become endemic in the Islamic world. Even while Jews were an integral part of Islamic life – as in eighth-century Baghdad, tenth-century Spain, twelfth-century Cairo, and sixteenth-century Turkey – the Christian world remained hostile towards them: they were the killers of Christ, and some Christians believed they re-enacted this ultimate evil by drinking Christian blood every Passover.

Although the Quran has positive as well as numerous harsh verses about Jews, the caliphs – except for the odd aberration – were enlightened secularists for their time. For them, the bottom line was that as long as Jews accepted Islamic political authority and the social and political limitations this imposed upon them, they were fully protected under Islamic law.

Islamist apologists of today may recoil at the thought, but for the many competing caliphates during the glory days of Islam, from the ninth through the twelfth centuries, good governance and the welfare of the population as well as stability were the key motivators, not jihad or sharia law.

Let us not pretend that prejudice against Jews did not exist in medieval Islamdom. It did, and at times this prejudice turned violent, but eras of cooperation and relative peace were also often characteristic of Jewish life under Islam. It was during the time of Maimonides that the forced conversion of Jews to Islam was initiated in both Muslim Spain (under the jihadi Mohads) and Yemen (where the Iraqi Abbasids fought against the Egyptian Ayyubids for control). As hard-line Islamic extremists gained ground in Spain and Yemen, Jews were targeted quite viciously.

According to Bernard Lewis, one of the foremost scholars of Islamic history, the anti-Semitic ideas of Christianity first entered the Muslim world because of Islam's conquest of Europe, which resulted in many Christians converting to Islam. Later, when Europe hit back and colonised the Middle East, its anti-Jewish ideas infiltrated the Arab world. "European anti-Semitism, in both its theological and racist versions, was essentially alien to Islamic traditions, culture, and modes of thought," writes Lewis. He notes that "prejudices existed in the Islamic world, as did occasional hostility, but not what could be called anti-Semitism, for there was no attribution of cosmic evil. And on the whole, Jews fared better under Muslim rule than Christians did."[3]

According to Lewis, it was Christian converts to Islam who brought anti-Semitism into the Arab world. Later, Greek Orthodox Christians who found themselves living under Ottoman rule are said to have introduced the notion of the blood libel into the Middle East.* "The blood libel was endemic in these parts [Greece] and was brought

---

* Blood libel is the allegation against a person or group that engages in human sacrifice and in which the blood of the victim is used in various rituals. Although Christians in Europe from the twelfth century onwards have levelled blood libel against Jews, the most recent high-profile claim was made in 1984, when the Saudi Arabian delegate to the UN Human Rights Commission conference on religious tolerance stated: "Jews have indeed been the victims of discriminations throughout the centuries. But why? Let them answer this question themselves. The Talmud says that any Jew who does not drink every year the blood of a non-Jew will be damned forever."

to the notice of Ottoman authorities through the usual disturbances it caused at Easter time. This was the first time this story became known in Muslim lands."[4]

In the mid-1800s, with the rise of European maritime power and the decline of Ottoman Turkey, there was a natural alignment between Christian Arabs and Christian Europeans. This contact brought numerous blood-libel charges against Jews living in the Ottoman Empire. Very often, it was business interests, not religion, that were at the root of the conflict. Christian businesses saw Jews as their main competitors in the Middle East, and it was easy to inflame Arab passions against the Jews. Lewis writes that anti-Semitism "was actively encouraged by Western emissaries of various kinds, including consular representatives on the one hand, and priests and missionaries on the other."[5] A famous example was the 1840 Damascus blood-libel case, in which the French consul backed the Capuchin monks who had accused the Jews of blood libel.

By the end of the century, there were calls for Christian-Muslim solidarity against the Jews. Soon, the allegations against the Jews of blood libel were coming from Muslim quarters, not Christian.

In 1856, another event inside the Ottoman caliphate caused Islamic clerics to suspect the hidden hand of the kuffar. At the end of the Crimean War, Turkey implemented the Reform Act, which gave equal status to all Ottoman subjects, irrespective of religious background, and forbade discrimination against non-Muslims. This was a huge step forward in the Ottoman effort to modernize as a European power and not remain the "sick man of Europe," as the Russians had referred to the six-hundred-year-old empire.

The old order, premised on the supremacy of Islam, yet providing protection to Jews and Christians as wards of the state, had stood for more than a millennium. Suddenly, however, Jewish citizens were deemed equal to Muslims, and the Islamist clergy as well as the privileged classes resented this. Murmurs of a Jewish conspiracy began to circulate. A memorandum by an Ottoman official reflects the angst of the Muslim population: "Today we have lost our sacred national rights won by the blood of our fathers and forefathers. At a time when the Islamic community is the ruling community, it has been deprived of the sacred right. This is a day of weeping and mourning for the people of Islam. As for the non-Muslims, this day, when they gained equality with the ruling community, was a day of rejoicing."[6]

Decades later, when the "Young Turks" overthrew Sultan Abdul Hamid II in 1908, their opponents, in order to discredit the supporters of constitutional reform, accused the revolutionaries of being supported by Jews. Even today, the Islamic world is rife with rumours that the father of the modern Turkish republic, Kemal Atatürk, who abolished the caliphate in 1924, was secretly a Jew. While the Ottomans were adjusting to the reality of an awakened and industrialized Europe, and attempting to modernize their society, the doors were meanwhile opening to all sorts of European ideas and philosophies: nationalism, Marxism, and, yes, anti-Semitism.

The first modern anti-Semitic literature in Arabic appeared in 1869, in the form of the confessions of a Moldavian rabbi who had converted to Christianity. Members of the Christian Arab community in Beirut published the Arabic translation, which supposedly revealed "the horrors of the Jewish religion." Later, in 1890, a Christian author, Habib Faris, published a book in Cairo called *The Talmudic Human Sacrifices*, accusing the Jews of ritual sacrifices, which were attributed to Talmudic teachings. Jews had lived among Muslims for nearly fourteen hundred years, yet it seems no one in Baghdad, Cordoba, or Cairo had heard of these "human sacrifices" until the Europeans came to enlighten us about our cousins. It must be added that the caliph was totally opposed to the distribution of these anti-Jewish texts; authorities closed down publishers and shuttered newspapers to prevent public disorder.

However, the publication that firmly established anti-Semitism in the Muslim consciousness was *The Protocols of the Elders of Zion*. The forgery was first translated into Arabic by an Arab Christian, and published in Jerusalem in 1926. From Jerusalem's Christian quarters to the offices of the city's Mufti (the spiritual and religious head of the city's Muslim community) was not too far a distance, and soon this piece of fiction became the ideological tool that motivated opposition to the trickle of European Jews who were beginning to settle in British Palestine. The book from Europe gave additional credence to the existing classical tales in Islamic literature about the devious nature of the Jew.

However, it was only after the end of World War II, when the rest of the world had dismissed *The Protocols* as a fake, that the tract found new life in the Middle East. *The Protocols* were reintroduced in Cairo in 1951, with a fresh Arabic translation. Defeat of the combined Arab armies in 1948 at the hands of Israel gave fresh impetus to Judeophobia. The baton of anti-Semitism was passed from Europe to the Arab world, and work began to blend the characterisation of Jews in *The Protocols* with their depiction in Islamic literature as untrustworthy sons of pigs and apes. The Jews were a secret society, it was said, a cabal that controlled the world. How else could we explain the inability of the combined armies of Egypt, Iraq, Jordan, Lebanon, and Syria to defeat the infant state of Israel?

After all, the argument went, had it not been for the Jewish conspiracy and Jewish control of the UN, the U.S.A., and the U.S.S.R., surely the Arab armies would have won. When asked why God had not intervened to help the Muslims, theologians answered that Muslims were being put through a test by Allah and if we returned to the path of seventh-century Islam, we would see the Jews defeated the way they were in the battle of Khaybar. If proof was needed of the devious and conniving methods of world Jewry, *The Protocols of the Elders of Zion* was produced as evidence.

It was in this climate of despair and failure in the Arab world of the late 1940s that the Islamist movement would discover its Lenin as well as its Trotsky in the same person – a man whose ideas still define the jihad launched on Western civilization by Osama bin Laden and his deputy Ayman al-Zawahiri.

Sayyid Qutb (also spelled Syed Qutub), who was born in 1906 and executed by the Egyptian dictator Gamal Abdel Nasser in 1966, is best known in the Arab world for his magnum opus, *Fi zilal al-Qur'an* (In the Shade of the Quran), a thirty-volume commentary on the Quran. However, it is Qutb's influence on the worldwide Islamist movement that is his claim to fame in the Muslim world and in the West. Even today, nearly fifty years after his death, Qutb's impact can be seen in the actions of al Qaeda. Nasser may have jailed Qutb and in the end eliminated him, but in doing so, the dictator also immortalized the dead jihadi.

In 1948, Sayyid Qutb went to the United States on a scholarship. While in Colorado, instead of absorbing the workings of a democracy, he began writing his first major book, *Al-'adala al-Ijtima'iyya fi-l-Islam* (Social Justice in Islam). America, it turned out, was not a pleasant experience for the ultraconservative Islamist from Egypt. Qutb believed in the Quranic edict "Men are the managers of women's affairs." What he saw in America's pre-feminist women of the 1940s challenged his manhood. On his return to Egypt, he had this to say: "The American girl is well acquainted with her body's seductive capacity . . . She knows seductiveness lies in the round breasts, the full buttocks, and in the shapely thighs, sleek legs, and she shows all this and does not hide it."[7]

Even after he returned to Egypt, Qutb was never able to find a woman of sufficient "moral purity and discretion" – essentially a desexualized woman chaste and religious enough to deserve his pious company – and resigned himself to bachelorhood. (Decades later, another jihadi terrorist would also find it difficult to find female companionship – the Fort Hood, Texas, shooter, Maj. Nidal Hasan. Like Qutb, Hasan "desired a virgin of Arabic descent – a woman in her 20s who wore the hijab, understood the Koran and prayed five times a day." The Fort Hood jihadi would fail to find such a virgin, even after he hired an Islamic matchmaker who introduced him to 150 single women.)[8]

During Qutb's long imprisonment in Egypt, during which he was regularly tortured by the Nasser regime, he wrote a manifesto of political Islam called "Maalim fil-Tareeq," which has now been translated as *Milestones*. This work represents the full expression of his radical anti-secular and anti-Western ideology, in which he expanded on his doctrine of armed jihad. He wrote:

> As to persons who attempt to defend the concept of Islamic Jihad by interpreting it in a narrow sense of the current concept of defensive war, and who do research to prove that the battles fought in Islamic Jihad were all for defence of the homeland of Islam – some of them considering the homeland of Islam to be just the Arabian peninsula – against the aggression of neighbouring powers, they lack understanding of the nature of Islam and its primary aim. Such an attempt is nothing but a product of a mind defeated by the present difficult conditions and by the attacks of the treacherous Orientalists on the Islamic Jihad. Can anyone say that Abu Bakr, Umar or Othman had been satisfied that the Roman and Persian powers were not going to attack the Arabian peninsula; they would not have strived to spread the message of Islam throughout the world? . . . It would be naïve to assume that a call is raised to free the whole of humankind throughout earth, and it is confined to preaching and exposition.

Qutb was blunt about his expectations of Muslims who lived in the West but remained loyal to its enemies.

> A Muslim has no country except that part of the earth where Shariah of God is established and human relationships are based on the foundation of relationship with God; a Muslim has no nationality except his belief, which makes him a member of the Muslim community in Dar-ul-Islam [the Muslim world]; a Muslim has no relatives except those who share the belief in God. . . . A Muslim has no relationship with his mother, father, brother, wife and other family members except through their relationship with the Creator, and then they are also joined through blood. . . . A Muslim can have only two possible relations with Dar-ul-Harb [the West]: peace with a contractual agreement, or war. A country with which there is a treaty [of subservience] will not be considered the home of Islam.[9]

In 1951, Qutb wrote an essay that clearly defined his view of the Jewish world. Titled "Ma'rakatuna ma'a al-Yahud" (Our Fight against the Jews), the essay was later included in a collection published in Saudi Arabia in 1970. The Saudi booklet bore the same title as Qutb's essay and was widely circulated in the Arab world, where it became the defining text on the Islamist view of Jews.

The 1970 Saudi version linked Qutb's work with the discredited *Protocols of the Elders of Zion*. Qutb's essay is pockmarked with footnotes by the Saudi editor, who uses *The Protocols* to prove Qutb's allegations against the Jews. For the editor, as for many contemporary Islamic authors, *The Protocols* were confirmation of anti-Jewish ideas rooted in Islamic tradition.

In his essay, Qutb not only dwelled on the nature of the Jew and the supposed Jewish goal of destroying Islam, he presented a simple answer to this challenge: Muslims must defeat the Jews. He wrote, "The Jews will be satisfied only with the destruction of this religion (Islam)."[10] He depicted Jews as the inevitable enemies of Islam and the creation of the state of Israel as the manifestation of Jewish revenge against Muslims for their humiliation in Medina fourteen centuries earlier.

Writing in the aftermath of the 1948 war with Israel, Qutb suggested that the Arabs were defeated because they failed to understand the Quran and did not follow its directives to Muslims regarding their relations with Jews. He wrote that there is no hope for Muslims in their struggle against Jews unless they have a Quranic understanding of their enemy's weakness. Qutb quoted from the Quran (Sura Al Hashr), which asks Muslims not to fear the Jews:

> They will not fight you together,
> except in fortified townships,
> Or behind walls,
> Strong is their fighting spirit amongst themselves;
> You would think they are united,
> But their hearts are divided.

In Qutb's viewpoint, God had promised punishment for the Jews for their evil-doing nature. God had inflicted such a punishment twice in destroying their Temples in Jerusalem and had promised punishments to the Jews throughout their history. Even Hitler, according to Qutb, was sent by Allah to rule over the Jews. He stressed that the only reason contemporary Muslims could not defeat the Jews was because they had not returned to the Quran for guidance.

This argument leaves some Muslims, like me, to wonder: If God made it possible for the Babylonians to destroy the first Temple, built by King Solomon (prophet Suleiman in the Quran), and defeat the Jews in 516 BC, why have Muslims not been able to do the same? After all, the Babylonians were not following the Quran, so why would Allah show this favour to polytheists and idol worshippers, but deny it to us Muslims? Have we not tried to emulate the Babylonians in 1948, 1956, 1967, and 1973? Yet each time we Muslims have ended up losing more territory than before. Is it possible Allah is sending us a message that we are ignoring?

In Sayyid Qutb's mind, there is no mistake: Arab defeat at the hands of the Jews is evidence that we Muslims are not following the laws of Allah as written by mere mortals in the corpus of jurisprudence called sharia. According to Qutb, if only we embraced sharia, then lo and behold, Israel would simply melt away before our eyes. And those pesky Jews would be driven out of the Holy Land the way they were expelled by the Babylonians and, five centuries later, the Romans.

Qutb states in the essay that it is God himself who determines the results of all wars. However, he does not reflect at all on the possibility that if the Muslim-Jewish conflict in the Middle East is stage-managed by Allah himself, then perhaps the verdict of the Divine is written on the wall.

Qutb insists that if Muslims returned to "proper" Islam (as interpreted by him), the ummah, the Muslim community, would triumph. The problem with that argument is that Hamas has taken that route but has not succeeded any more than have the secular Palestinians of Fatah or the Popular Front for the Liberation of Palestine (PFLP). In fact, by following the guidelines of Qutb and his followers, such as the late Sheikh Yassin and the exiled Khaled Meshaal, the Muslims of Gaza are today worse off than their compatriots in the West Bank.

If a Muslim were to take Sayyid Qutb's essay as a guide to understanding Jews (and many Islamists do), he or she would be hard pressed not to view world history as one endless battle that can be won only by completely annihilating the Jewish people. Repeatedly, Qutb depicts

Jews as the eternal enemy of Islam, with whom Muslims are locked in a divinely ordained battle to the end. The essay leads to four conclusions:

- The Jews have opposed Islam as enemies of the Prophet from the moment the "Islamic State" was established in Medina.
- It was the Jews who were instrumental in creating the Shia-Sunni divide in Islam.
- The Jews will only be satisfied once the religion of Islam has been destroyed.
- The war between Muslims and Jews has been raging for fourteen centuries and will continue in all corners of this earth.

Among Qutb's many allegations against the Jews, the one that is most dangerous and that has done tremendous damage within Islam is the charge that the Shia-Sunni divide is the result of a Jewish conspiracy and that Shia Muslims are a product of Jewish machinations, and thus their fifth column inside Islamdom.

Qutb also writes about how the Jews conspired to sow dissension among the factions vying for power after the death of Prophet Muhammad, discord that led to the murder of the third caliph, Uthman bin Affan, by a rioting mob. He writes in the essay that the man who incited the people and set them loose to kill caliph Uthman was Jewish.

Sayyid Qutb is prone to lie with a sense of self-righteousness that is the hallmark of most Islamists. The person he accuses of being the Jew who incited the killing of Uthman and of fomenting the schism in Islam was a man named Abdullah ibn Safa. By all accounts he was a Yemeni Jew who had converted to Islam. So what? All the Muslims involved in this first civil war of Islam – the Muslims backing Uthman and those opposing him – were not born in Islam. Some, like Caliph Uthman, were former pagans, while others had come to Islam from Christianity, Judaism, and Zoroastrianism. To use the Jewish ancestry of Abdullah ibn Safa (who the Shias, besides, claim is a fictitious character) as a sign of Jewish deviousness, when other converted Jews were supporting Uthman, is unadulterated Judeophobia that has gone unchallenged for centuries. Qutb's essay epitomizes the Islamist tradition of passing the buck to the kuffar. No matter how badly we Muslims bungle our diplomacy, there is always the Jew to blame for the mess we create. One could argue that if a Jew can be blamed for the murder of Caliph Uthman, then a Jew can also be blamed for the Darfur genocide or the Muslim-on-Muslim slaughter in Pakistan.

Sayyid Qutb's Jew-hatred has had dreadful consequences in the Muslim communities where Shia and Sunni Muslims peacefully coexisted for centuries on the Indian subcontinent, where the descendants of the Prophet Muhammad took refuge among Hindu kingdoms as they were hunted down by the Umayyad Arab caliphate in Damascus. Today, the anti-Semitism spread by Islamists like Qutb and their Saudi sponsors has mutated into hatred of the Shias, since it is hard to find a single Jew in all of Pakistan. Among the slanderous myths that have come from *The Protocols* and been tweaked to apply to Shia Muslims are the following:

- Shias slaughter young Sunni children and use their blood and meat during the feast offerings at the time of Ashura to commemorate the martyrdom of Imam Hussein, grandson of the Prophet.
- Shias inject their semen into food they serve to Sunnis.
- Shias disembowel their dead seniors, extract a clear liquid, and use it in the preparation of food to be served to other Muslims during the holy month of Muharram.
- During the celebration of Nawroz (when Shias in Pakistan and Iran gather to read Sufi prayers), Shia Muslims indulge in incestuous orgies.

These are some of the lies being propagated by Sunni Islamist groups, such as Sipah-e-Sahaba, that are allied to the Taliban and al Qaeda, where the teachings of Sayyid Qutb are introduced by the so-called Arab Afghans who come to Pakistan and Afghanistan armed with

The Protocols, Milestones, and Qutb's essay "Our Fight against the Jews." When they can't find any Jews to blame, the next best thing for them to target is Shia Muslims. It is not uncommon to hear Arabs from Sunni-dominated societies say that they are "free of the swines and the Shias."

In sweeping statements that depict Jews as a monolithic organism stretching from seventh-century Medina to his own day, Qutb claims that this enemy of Islam is waging a two-pronged attack against Muslims – one physical and the other religious. Qutb accuses Jews of being both cowardly and conniving, and of creating confusion in the minds of Muslims about their new faith, Islam, by sowing doubt about their faith, and by hatching plots to make Muslim fight fellow Muslim.

There is no doubt that the debate about Islam and Judaism that took place in Medina in 622 between Prophet Muhammad and the Jewish rabbis of the city must have been intense. It is within the realm of possibility that the Jewish leadership of Medina resisted the emerging force of Islam, resulting in conflict and bitterness. However, Sayyid Qutb takes a ludicrous leap by suggesting that the war against Islam is one long continuous and continuing struggle, and he fails to acknowledge that by the eighth century, Jews had become an integral part of Muslim societies.

Even the rise of the Muslim intelligentsia in the twentieth century is attributed by Qutb to a Jewish conspiracy. He accuses the Jews of installing regimes in the Muslim world in order to conspire against the Muslim community. He writes that in addition to installing favourable governments in the Muslim world, the Jews have sent "a massive army of agents in the form of professors, philosophers, doctors and research-ers – sometimes also writers, poets, scientists and journalists – carry-ing Muslim names, because they are of Muslim descent!!. And some of them are from the ranks of the Muslim religious authority."[11]

Qutb is earnest in his belief that a secret Jewish hand is behind every Muslim who wishes to break free from the clutches of Islamism and the authority of clerics. He accuses these traitorous, renegade Muslims, who supposedly dance to the tune of the Jews, of intending "to break the creed of the Muslims, in all ways – through research, learning, literature, science and journalism; by prying the principles of the creed and Sharia."[12] Of Muslims who desire secularism, a separation of religion and state, an equality of men and women, Qutb says they are Muslims in name only.

It is little wonder that Islamist followers of Qutb today consider the founder of the Turkish republic, Kemal Atatürk, to be a Jew. Why? Because he modernized the country. Any Muslim who dares to dream of technological progress and material happiness is slapped with the same label, as if deprivation and stagnation were the necessities of Islam, not the belief in oneness of God and Muhammad as his Messenger. Consumed by his fundamentally ingrained hatred of Jews, Qutb blames them for everything that in his view is wrong with the world today. At the end of his notorious essay, he writes: "Behind the doctrine of atheistic materialism was a 'Jew'; behind the doctrine of animalistic sexuality was a Jew; and behind the destruction of the family and the shattering of sacred relationships in society was also a Jew" – the three being Karl Marx, Sigmund Freud, and Émile Durkheim.[13]

Sayyid Qutb's essay has had a lasting effect on the Islamist psyche. Here is a sampling of what passes for acceptable speech on Egyptian TV today. On Al-Rahma TV on October 31, 2009, Egyptian cleric Hazem Shuman said about Jews: "Your turn has come at last, you offspring of apes and pigs, you most accursed creatures created by Allah, you people who have harmed the Prophet again and again. . . . I have a message for every Jew on the face of the earth. The army of Muhammad will return. O offspring of apes and pigs, the day of vengeance is nearing. O most accursed creatures created by Allah, those who swore before the Prophet Muhammad to die, are returning.

Wait for us and you will see, you most accursed creatures." And on Cairo's Al-Nas TV, on December 29, 2009, Egyptian cleric Muhammad Hussein Yaqub said, "The Jews are our enemies. Allah will annihilate them at our hands. This is something we know for certain. We know this for certain – not because I say so, but because Allah said so. 'You shall find that the people strongest in enmity to the believers are the Jews and the polytheists.'"

Defenders of Qutb often gloss over his ideological war against the West and the Jews, claiming they follow the man because of his magnificent multivolume magnum opus, In the Shade of the Quran. Others say he cannot be blamed for what his followers do, but this is a weak excuse for someone whose terrorist tentacles reach from the past well into the future. Today's jihadi terrorists, led by Ayman al-Zawahiri and bin Laden, are not that far from the guru of world Islamism. One of Sayyid Qutb's closest supporters was his brother Muhammad, who became a professor of Islamic studies in Saudi Arabia while editing and publishing his late brother's writings. The notorious Ayman al-Zawahiri was one of his students before becoming a member of the Egyptian Islamic Jihad and, later, mentor and deputy to Osama bin Laden and a leading member of al Qaeda. Bin Laden, too, was acquainted with Qutb's brother. A friend of Osama's claims that bin Laden regularly attended weekly public lectures by Muhammad Qutb at the university, and that both men "read Sayyid Qutb."[14]

Sayyid Qutb worked on his Islamist goals in the years after the Second World War, but his ideology was not born in isolation. Much of the anti-Semitism that even today weaves itself through the Islamic centres of North America and Europe has its origin in the period leading up to the war. Qutb was the inheritor of a fascist ideology nurtured in the 1930s by another character whose shadow looms long over the Middle East – the Grand Mufti of Palestine, an ally of Adolf Hitler. While tens of thousands of other Muslims were dying fighting the

Nazi war machine, the mufti and his allies, the Muslim Brotherhood, backed the Third Reich and eagerly waited for Rommel's Afrika Korps to advance from Egypt into British Palestine and annihilate the Jewish population.

CHAPTER THREE

Allah, Hitler, and the Mufti

Hitler's Third Reich was on its last legs as the first units of the Soviet Red Army reached the Vistula River outside Warsaw on September 13, 1944. In August, Paris had been liberated by the Free French and the United States 4th Infantry Division. Nevertheless, the defeat of the once mighty Wehrmacht was of little solace to the prisoners in concentration camps awaiting execution by the SS, including four women nabbed by the Gestapo for aiding the French Resistance.

The same morning the Red Army reached the Vistula, a thousand kilometres to the west of Warsaw, as the sun rose over the concentration camp at Dachau, a shackled Nora Baker and three other women faced the firing squad. Friedrich Wilhelm Ruppert, the SS trooper in charge of executions, made the women kneel before he gave the orders to shoot. Eyewitness accounts say that one by one the troopers shot Madeleine Damerment, Eliane Plewman, and Yolande Beekman. However, when it came time to shoot Nora Baker, the SS had a special treat for the darker-skinned woman, who pretended to be French and was suspected by the Germans of being Creole. Ruppert stepped forward and hit Nora Baker with his gun butt. When she fell to the ground, he kicked her till she bled. After the thirty-year-old screamed one last word in defiance – "*Liberté*" – the SS trooper shot her in the back of the head. Nora Baker was not her real name and she was not Creole, but of Indian ancestry.

Nora Baker, the woman the Nazis had captured in Paris as a radio operator working for British Intelligence and the French Resistance, was in fact an Indian princess, a Muslim by the name of Noor Inayat Khan. She was the great-great-granddaughter of Tipu Sultan, the last Muslim sovereign of South India, who died fighting the British in 1799. Ironically, the sultan's descendant would die fighting for the British.*

Noor Inayat Khan was not the only Muslim who died fighting the Nazis. Tens of thousands of my people gave their lives to stop the Holocaust and destroy Hitler's killing machine. If India's Princess Noor represented heroism and valour in covert military action, other Muslims, like the Albanian family of Destan and Lime Balla, represented silent courage that earned them honourable mention in Jerusalem's Yad Vashem – Israel's official memorial to the Jewish victims of the Holocaust – as "Righteous Among the Nations." Decades later, Lime Balla would write:

> In 1943, at the time of Ramadan, seventeen people came to our village of Shengjergj from Tirana [capital of Albania]. They were all escaping from the Germans. At first I did not know they were Jews. We divided them among the villagers. My family took in three brothers by the name of Lazar. We were poor – we didn't even have a dining table – but we never allowed them to pay for the food and shelter. I went into the forest to chop wood and haul water. We grew vegetables in our garden so we all had plenty to eat. The Jews were sheltered in our village for fifteen months. We dressed them all like farmers, like us. Even the local police knew that the villagers were sheltering Jews. I knew they spoke many different

---

* Sixty years after Inayat Khan's death, Canadian author Shauna Singh Baldwin would immortalize her in the book *The Tiger Claw* (Random House of Canada, 2005).

languages. In December 1945, the Jews left for Pristina where a nephew of ours, who was a partisan, helped them. After that we lost all contact with the Lazar brothers. It was not until 1990, forty-five years later, that Schlomo and Mordecai Lazar made contact with us from Israel. All of us were Muslims. We were sheltering God's children under our Besa.[1]

As Nazis hunted Jews across Europe, Muslims were not only saving Jewish lives by offering refuge and protection. One Muslim family saved a Jewish treasure that was centuries old.

Meet Dervis Korkut of Bosnia, who, in 1942, was the curator of the Sarajevo Museum that housed the renowned "Sarajevo Haggadah." This superbly illuminated fourteenth-century volume was the best known and most admired of Haggadahs in the world.[*] (The Haggadah is used as a guide to the Exodus story recounted at the Seder.) When the commanding officer at Sarajevo, Gen. Johann Hans Fortner, came looking for the famous Haggadah to confiscate the historic text, he was told that another, unidentified Nazi officer had already taken it away.

In fact Dervis Korkut had hidden the 109 bleached calfskin pages elsewhere in the museum. He later entrusted the Haggadah to a Muslim family, who kept it in their farmhouse, deep in the hills of Bosnia, for the duration of the war.

Rescuing the Haggadah was not Korkut's only act of solidarity with the Jewish people. In 1941, when the Nazis occupied Yugoslavia, the SS began recruiting Balkan Muslims, hoping to capitalize on their supposed anti-Jewish attitudes. Dervis Korkut submitted a courageously worded position paper to the government titled "Anti-Semitism Is Foreign to the Muslims of Bosnia-Herzegovina."

---

[*] In 2008, Pulitzer Prize–winning author Geraldine Brooks wrote a novel based on the story of this Haggadah, titled *People of the Book* (Viking).

Korkut and his wife, Servet, would also save the life of Mira Papo, a Jewish woman who was part of a communist partisan unit being hunted by the Nazis. As the Nazis closed in on her, Mira was introduced to Korkut, who smuggled her into his home. She was given the name Ameera and dressed in Muslim attire to avoid suspicion. Neighbours were told that Ameera had come from a village to work as a nanny for the Korkuts' newborn son. Mira "Ameera" Papo lived with her Muslim family for four months, until she was spirited out of Sarajevo by family friends. In 1994, Dervis and Servet Korkut were posthumously honoured by Israel as "Righteous Among the Nations" and their names engraved at the Yad Vashem.

The story does not end there. During the Kosovo war of 1999, the Korkuts' daughter Lamija Jaha and her husband became refugees in Macedonia after fleeing the Serbian assault on Pristina. Because of what her parents had done for Mira Papo and the Sarajevo Haggadah, Lamija and her family were accorded residency in Israel, where she now lives among the Jews.

There were many more Muslims who fought the Nazis. Among them was Palestinian Hazim Khalidi, a graduate of the London School of Economics who volunteered in the Indian army's Palestine Regiment and saw action in Syria and Libya. Few people have heard of the Palestine Regiment, a unit in which Jew and Muslim fought side by side against Hitler's Afrika Korps in Libya.

At the time of Kristallnacht, in 1938, the only Muslim monarch in Europe, King Zog of Albania, issued four hundred passports to German Jews so that they could escape Germany as Albanian citizens. Another Muslim monarch, the Arab King of Morocco – a direct descendant of Prophet Muhammad – went out of his way to protect the lives of his Jewish subjects. When the German-influenced Vichy government of France announced that it had prepared 200,000 yellow stars for the Jews of Morocco, King Mohammed v replied that he would need fifty more for himself and other members of his royal family. He refused to make any distinction between his Muslim and Jewish citizens.

Muslims from places as diverse as Uzbekistan, Azerbaijan, and Tajikistan in central Asia and France's Tirailleurs Senegalese in Africa fought and gave their lives to end the Holocaust. Tens of thousands of Indian Muslims fell in such far-off battlegrounds as Singapore and the Sahara. Muslims contributed to the victory in battles from Stalingrad, where Hitler's advance into the Soviet Union was blunted, to North Africa, where they helped send Hitler's Desert Fox, Erwin Rommel, scurrying back to his den in Berlin.

In the cemeteries of El Alamein, Egypt, lie the dead Muslims – the Muhammads, the Khans, and the Ismails – who gave their lives so that Nazism could be defeated. The cemeteries of Stalingrad bear the names of the young central Asian Muslims whose tombstones remind us of the human spirit that came together to stop the Nazi war machine.

But while the Muslim King Zog of Albania smuggled Jews out of Germany and King Mohammed of Morocco was giving them protection, there were other Muslims actively serving Nazi Germany.

Most were recruited from among the Muslim soldiers of the Red Army taken prisoner during the Nazi invasion of the Soviet Union in 1941–42.

The architects of this recruitment of Muslims into the Nazi army were two men with very different backgrounds. The first was a Muslim German of Uzbek ancestry, Veli Kayum Khan, who had fled communism and made Germany his home in 1922. Khan was the head of Operation Tiger B, assigned to form an exclusive Muslim regiment to aid the Nazi war effort on the Eastern Front. He was armed with an Islamic endorsement from one of the most prominent figures of the Muslim world, the Grand Mufti of Palestine.

Operation Tiger B soon expanded, and the Wehrmacht established the 450th Infantry Battalion. By 1943, Veli Kayum Khan's efforts would result in three more regiments that were all amalgamated to form a new division under the SS known as the East Turkestan Armed Formation.[2]

The Muslim soldiers in this division wore the regular German army uniforms but with one addition: an armpatch outlining the historic Chah-I-Zindeh mosque in Samarkand, with the phrase, Biz Allah Bilen (God be with us) under the mosque emblem.

Veli Kayum Khan may have spoken the Turkic languages of the former Soviet soldiers, but it is unlikely he would have met the same success in his recruitment without the Islamic endorsement by the Grand Mufti of Palestine.

Hajj al-Husayni was a guest of the Führer assigned the task of whipping up anti-Jewish sentiment among Muslims around the world. While Muslims from India to Senegal were dying fighting the Wehrmacht, Mufti Hajj al-Husayni was photographed with Hitler and often dined with Himmler. The Nazis even had him preside over the opening of the Islamische Zentral-Institut (Islamic Central Institute) in Berlin in December 1942.

Hajj Al-Husayni's flirtation with Hitler could be dismissed as trivial in the larger scheme of things, but his fascination with fascism did not end with the fall of Berlin. He was lucky. He had the distinction of being the only former associate of Hitler who escaped and was never tried as a war criminal. While prominent Nazis were hunted down and tried, Hajj al-Husayni, with 50,000 marks in his pocket from the German Foreign Office, was allowed to escape, first to France – where he was put up in the Villa Les Roses in the Parisian suburb of Louveciennes with a chauffeur, two bodyguards, and his secretary – and then to Egypt, where he was granted asylum. Unwilling to risk offending the large Muslim population in Egypt, and to avoid any problems in Palestine, which was still under British mandate, Britain looked the other way as the mufti ended up in Cairo.

Yugoslavia, where the mufti had organized the Muslim SS division responsible for the murder of thousands of Marshal Tito's partisans, demanded that Hajj al-Husayni be tried for war crimes. Britain, reeling after the surprise defeat of Churchill two months after he won the war, was now governed by Clement Atlee's Labour Party. The last thing Atlee's government wanted was unrest in the colonies. Britain wanted out of both Palestine and India, and in both places, partition was in the air and Muslims were restless. Not wanting to offend the Muslims – assuming wrongly that they were at the beck and call of a pro-Hitler mufti – London made a feeble request to France, asking them to hand over al-Husayni. The French balked, and the British simply dropped the matter.

Behind the scenes, al-Husayni was pulling the strings of his Egyptian connection, the Muslim Brotherhood. In Egypt, there existed a reservoir of sympathy for the Nazis. Men like Anwar Sadat, who would become president, and many other Egyptian army officers had openly expressed sympathy, and some had worked for the Germans as spies. In this climate, the Brotherhood, with its pro-Nazi leanings, took up the cause of Hajj al-Husayni. They sent a telegram to the British ambassador in Cairo asking him to ensure the well-being of the mufti, referring to him as the sole representative of Palestine. Simultaneously, the Brotherhood sent telegrams and delegations to the French ambassador to convey their thanks to Paris.

With both London and Paris unwilling to bring the mufti before a war crimes tribunal, Yugoslavia approached the United States to apply pressure. When America asked Paris to hand over Hajj al-Husayni, the head of the Muslim Brotherhood sent a protest memorandum to the Americans that read: "We, in the name of the Muslim Brothers and all Arabs and Muslims, would like to warn your government not to continue this unjust Zionist policy. . . . We would also like you to confirm to your government our preparedness to sacrifice ourselves for the sake of rescuing our brethren, wherever necessary."[3]

This posturing by the Muslim Brotherhood actually worked. Soon, the year-old Arab League, not wanting to be seen as abandoning an Arab leader, also added its name to the call to save the Grand Mufti from prosecution. In June 1946, al-Husayni managed to quietly slip out of France and into Egypt, where King Farouk readily granted him asylum. Britain once more half-heartedly asked Cairo to extradite the mufti, but the Egyptians knew this was more of a formality than an order. Like the French, they too shrugged off the British, whose strength as an empire had been sapped beyond recognition.

Today, when European governments kowtow to Islamo-fascists, fearing a backlash, one is reminded of the lack of will to prosecute the Grand Mufti of Palestine in 1945.

In Egypt, where he was treated as a hero, Hajj al-Husayni expressed no regret for his role in the deaths of thousands of Yugoslav partisans. This was not the first time the Arab Street has cheered a mass murderer. When the Egyptian government criticized those who had backed Hitler, including al-Husayni, his allies in the Muslim Brotherhood came to his defence. They declared that the mufti had committed no wrong by aligning himself with the Nazis. In fact, they claimed, Hajj al-Husayni was simply carrying out jihad.

Between the Zionists, who grossly exaggerate the mufti's role in the Holocaust, if any, and his apologists, who, depending on the audience, either dismiss any culpability on his part or express regret at Hitler's ignominious failure, one thing is clear: the Mufti worked for Hitler. The nature and purpose of their relationship can be judged by the minutes of their meeting in 1941.

Minutes of the meeting between German Chancellor Adolf Hitler and Grand Mufti Haj Amin al-Husseini:

Zionism and the Arab Cause (November 28, 1941)

The Grand Mufti began by thanking the Führer for the great honor he had bestowed by receiving him. He wished to seize the opportunity to convey to the Führer of the Greater German Reich, admired by the entire Arab world, his thanks for the sympathy which he had always shown for the Arab and especially the Palestinian cause, and to which he had given clear expression in his public speeches. The Arab countries were firmly convinced that Germany would win the war and that the Arab cause would then prosper: The Arabs were Germany's natural friends because they had the same enemies as had Germany, namely the English, the Jews, and the Communists. They were therefore prepared to cooperate with Germany with all their hearts and stood ready to participate in the war, not only negatively by the commission of acts of sabotage and the instigation of revolutions, but also positively by the formation of an Arab Legion. The Arabs could be more useful to Germany as allies than might be apparent at first glance, both for geographical reasons and because of the suffering inflicted upon them by the English and the Jews. Furthermore, they had had close relations with all Moslem nations, of which they could make use in behalf of the common cause. The Arab Legion would be quite easy to raise. An appeal by the Mufti to the Arab countries and the prisoners of Arab, Algerian, Tunisian, and Moroccan nationality in Germany would produce a great number of volunteers eager to fight. Of Germany's victory the Arab world was firmly convinced, not only because the Reich possessed a large army, brave soldiers, and military leaders of genius, but also because the Almighty could never award the victory to an unjust cause.

In this struggle, the Arabs were striving for the independence and unity of Palestine, Syria and Iraq. They had the fullest confidence in the Führer and looked to his hand for the balm on their wounds which had been inflicted upon them by the enemies of Germany.

The Mufti then mentioned the letter he had received from Germany, which stated that Germany was holding no Arab territories and understood and recognized the aspirations to independence and freedom of the Arabs, just as she supported the elimination of the Jewish national home.

A public declaration in this sense would be very useful for its propagandistic effect on the Arab peoples at this moment. It would rouse the Arabs from their momentary lethargy and give them new courage. It would also ease the Mufti's work of secretly organizing the Arabs against the moment when they could strike. At the same time, he could give the assurance that the Arabs would in strict discipline patiently wait for the right moment and only strike upon an order from Berlin.

. . .

In these circumstances he was renewing his request that the Führer make a public declaration so that the Arabs would not lose hope, which is so powerful a force in the life of nations. With such hope in their hearts the Arabs, as he had said, were willing to wait. They were not pressing for immediate realization of their aspirations: they could easily wait half a year or a whole year. But if they were not inspired with such a hope by a declaration of this sort, it could be expected that the English would be the gainers from it.

The Führer replied that Germany's fundamental attitude on these questions, as the Mufti himself had already stated, was clear. Germany stood for uncompromising war against the Jews. That naturally included active opposition to the

Jewish national home in Palestine, which was nothing other than a center, in the form of a state, for the exercise of destructive influence by Jewish interests. Germany was also aware that the assertion that the Jews were carrying out the function of economic pioneers in Palestine was a lie. The work there was done only by the Arabs, not by the Jews. Germany was resolved, step by step, to ask one European nation after the other to solve its Jewish problem, and at the proper time direct a similar appeal to non-European nations as well.

. . .

The aid to the Arabs would have to be material aid. Of how little help sympathies alone were in such a battle had been demonstrated plainly by the operation in Iraq, where circumstances had not permitted the rendering of really effective, practical aid. In spite of all the sympathies, German aid had not been sufficient and Iraq was overcome by the power of Britain, that is, the guardian of the Jews.

. . .

The Führer then made the following statement to the Mufti, enjoining him to lock it in the uttermost depths of his heart:

1. He (the Führer) would carry on the battle to the total destruction of the Judeo-Communist empire in Europe.

2. At some moment which was impossible to set exactly today but which in any event was not distant, the German armies would in the course of this struggle reach the southern exit from Caucasia.

3. As soon as this had happened, the Führer would on his own give the Arab world the assurance that its hour of liberation had arrived. Germany's objective would then be solely the destruction of the Jewish element residing in the Arab

sphere under the protection of British power. In that hour the Mufti would be the most authoritative spokesman for the Arab world. It would then be his task to set off the Arab operations which he had secretly prepared. When that time had come, Germany could also be indifferent to French reaction to such a declaration.

Once Germany had forced open the road to Iran and Iraq through Rostov, it would be also the beginning of the end of the British world empire. He (the Führer) hoped that the coming year would make it possible for Germany to thrust open the Caucasian gate to the Middle East. For the good of their common cause, it would be better if the Arab proclamation were put off for a few more months than if Germany were to create difficulties for herself without being able thereby to help the Arabs.

He (the Führer) fully appreciated the eagerness of the Arabs for a public declaration of the sort requested by the Grand Mufti. But he would beg him to consider that he (the Führer) himself was the Chief of State of the German Reich for five long years during which he was unable to make to his own homeland the announcement of its liberation. He had to wait with that until the announcement could be made on the basis of a situation brought about by the force of arms that the Anschluss had been carried out.

The moment that Germany's tank divisions and air squadrons had made their appearance south of the Caucasus, the public appeal requested by the Grand Mufti could go out to the Arab world.

The Grand Mufti replied that it was his view that everything would come to pass just as the Führer had indicated. He was fully reassured and satisfied by the words which he had

heard from the Chief of the German State. He asked, however, whether it would not be possible, secretly at least, to
enter into an ágreement with Germany of the kind he had just
outlined for the Führer.

The Führer replied that he had just now given the Grand
Mufti precisely that confidential declaration. The Grand Mufti
thanked him for it and stated in conclusion that he was taking
his leave from the Führer in full confidence and with reiterated
thanks for the interest shown in the Arab cause.[4]

The meeting between Hitler and the mufti produced immediate
results. Soon after, Hajj al-Husayni was allowed to hire a staff of sixty
Arabs in Germany to run an Arabic-language radio service for the Nazi
shortwave Oriental Service that targeted the Arab world, Turkey, Iran, and
India. Broadcasting out of Zeesen, south of Berlin, the programming skil-
fully intermingled anti-Semitic propaganda with verses from the Quran
and the Hadith depicting Jews as the enemies of Muslims until the end of
time. The Hadith narrating of how, at the end of times, stones and trees
would supposedly speak to Muslims and say "There is a Jew hiding behind
me" would most certainly have figured prominently in his radio chats.

But Hitler had bet on the wrong horse. There may have been isolated sympathy for the Nazis in some parts of the Muslim world, Egypt
in particular, but there was no sign of this in Iran, Turkey, or India, not
even in the mufti's native Palestine. It was only in Bosnia, where the
mufti raised the now infamous Muslim SS division, that he had some
success and managed to hold sway over the mosque establishment,
as well as with Muslim POWs of the Red Army. While addressing the
imams of the 13th Waffen SS Mountain Division in October 1944, Hajj
al-Husayni dwelled on the convergence between national socialism and
Islam. He summarized this as follows:

- Monotheism – unity of leadership, the leadership principle;
- A sense of obedience and discipline;
- The battle and the honour of dying in battle;
- Community, following the principle: the collective before the individual;
- High esteem for motherland and prohibition of abortion;
- Glorification of work and creativity: "Islam protects and values productive work, of whatever kind it may be";
- Attitude towards Jews – "in the struggle against Jewry, Islam and National Socialism are very close."[5]

Despite his calls to Arabs to support the Nazis, Hajj al-Husayni's pleas fell on deaf ears. When American troops landed in North Africa to engage Rommel's Afrika Korps, the Mufti moaned on the radio: "The Americans are the willing slaves of the Jews . . . as such the enemies of Islam and the Arabs."[6]

—

The path that took a Muslim cleric from the Middle East into the bosom of the Third Reich is the story of a man who served three colonial masters – the Ottomans as a military officer, the British as one of their appointed muftis, and Hitler as an ally.

Born into a well-known landowning family in 1897, Mohammed Amin al-Husayni's father was the mufti of Jerusalem and a prominent early opponent of Zionism. The al-Husayni clan were formidable power brokers in Palestine during the Ottoman period; thirteen of its members sat as the mayor of Jerusalem between 1864 and 1920.

Young Amin al-Husayni first attended an Islamic school, but later went to one of the Ottoman government institutions, where he learned to speak fluent Turkish. As the son of a cleric whose elder half-brother was already a mufti, in 1912 young Amin was sent to study Islam at the prestigious Al-Azhar University in Cairo. He never graduated.

After dropping out of Al-Azhar, he returned to Jerusalem in 1913 before going to Istanbul to join the Military Academy. Here, too, he could not complete his education because of the outbreak of World War I, in which Turkey joined Germany against Britain, France, and Russia. After being commissioned as an artillery officer, al-Husayni was assigned to the Forty-Seventh Brigade stationed in and around the city of Smyrna. It was during the Ottoman caliphate's darkest hours that the future Grand Mufti of Palestine would commit treason and betray his oath. A sworn pan-Islamist who would later invoke Islam in every action he took, he had no problem whatsoever selling out the very caliphate of Islam he had sworn to defend in exchange for British favours.

In November 1916, while his own Ottoman army was fighting the British, al-Husayni took a three-month disability leave and moved to Jerusalem. While pretending to convalesce, and still in the pay of the Ottoman army, Hajj al-Husayni secretly severed his allegiance after being bought off by the British, who made him an officer in the army of their ally, Sharif Hussein bin Ali, who later became king of Hejaz.

By 1917 the British army under General Allenby had defeated the Ottoman Turkish forces, and, with the aid of the Arab irregulars, occupied Palestine and Syria. For the first time since the Crusades in 1099, Jerusalem had fallen to a largely Christian army; this time with the aid of the native Muslim population. Seven hundred years after the Kurdish general Saladin had liberated Jerusalem, the city was back under the flag of a European power. Ironically, it was Muslims who helped defeat the caliphate.

After the war ended with the defeat of the Ottoman Turks, it dawned on the Arabs of Palestine that liberation at the hands of colonial powers would not entail freedom. As Arab political scientist Samir Amin famously declared decades later, "The Armies of the North can never bring freedom to the peoples of the South." The Palestinians who had been part of the Ottoman caliphate for more than four hundred years and had elected members to the Ottoman Parliament in 1877, 1908, 1912, and 1914 now found themselves locked inside a cage of their own making.

When World War I ended, the Arabs began to riot, demanding the rescinding of the Balfour Declaration of 1917 that promised the Jews a homeland in Palestine. True to their tradition, the British set up a royal commission to look into the riots. Hidden in the details of this commission's report can be found the role of Hajj al-Husayni and his collaboration with the British.

The commission's report, filed on July 1, 1920, argued that the disturbances were caused by the Arabs' disappointment over unfulfilled promises of independence that the British had made during the war to Sharif Husein ibn Ali of Mecca, as well as their belief that the Balfour Declaration implied the denial of their own right to self-determination. It said the Arabs feared that establishing a Jewish national home would lead to such substantial Jewish immigration that the Arabs would become subjects of the Jewish community. The report concluded that the British must rule with a firm hand, meaning the policy of the Balfour Declaration would not be reversed, but also confirming that the Arabs would be treated fairly.

Buried in the report was the name of the English officer who had recruited Hajj al-Husayni. Capt. C.D. Brunton told the commission that he found al-Husayni very pro-English and that he had facilitated the dropping of British War Office pamphlets from the air promising the Palestinian Arabs peace and prosperity under English rule – "the recruits [were] being given to understand that they were fighting in a national cause and to liberate their country from the Turks."[7]

Hajj al-Husayni wasn't the first or the last Arab leader to demonstrate political short-sightedness. After first collaborating with the British, he now led the anti–Balfour Declaration riots. As a result, in April 1920, the British authorities sentenced him to ten years in prison. The future mufti escaped to Syria, but when the Damascus regime collapsed, the fugitive al-Husayni fled to Transjordan.

In the 1918 British elections, former Home Secretary Herbert Samuel, who was one of the country's prominent Zionists, lost his seat in parliament. Samuel's ideas had helped shape the Balfour Declaration. In addition, it was Samuel's idea to offer thousands of Russian Jewish refugees during the war years a choice of being conscripted into the British army or returning to Russia for military service. Many of these new British soldiers of Russian Jewish background became part of the British army that defeated the Ottomans and occupied Palestine and Jerusalem.

After losing his seat in Parliament, Samuel was appointed Britain's first high commissioner to Palestine. In a twist of fate, by helping defeat the Ottomans, Hajj al-Husayni and his anti-Zionist jihadis had helped make one of the leading Zionists the de facto ruler of British Palestine.

Herbert Samuel went to Palestine with the full weight of the British Empire behind him and the collective expertise of the empire's fine-tuned statecraft for ruling colonies. As few as fifty thousand British civil servants governed five hundred million souls in India for more than a century. Palestine, by comparison, was no big deal. One of the first acts of the new high commissioner was to pardon Hajj al-Husayni and bring him back from Transjordan into the British fold in Jerusalem. Samuel knew how valuable al-Husayni, the head of a prominent family, was to the British administration.

In March 1921, the mufti of Palestine, Kamil al-Husayni – Amin al-Husayni's half-brother – died, leaving the position vacant. To fill the vacancy, the British administration arranged an election, in which they would select from the top three vote-getters.

When the elections were held in April, al-Husayni received the least number of votes among the four candidates. The top three vote-getters all belonged to a rival clan of the Husaynis, the Nashashibis. For the first time, no al-Husayni was in the running for the position of mufti.

The shocking defeat of the heir apparent caused widespread distress among the Husayni clan, who began a territory-wide campaign of petitioning the British, demanding that the high commissioner set aside the election results and appoint Hajj al-Husayni as mufti.

Jerusalem mayor Raghib al-Nashashibi bitterly opposed any accommodation for al-Husayni. The two leading families of Palestine were sworn enemies of each other. (Later, this feuding proved extremely costly to the Palestinian people, just as today Fatah and Hamas are perennially at each other's throats. It is remarkable how feudalism and clan-based tribalism has played such an important role in the tragedy of Palestine.)

As the feuding reached fever pitch, the British stepped in to resolve the problem with a stroke of good old colonial arm-twisting. High Commissioner Samuel summoned the Nashashibi front-runner and persuaded him to withdraw. This automatically promoted Amin al-Husayni to third position, thus allowing the British diplomat to appoint his man as a symbolic chief of the Palestinian Arabs.

Thus was born the mufti of Palestine, Hajj Amin al-Husayni, delivered by Caesarean section under the direction of a British Zionist architect of the Balfour Declaration. Because he lacked Islamic credentials, Hajj al-Husayni received the title not of Grand Mufti, but merely Mufti of Jerusalem and Palestine. Nevertheless, his followers openly addressed him as the Grand Mufti, a title that has stayed with us ever since.

Subsequently, in 1922, the British high commissioner created the Supreme Muslim Council and had the Grand Mufti elected as its president. This was a significant development, for the council was given control of funds, amounting to tens of thousands of pounds annually. In addition, the Grand Mufti controlled all the Islamic courts in Palestine and exercised his authority to appoint teachers and preachers. Effectively, the mufti began to control the lives of the people in British Palestine with unmatched authority. In return, the mufti offered near-total cooperation to the British colonial powers while keeping Palestinian demands in check from 1921 to 1936.

The Grand Mufti's rise to power in Palestine must be seen in contrast to events in the rest of the Muslim world, where – from Egypt to Turkey and Indonesia to Iran – the population was emerging from under the weight of religious leadership and embracing a more secular approach to Islam and the community. In the words of Bernard Lewis, rather than the nation being a sub-unit of Islam, Islam became a sub-unit of the nation in which citizenship was not based on religion.[8]

In the 1920s, most of the Muslim world did not live under sharia law. In Turkey, Kemal Atatürk had separated religion and state in 1924, while next door in Iran, Reza Shah Pahlavi was introducing laws to enable a break with medievalism. Farther east, in India, the Muslim leadership – represented by Muhammad Iqbal, the philosopher-poet; Muhammad Ali Jinnah, who became the founder of Pakistan; and Sir Sultan Mohamed Aga Khan, one of the founders of and the first president of the All-India Muslim League – were all Muslim modernists.

The Islamic traditionalists were deeply troubled by these steps towards modernity in the Muslim world. They saw these developments as a threat to their own power. To counter the march of history, the clerics would tell their congregations that science, technology, and European ideas were satanic, indeed an attack on Islam itself. Atatürk was labelled a Jew; Reza Shah a Shia, and thus a Jew; and the Aga Khan a British stooge. This resistance to modernity gave birth to the contemporary Islamist movement, whose leading protagonists were Hasan al-Banna, who founded the Muslim Brotherhood in Egypt, and Syed Maududi, who established the Jamaat-e-Islami, in India. (I will later examine Maududi's role as the creator of the Islamist monster let loose in Pakistan. The Jamaat-e-Islami in India and in Pakistan became the vessel in which Saudi-funded Islamic extremism was nurtured.)

At a time when the Muslim world yearned to move forward and embrace the twentieth century, al-Banna, al-Husayni, and Maududi demanded a return to governance under sharia law as a rebuttal to Western civilization, which they viewed as essentially a Jewish conspiracy against Islam. However, until the 1930s, the Grand Mufti, despite his own Islamist leanings, was happily sucking up to the British colonial authorities while strengthening the grip of his Supreme Muslim Council over the Arab population of Palestine. The obvious hypocrisy of being anti-West while seeking help from the West is still the norm in Arab diplomacy and politics.

In 1922, when protests against steady Jewish immigration and Zionist land purchases erupted across Palestine, the Mufti refused to be associated with the demonstrating crowds and kept his distance from the movement, unwilling to risk his close ties to Sir Herbert Samuel, to whom he owed his title, wealth, and power. Not only did the mufti let down the Palestinians in the protests of 1922, he also brought together other notables of the landed aristocracy to put an end to the peaceful protest of the Palestinians who had stopped paying taxes to the British administration.

The mufti's leadership in 1922 should be seen in contrast to the anti-British home rule movement in India, where in 1921, after assuming leadership of the Indian National Congress, Gandhi led nationwide campaigns to achieve swaraj, or self-rule. While Gandhi led Indians from the front, the mufti sabotaged Palestinians from the rear. Gandhi was arrested in March 1922, tried by the British for sedition, and sentenced to six years' imprisonment. By contrast, the mufti put himself and the interests of the elites above those of the ordinary Palestinian.

The mufti's instinct for self-preservation was the dominant motivating factor during the 1920s. When the British offered to create an elected representative assembly in 1922, al-Husayni turned it down. In contrast, in India, Gandhi, as well as the Muslim leadership, embraced the idea and laid the foundations for a democracy that today is the largest in the world. Said K. Aburish, author of *A Brutal Friendship: The West and the Arab Elite,* writes, "Beyond acting as an instrument of appeasement and neutralizing both the people's passions and their passive resistance plans, the Mufti's activities between 1922 and 1927 appear to have centered on enhancing his position and that of his already powerful family."[9]

In 1928, a Jew placed a religious exhibit in front of the Wailing Wall in a way that was objectionable to a nearby Muslim. The minor altercation developed into large-scale clashes between Arabs and Jews. These riots seem to be the turning point for the mufti. The controversy involved the question of sovereignty over the Al-Aqsa Mosque and the Dome on the Rock, both built over the Jewish Temple a millennium earlier and under the administration of Muslims. Arabs feared a Jewish takeover of the site they consider the third-holiest shrine in Islam.

While the British worked on yet another White Paper, the mufti turned the issue into an international Islamic campaign, asking Muslims worldwide to help him save the Dome from the hands of the Jews. If he had any illusions that the British would honour their private promises to him, an exchange in London in May 1930 revealed the true attitude of Britain towards Palestine. The mufti and a number of Palestinian "notables" met with Labour prime minister Ramsay MacDonald and his socialist secretary of state for Dominion affairs, Lord Passfield (formerly Sidney Webb, the well-known Fabian and author), to review the ramifications of the bloody clashes between Jews and Arabs that had occurred in 1928–29, and look at the options available to resolve the Palestine Question.

The mufti and his team argued their case on the basis of Article 4 of the League of Nations Covenant, under which the British were awarded the mandate in Palestine. Article 4 recognized the mandated territories as "independent states," yet the British wouldn't budge on the question of creating a Jewish national home in Palestine. In fact, MacDonald brushed aside the Arab argument as "irrelevant." Lord Passfield rubbed salt into the wound by lecturing his Palestinian guests: "Your position is inferior to that of a colony and it is our duty under the Mandate to endeavour that you should rise to the point of a Colony." Shocked, the mufti asked, "Do you mean we are below the Negroes of Africa?" Passfield reassured him that they were not, but that they were "less than" some other colonies. Raghib al-Nashashibi lamented, "We had a government of our own in which we participated. We had Parliaments" (referring to the Ottoman Parliament before the British occupation). Sitting next to him was Hajj al-Husayni, the very man who had contributed to the defeat of the Parliament the two Palestinians were now moaning about. The arguments of the Palestinians fell on deaf ears. They were admonished by the British prime minister to "get back into the Iron Cage."[10]

However, when Lord Passfield came out with his White Paper, the Arabs were overjoyed. To the outrage of the Zionists in the cabinet and among the Jewish population, he recommended that all Jewish immigration to Palestine be suspended. Prime Minister MacDonald was forced to distance himself from the paper in a "letter of clarification" to Chaim Weizmann, president of the World Zionist Organisation. Among Arabs the letter became known as the "Black Letter" that killed the White Paper. Seeing a dead end, the mufti turned to the Muslim world and organised an International Islamic Conference to drum up support for his cause.

In December 1931 the General Islamic Congress met in Jerusalem. Prominent among the delegates were Rashid Rida, the Egyptian

Salafist; Muhammad Iqbal, the Indian philosopher-poet; and Shawkat Ali, the head of India's Khilafat Movement that had rallied in defence of the Ottoman caliphate, the very institution the mufti had helped defeat. Turkey and Saudi Arabia stayed away. But even after days of deliberation, the only thing that emerged beyond rhetoric was the decision to establish an Islamic university in Jerusalem, as if Al-Azhar and the countless other madrassahs were not enough. While the frustrations of the Palestinian people grew, the conference of world Muslims offered them mere platitudes and prayers. The delegates had obviously forgotten that a large number of Palestinians were Christians.

By the time the Palestinian uprising began in 1936, the Nazi hatred of the Jew had been incorporated into the existing Muslim narrative that the Jews were untrustworthy and rejected by God himself. The spurious Jew-hating Hadith were being blended with *The Protocols*, and Muslims were picking up the nastiest strains of Christian anti-Semitism from the scores of Muslim-Christian associations that had sprouted up to counter the Jews.

As early as 1933, there are records of the mufti visiting the German consul in Jerusalem and assuring him, "The Muslims inside and outside Palestine welcomed the new regime of Germany."[11] In return, Germany helped out the mufti with funds.

In September 1937, Adolf Eichmann and two SS officers carried out a mission to the Middle East accompanied by the head of the Hitler Youth, Baldur von Schirach, who later funded an "Arab Club" in Damascus where German Nazis trained recruits for the mufti's growing army of insurgents. In his seminal study on the mufti, Klaus Gensicke writes, "The Mufti himself acknowledged that at that time it was only due to German funds he received that it had been possible to carry through the uprising in Palestine. From the outset, he made high financial demands which the Nazis to a great extent met."[12]

In the 1930s, about two decades after the Balfour Declaration, there was growing evidence of a convergence of German and Arab enmities that allowed for Nazi-style anti-Semitism to penetrate the Arab world. Although technically the Arabs were also Semites, the Arab hatred for the British and the French was good reason for the Nazis to accommodate them. Soon, a covenant between anti-Zionist Arab leaders and the Nazis began to emerge. Leaders on both sides chose to either finesse or ignore the implications of the kind of anti-Semitism featured in Hitler's *Mein Kampf.* An article in the Nazi Party newspaper in 1937 explained that Arabs had been at least partly "Aryanized" through mixing with Armenians and Circassians, while some Nazis went on to suggest that *Mein Kampf* be amended to clarify that only Jews, and not Arabs, were meant as objects of Hitler's rage and disdain.[13]

The Nazis also used radio propaganda in the Arab world, where attacks on their common enemy, the Jews, were a major feature of broadcasts. Murderous anti-Jewish riots in Iraq in 1941 and in Egypt, Syria, and Libya in 1945, and massacres in Aleppo and Aden in 1947 demonstrated how the anti-Semitic propaganda of the Nazis, the activism of the mufti, and increasing tension over the emergence of a Jewish state in Palestine combined to completely erase the distinction between anti-Zionism and anti-Semitism. New forms of Arab nationalism also left less room for tolerance of minority groups than had existed in the Ottoman Empire.

In addition, the odd relationship that had developed between the Nazis and some Arab countries continued after the war. Egypt, for one, became a refuge for runaway Nazis. Nazi war criminal Johann von Leers, an expert in anti-Semitic literature, was one of a number of Nazis welcomed by Egypt for their "expertise in Jewish affairs." Von Leers was warmly received by none other than Mufti Hajj Amin al-Husayni. In his welcome speech the mufti remarked, "We thank you for venturing to take up the battle with the powers of darkness that have become incarnate in world Jewry."[14]

The much talked about Arab Revolt in Palestine between 1936 and 1939 was multifaceted and was triggered by a growing frustration among the Palestinians about their future. The immediate trigger for the revolt was the killing of two Arabs near Petah Tivka on April 15, 1936, in retaliation for an ambush by Palestinians on a Jewish convoy in which two Jews had died.

As time passed, the British asked their allies in the Arab world to intervene, seeking help from the leaders of Transjordan, Egypt, Iraq, and Saudi Arabia to help end the strikes that had paralyzed the economy. Notwithstanding the harsh measures taken by the British authorities, the mufti chose to come to the table to highlight the plight of the most vulnerable among the Palestinians. The economic interests of Arab orchard farmers played a role as well. The Spanish Civil War was at its peak, causing citrus prices to soar in Europe. If the strike by Palestinian farmers continued, they would not benefit at all from the shortages created by the war in Spain.

As soon as the hostilities ceased, the British acted. Within a month, a royal commission was set up to examine the underlying causes of the disturbances in Palestine. William Robert Wellesley, Earl Peel, who had been Britain's secretary of state for India in 1922, headed the commission. The earl arrived in Jerusalem in November 1936, got down to work immediately, and stayed in Palestine less than three months. For most of his stay, the Arabs boycotted the commission, feeling it had come with a preconceived notion about the conflict. However, the 400-page Peel Commission report contained a surprising admission. It stated in unequivocal terms that the British Mandate could no longer be maintained and needed to be replaced by new treaty arrangements between the parties. For the first time, the notion of a single state based on the Balfour Declaration was abandoned. The report described the dilemma faced by the British in unflattering terms.

"An irrepressible conflict has arisen between two national communities within the narrow bounds of one small country. There is no common ground between them. Their national aspirations are incompatible. The Arabs desire to revive the traditions of the Arab golden age. The Jews desire to show what they can achieve when restored to the land in which the Jewish nation was born. Neither of the two national ideals permits of combination in the service of a single State."

Instead, the Peel Commission proposed a "partition" of Mandate Palestine into an Arab state and a Jewish state. In hindsight, this was a bonanza for the Arabs. Most of Mandate Palestine (70 per cent) was to remain in the Arab state, including all of the Negev to Nablus in the north and Gaza in the west. The Jewish homeland (20 per cent) was restricted to the northwest and included the Galilee, Tel Aviv, and Haifa, while a corridor from Jaffa to Jerusalem would remain under a fresh British mandate. There was one catch: the Arab area was to be merged with Transjordan, which was originally part of the Palestine Mandate and had been carved out as a separate kingdom in 1922.

Surprisingly, the Zionists gave the proposal a qualified approval, but true to tradition, the Arab leadership rejected the plan. Hajj al-Husayni, who presided over the Arab Higher Committee, called for a wholesale rejection of the plan and the creation of an Arab state in all of Palestine. (Hamas still clings to this hope.) With war clouds gathering in Europe, terror was introduced for the first time as a weapon in the conflict. On September 26, 1937, a senior British civil servant, Lewis Andrews, was assassinated in Nazareth. Although the Arab Higher Committee condemned the killing, the British administration outlawed the group and all the strike committees across Palestine. Leading politicians were arrested and some were deported to distant Seychelles in the Indian Ocean.

The mufti went into hiding in the Al-Aqsa Mosque compound while the British proscribed the Supreme Muslim Council, dismissed him from his positions, and impounded all the endowments that al-Husayni represented. The mufti's remarkable double role as a spokesman for the Arab cause and a salaried official of the British Crown had come to an end.

Within weeks, Hajj al-Husayni scurried off to Lebanon – disguised as a woman – escaping the British dragnet in much the same way as, decades later, Mullah Omar and Osama bin Laden wore burqas and gave the slip to the Americans. From Lebanon, where he was briefly arrested by the French, al-Husayni tried to control the uprising in Palestine, but the movement had fallen from the hands of the "notables" to the peasantry and working class. The mufti became less relevant, and the movement even more incoherent than before. Leadership passed into the hands of local committees that had little direction. The rebel leadership lacked a coordinated, detailed program.

Many Palestinians were caught between the rebels and their enemy, the British army. Among the wealthy families, it was fashionable to escape to neighbouring countries to avoid facing a political rebellion. This time-honoured practice of the Arab bourgeoisie's bailing out in times of difficulty was repeated in 1947–48 with devastating consequences. Others, like Fakir al-Nashashibi, would create the Arab Peace Corps to fight the rebels with British assistance. Palestinian-on-Palestinian violence was on the rise, much like the ongoing Hamas vs. Fatah brutality of today.

Some of the mufti's rebels tried to silence any opposition from within the community. Brutal measures were adopted, and it is said that Palestinians killed more of their own people in the 1936–39 rebellion than the British or the Jews did. Thus, a new dimension was added to the Palestinian narrative during this uprising. In the areas controlled by the mufti's men, sharia laws were introduced, along with strict dress codes that were enforced with unreasonable harshness and zeal. Any Muslim Palestinian declared "un-Islamic" by the mufti's rebels was dealt with with insane violence. Anyone professing opposition to the rebellion was declared a traitor; anyone who argued in support of the Peel Report's partition plan was targeted in worse ways than used by the Taliban of today.

In Yehoshua Porath's painstaking study of the Palestinian rebellion, he gives a disturbing account of the brutality faced by any Arab considered sympathetic to either the British or the Jews. He writes that Palestinians who sought a compromise with the Jews "were not always immediately murdered; sometimes they were kidnapped and then taken to the mountainous areas under rebel control. There they were thrown into pits infested with snakes and scorpions. After spending a few days there, the victims, if still alive, were brought before one of the rebel courts and usually sentenced to death, or a special dispensation if not severe flogging. The terror was so daunting that no one, including the ulema (clerics) and priests, dared to perform the proper burial services."[15]

The Muslim Brotherhood and the Nazis were also involved, providing financial and military support and supplying the ideological and theological justification for the movement, whose failure was a result of the "all or nothing" goal of the Islamists and the anti-Jewish agenda of the Germans. The real victims of this lawlessness and lack of restraint were the Palestinian people, a condition that haunts their lives even today. An inept leadership that so easily brutalizes its own people and is driven by hate of "the other," in this case the Jew, rarely succeeds. In the case of the Palestinian rebellion, lawlessness led to a fascist stream that at one stage enforced how people dressed or covered their heads. A good illustration of this is found in a biography of the mufti published in Germany in 1943. The Nazi author talks about the Palestinian "liberation struggle."

In a tree-lined street in Jerusalem's Old Town the police find two Arabs lying face-downwards, clearly struck down by bullets through the back, and entry wounds carefully covered with the head gear known in Europe as the "Fez" and in the East as the "tarbush." One of the dead is a well-known lawyer, the other a prosperous landlord. . . . Both are Arabs, shot by fellow Arabs. Their crime was to have ignored the recent instruction from the "insurgent general," which had been posted on every corner in Jerusalem, "In the name of Allah the Beneficent, the Merciful! The Headquarters of the Arab revolution reminds all the Arabs and Palestinians that the 'tarbush' is not the true national headgear of the Arabs. The Arabs must immediately remove their tarbushes, the garb of the former oppressors and wear the national kaffiyeh."[16]

In his account of the Palestinian struggle for a homeland, *The Iron Cage,* Arab-American scholar Rashid Khalidi writes about how the rebellion was also a rejection by the freedom fighters of the Palestinian elites. "Hajj Amin al-Husayni was acting out of fear of forces he did not fully control, but that his actions, and his earlier inaction, had helped to unleash: these were represented by the scattered rebel bands in the hills of Palestine." In a statement issued by these rebels, they say the Palestinians were subject neither "to the Nashashibis or to the Hosannas, nor to the Arab kings, who ruled by the grace of Britain."[17]

Khalidi outlines how the Palestinian leadership became so weak that they were soon being dictated to by the defeated rebels. While others in the Arab Higher Committee counselled the mufti to accept the British initiative, he sided instead with the ragtag army of hill-bound rebels that were assaulting fellow Palestinians who showed any opposition to them. By the time hostilities broke out in Europe, the Palestinian uprising had petered out into an aimless enterprise, while the Jewish community had consolidated their gains, with steady immigration and a zealous self-sufficiency in their economy, as well as military strength.

When Nazi tanks rolled into Poland in September 1939, France's coy relationship with the mufti, which had allowed him to needle the British in Palestine, had to change. Both France and Britain declared war on Germany, and the two countries were now allies. The French conveniently drove Hajj al-Husayni to Iraq under a promise made to Baghdad that he would not meddle in the fractious politics of that country.

By 1941 the Nazi juggernaut was knocking on the doors of the Middle East. From the north Hitler was aiming to break through the Caucasus and enter the Muslim Soviet republics where Turkey and Iran meet. From the south he was hoping Rommel's Afrika Korps would be able to take Egypt and Palestine. The disastrous Nazi defeat at Stalingrad and the mauling of Rommel at El Alamein had not yet happened. In this environment of heady Nazism, pro-German Arabs staged a coup in Iraq, putting Rashid Ali al-Kaylani in charge, displacing the pro-British prime minister Nuri Said. For Hajj al-Husayni, the stars had aligned as he had hoped. The mufti's home became the mecca of the pro-German Iraqi army officers and their political allies. The rebellion was short lived, however, as British and Transjordanian troops invaded Iraq in May 1941 to ensure that the Nazi-inspired government in Baghdad had no time to consolidate.

The daunted Iraqi army was routed by the British forces. While the Iraqi officers were charged and executed, the wily mufti escaped. He and Rashid al-Kaylani sneaked into Iran and then across the border to Turkey, where they found favour with the German ambassador. By November that year, both the Grand Mufti and al-Kaylani were safe in Berlin as guests of the Führer. The rest is history.

In Germany, the mufti befriended senior members of the Third Reich. That he was ultimately the only person to live to make a political comeback suggests he learned nothing from the events of the Second

World War. Back in Egypt, he restarted the engines of hate as if nothing had happened.

With no sense of guilt, and not being held accountable for the deaths of thousands, the mufti in the Cairo of 1945 was ready for his second act, in which he worked to turn the genuine national aspirations of the Palestinian people into the Jew-hatred he had learned in Berlin.

In postwar Egypt, Hajj al-Husayni was able to inspire other Islamists to take up the cause of anti-Semitism, chiefly through the Muslim Brotherhood and the work of the young Egyptian radical Islamist Sayyid Qutb, who would describe Hitler's coming to power as an expression of Allah's will and a reflection of the Divine's decision to punish the Jews. In his essay "Our Fight against the Jews," Qutb wrote: "And the Jews did indeed return to evil-doing, so Allah gave to the Muslims power over them. The Muslims then expelled them from the whole of the Arabian Peninsula. . . . Then the Jews again returned to evil-doing and consequently Allah sent against them others of his servants, until the modern period. Then Allah brought Hitler to rule over them."[18]

—

Since Israel is held responsible for all the ills of the Muslim world, we Muslims need to come to terms with whom we hold responsible for the creation of Israel in its current form. We are told that even if a Palestinian state is created, it will be no more than a Bantustan country, a mere fraction of what the Palestinians deserved as a reward for their leaders betraying their fellow Muslim Ottomans and helping the British conquer Jerusalem. There is no doubt that the global Zionist movement worked methodically on a long-term plan to create a Jewish state, but its current borders are more a result of Palestinian obstinacy than Jewish "cunning" or their supposed stranglehold on the world.

This idea needs some examination. To begin with, from an Islamic perspective, it is the Palestinian leadership that should face the wrath of all Muslims, because it is they who chose not to fight the "kuffar" army of the latter-day "crusaders" – the British – as they advanced to occupy Palestine. The fact is, in 1917, the invading British were welcomed by the leadership of the Palestinians as they conquered Jerusalem and the rest of Palestine, which then came under the British Mandate. If Muslims around the world wish to get to the cause of the current mess, they should examine the role of the men who betrayed the Ottoman caliphate and helped the British occupy Palestine. If there are Muslims who are willing to admit this was a monumental mistake that is at the root of the problem today, then those voices have not yet been heard. Applying Islamist logic, if Jerusalem is as holy to Islam as we Muslims claim it is, shouldn't we be willing to consider the thought that our suffering today is the wrath of Allah for facilitating the occupation of Jerusalem by a European Christian power?

Staying with Palestine, let us examine how the Muslim leadership dug one grave after another, kept falling into them, and kept blaming others for our demise. After facilitating the defeat of the Ottoman army by the invading British, the Arab leadership in Palestine was in for a rude shock. On November 2, 1917, the British government issued the Balfour Declaration, which stated, "His Majesty's government view with favour the establishment in Palestine of a national home for the Jewish people, and will use their best endeavours to facilitate the achievement of this object, it being clearly understood that nothing shall be done which may prejudice the civil and religious rights of existing non-Jewish communities in Palestine, or the rights and political status enjoyed by Jews in any other country."

Overnight, the Arabs of Palestine had been demoted. They were now not who they were, but who they were not: the "existing non-Jewish population." The reward for betraying their fellow Muslims of the Ottoman army was delivered to the Arabs even as the war was progressing and European powers were hovering over Turkey like vultures ready to feed on the carcass of a wounded lion. While Muslims in India rallied to save the Turks from a calamity, Muslims of the Arab world celebrated the defeat of the Turks. The Arab leadership had aligned themselves with the British and French and were now waiting to grab a share of the war booty. The most they would get, though, was borders drawn with geometry sets of the Anglo-French colonizers who came up with a treaty known as the Sykes-Picot Agreement that fathered the French Mandate of Syria and British Mandate of Palestine.

Once the League of Nations awarded Britain a mandate over Palestine, the writing was on the wall. Britain was bound by the Balfour Declaration and a commitment to the creation of a Jewish national homeland in Palestine, while the Arabs, who had relied only on oral promises, woke up to the realization that they had been had. However, before a Jewish homeland could be carved out of Palestine, Britain had other matters to settle. It would lop off more than three-quarters of the Palestinian territory east of the Jordan River and create a country called Transjordan (now Jordan), which it would then hand over to the runaway royal family of the Kingdom of Hejaz as a gift for their services in defeating their fellow Muslims, the Ottomans. The Palestinians who lived east of the Jordan River suddenly ended up with a new king and a new nationality.

From then until the creation of Palestine in 1948, and until today, many opportunities that could have brought about a functional, sovereign, dynamic Palestinian state were missed or squandered via a policy of "all or nothing" that is even today the doctrine of Hamas and Iran. Let us have a look at three of these.

The Faisal-Weizmann Agreement of 1919: This agreement was signed on January 3, 1919, by Chaim Weizmann, later president of the World Zionist Organization, and Emir Faisal, son of the king of Hejaz, as part of the Paris Peace Conference. (The two men had met in June 1918, when Arabs were helping the British advance from the south against the Ottoman Empire.) Weizmann and Faisal agreed to a Jewish state in Palestine alongside an Arab kingdom that Faisal hoped to establish. However, Faisal attached a handwritten note to the agreement saying it was conditional upon the acceptance of British wartime promises to the Arabs of independence in a vast area of the Ottoman Empire. A few weeks before Faisal signed the agreement, he had stated:

> The two main branches of the Semitic family, Arabs and Jews, understand one another, and I hope that as a result of inter-change of ideas at the Peace Conference, which will be guided by ideals of self-determination and nationality, each nation will make definite progress towards the realization of its aspirations. Arabs are not jealous of Zionist Jews, and intend to give them fair play and the Zionist Jews have assured the Nationalist Arabs of their intention to see that they too have fair play in their respective areas. Turkish intrigue in Palestine has raised jealousy between the Jewish colonists and the local peasants, but the mutual understanding of the aims of Arabs and Jews will at once clear away the last trace of this former bitterness, which, indeed, had already practically disappeared before the war by the work of the Arab Secret Revolutionary Committee, which in Syria and elsewhere laid the foundation of the Arab military successes of the past two years.[19]

As news reached Damascus, violent protests broke out among the Palestinians. Protest notes were sent out from Nablus and other cities to the Arab delegation in Paris, rejecting any agreement with the Zionists regarding the creation of a Jewish homeland. The possible rapprochement between Muslim and Jew was snuffed out before it could even be discussed. Faisal, and, in future, his transplanted royal family, would have to live with the label of "traitor."

The Peel Commission Plan of 1937: After the Arab revolt in Palestine erupted in 1936, it became clear to the British that the possibility of implementing the Balfour Declaration, as it stood, was an impossible task. The Arabs were not simply the "other" – the "non-Jewish" residents of Palestine. Rather, they were the overwhelming majority of its population. The maxim "Palestine is a land without people for a people without a land" turned out to be no more than a slogan, devoid of any truth. By rebelling against British colonial rule, and with acts of violence against the Jews, the Palestinians had succeeded in demonstrating beyond a shadow of a doubt that without their consent, no solution would have any chance of success.

As violence abated in late 1936, the British appointed a royal commission of inquiry headed by Earl Peel to examine the underlying causes of the Arab revolt and to make policy recommendations to London. The Peel Commission was mandated to propose changes to the British Mandate of Palestine.

On July 7, 1937, the commission issued its report, recommending that the Palestine Mandate be abolished and mooting the idea of two separate states: the Jewish state was to receive a small portion in the west and north, from Mount Carmel to south of Be'er Tuvia, as well as the Jezreel Valley and the Galilee, while the Arab state was to receive most of the territory in the south and mid-east, which included Judea, Samaria, and the sizable Negev desert.

Today, one look at the proposed partition plan should convince any Muslim that the travails of the Palestinians are rooted in their own political and religious leadership, not a Jewish conspiracy. What the Arab leadership rejected in 1937 should be remembered by all Muslims as a betrayal of their trust and support. The problem is, few Muslims are aware that the Arabs gave up almost 80 per cent of Palestine in rejecting the Peel Commission Report. They continued down the path of "all or nothing," a strategy that some still cling to in Hamas and Iran, much to the chagrin of progressive Muslims everywhere.

The UN General Assembly Partition Plan of 1947: The Holocaust and its aftermath added a new dimension to the Arab-Jewish conflict in British Palestine. Holocaust survivors subsisted in displacement camps in Europe, and most, if not all, wanted to move to Palestine. When President Truman came out in support of resettling the Jews, the secretary-general of the newly formed Arab League declared that such a move would touch off a new war between Christendom and Islam, one that would rival the Crusades in scope.

The enormity of the Holocaust had not yet entered the Arab consciousness – denial is still common – and neither had the fact that because of the Grand Mufti of Palestine's alliance with Hitler, world opinion had swung in favour of the Zionist claim and the desire for a Jewish state in Palestine. Instead of adjusting its tactics to accommodate the new reality, the Arab League acted as if nothing had changed since the end of the 1936–37 intifada. Soon the Arab High Command, or AHC, was recreated as the supreme body representing the Palestinians. Here too, however, the haggling between "notable" families ensured there would be no unified voice. In 1946, the AHC was disbanded by opponents of the Husseini family, who created the Arab Higher Front (AHF). A few months later both the AHC and the AHF were dissolved by the Arab League, and the Arab High Executive (AHE) was created with its top position reserved for the Grand Mufti, fresh from his date with the devil in Berlin. By January 1947, the AHE was renamed the Arab Higher Command.

As the Arabs squabbled and uttered empty threats of jihad, the Zionists organized militias, acquired arms and ammunition, and did everything to circumvent the ban on Jewish immigration to Palestine that the British imposed during the war. Meanwhile, London was desperate to get rid of the Middle Eastern albatross that had hung around its neck since 1917 as it struggled to survive after World War ii. In April 1947, Britain asked the United Nations secretary-general to convene a session of the General Assembly to take Palestine off its hands. Within weeks, the General Assembly created the United Nations Special Committee on Palestine, or UNSCOP, with the mandate to recommend a solution to the Palestinian problem.

For two and a half months, the eleven-member committee, consisting of India, Holland, Sweden, Iran, Czechoslovakia, Yugoslavia, Canada, Australia, Peru, Guatemala, and Uruguay, went on a fact-finding mission. None of the superpowers were represented, but three of the delegates had strong Muslim leanings. The delegates of Iran and India were Muslim, and the Yugoslav delegate had to take the substantial Muslim minority in his country into consideration.

From the outset, the reaction to the UN committee was predictable. While the Zionists welcomed the UN mission, the Arab Higher Command issued a statement saying the UN delegation was "pro-Zionist." The Arabs announced a total boycott and said they would censure anyone who talked to the delegation – a time-tested weapon that has been used by every level of Arab leadership for generations and that always ensures they shoot themselves in the foot rather than deal with the challenge their people face. (Nevertheless, they met the delegation in private and off the record.) As the fate of the Palestinians was being decided, none of their leadership wanted to be seen as weak, thus leaving the field open to the Zionist leadership, who pulled out all the stops to impress upon the delegates the righteousness of their cause and their willingness to compromise.

As the UN delegation toured Palestine, it was met at every Jewish city and settlement by cheering crowds and flower-bearing children. The team members were given presentations of the Jewish case with simultaneous translations into Spanish, Swedish, Persian, and any other language required. In contrast, the UN team's visits to Arab centres were always met with hostility and protest. At one Arab school, the children were told not to even look at the visitors. Residents of another village were evacuated to protest the arrival of the UN team, who were then greeted by a delegation of children who cursed the visitors.

The Arab tactic backfired to such a degree that even the two Muslims on the UN team were dismayed. Iran's delegate was heard to say, "What asses these Arabs are. The country is so beautiful and, if it were given to the Jews, it could be developed into Europe." The Indian delegate, though, was sympathetic to the Arab cause and complained privately that the Arab boycott was having a "disastrous effect on his [UN] colleagues."[20] Another telling comment about the antics of the Arab leadership came from the Swedish deputy head of UNSCOP, Paul Mohn. Recalling his meeting with Arab leaders in Lebanon, Mohn wrote in his memoirs that "there is nothing more extreme than meeting all the representatives of the Arab world in one group . . . when each one tries to show that he is more extreme than the other."[21]

UNSCOP voted to recommend to the UN General Assembly a partition of British Palestine into an Arab state and a Jewish state.

While all this was unfolding, another colony, India, the jewel in the empire, had been partitioned into the Muslim state of Pakistan and the secular Republic of India after the two sides had come to an agreement. However, in Palestine there was no such agreement. The Zionists and the Jewish Agency welcomed the UN's findings, but the Arab reaction was again predictable. Jamal Husseini, the Palestinian representative at the UN, slammed the majority finding of UNSCOP, warning that "blood will flow like rivers in the Middle East."

After months of lobbying by both sides, on November 29, 1947, the UN General Assembly voted by two-thirds majority to pass Resolution 181, which called for the creation of a Jewish state on 55 per cent of Palestine and an Arab state on the rest of the territory, with Jerusalem and its suburbs to be governed by the United Nations in trust. As expected, the Jews rejoiced while the Arab leaders called for a "worldwide jihad in defence of Arab Palestine."

By the time the deadline for the British to pull out of its Palestine Mandate approached, Arab countries were preparing to declare war on the new state of Israel. The armies of Lebanon, Egypt, Iraq, and Jordan, along with smaller contingents from across the Arab world, poured into Israel to attack it from every flank. Israel repulsed all of them, thus ensuring a long, tragic existence for the Palestinians. For all the bravado and fiery speeches of the Arab leaders, all they ever produced was hot air about their medieval machismo.

Much has been written about the 1948 war, which is rightfully mourned as the al-Naqba – catastrophe – by the Palestinians and celebrated as a new beginning by the Jews. However, Muslims should take a look at the map of Palestine approved by the UN in 1947 and ask the question: Who should we blame for putting Jerusalem under Israeli jurisdiction? We cannot blame Israel or the UN. Israel after all had accepted the 1947 partition plan that would have left Jerusalem under UN trusteeship. The blame falls squarely on the Arab countries who rejected the UN resolution. Should we Muslims not take ownership of the errors of the Arab leadership and learn from past mistakes to ensure we don't repeat them?

By the time the last of the ceasefires were enforced, the state of Israel had expanded its borders beyond the areas sanctioned by the UN, while hundreds of thousands of Palestinians were forced out of or willingly fled their villages and towns to the safety of refugee camps. If the UN partition plan had been accepted, would the Palestinians today not have had their own state, with Jerusalem as an international city?

The proposed partition maps of the Peel Plan and the UN General Assembly that the Arabs and their Muslim allies rejected must be seen in light of where we are today, or even where we were at the end of the Six Day War of 1967. These maps should show us Muslims the folly of our choices, but very few of us are willing to take responsibility for or admit to the mistakes of earlier generations. We seem to find more solace in blaming our misery on the Jew.

After the "al-Naqba," the Islamist baton would move from Hajj al-Husayni to Sayyid Qutb, who would carry it through the postwar years until his death in 1966. In the previous chapter I dwelled on how Qutb internationalized the jihadi movement by suggesting that the only way to defeat Israel and the Jews was to return to the fundamentalist doctrine of Hasan al-Banna, the founder of the Muslim Brotherhood. Today, that Islamist baton is firmly in the hands of al-Banna's grandson, the charming, sweet-talking Swiss-born Tariq Ramadan. The language may have developed a level of sophistication, but the message remains the same: the Jews and the state of Israel are the reason why Muslims are stuck in a quagmire of despair.

CHAPTER FOUR

Is Israel Fuelling Anti-Semitism?

Few Muslims dare to state publicly that Israel has a right to exist as a Jewish state. Those of us who do, incur huge risks. Not only are we wrongfully portrayed as endorsing Israel's continued occupation of Palestinian territories, but it is claimed we are the ultimate enemies of Islam: Muslims who have betrayed our faith and who have acted against Allah's covenant and his fabled curse on the Jews.

This religious blackmail by the Islamist hate-mongers has forced countless Muslims who believe that both sides in the Israeli-Palestinian conflict have valid claims to maintain a troubling silence. Those of us who defend Israel's right to exist without the sword of Damocles hanging over its head have not surrendered our right to criticize the Jewish state when it deserves criticism.

In my case, I have straddled the fence and remained conflicted for decades. I felt delighted as a teenager to shake the hand of Leila Khaled when she came to Pakistan.* As a student at Karachi University,

---

* Leila Khaled is a Palestinian Marxist and a member of the Popular Front for the Liberation of Palestine. She came to public attention after her role in the 1969 hijacking of a TWA flight from Rome to Athens, which was diverted to Damascus. She acquired an iconic status among revolutionary movements around the world. Songwriter Julian Cope included a love song to her, "Like Leila Khaled Said," on his 1981 album *The Teardrop Explodes*.

I raised funds for the Popular Front for the Liberation of Palestine; in Toronto I demonstrated outside the Israeli consulate. But never once in my entire life have I had even an iota of anti-Semitism in my soul. While I met my first Palestinian in 1967, at Karachi University, my first friendship with a Jew had to wait until 1993, in Toronto, when I was hired by Julius Deutsch, a fascinating trade unionist. (He passed away in early 2010.) In lengthy chats with him, I was surprised to learn there were Jews in the same boat as me: supportive of Israel, but critical of its tactics in resolving the Palestinian question. Deutsch, son of German Jews who fled to Sydney after World War II, became my doorway to understanding the complex nature of the Middle East crisis. I learned from this Jew that things are rarely ever black and white and that the truth is usually found in the grey areas of overlapping narratives.

During those heady days of the Oslo Accords in the early 1990s, there was one thing that this Muslim and his Jewish friend and boss agreed upon: since Israel was the dominant power, it carried a bigger responsibility to move along the path to peace, and that failure on this road would further fan Muslim anti-Semitism. It was on the encouragement of Julius Deutsch that I ran for a seat in the Ontario Legislature, spoke for gay rights inside a mosque, and defended Israel's legitimacy in a Muslim community centre.

Years later, Irshad Manji, a well-known Canadian author, accused me of being anti-Jewish simply because in a conversation I had judged her book as catering exclusively to an Israeli audience. Manji is a bright woman, but like so many others on both sides of this dispute, she could not understand how one could be both pro-Israeli and pro-Palestinian at the same time, and with a clear conscience.

Muslims need to reconcile themselves to the fact that Israel is a country created by the United Nations General Assembly with the support of a two-thirds majority. Questioning Israel's moral and legal right to exist as a state within secure borders that are recognized by its neighbours should cease to be a subject of endless debate.

The Jews are an ethno-religious group with roots going back more than three thousand years. Since most national groups – from Arabs to Indians, Japanese to Germans – have a homeland, why not the Jews? I believe it is fundamentally anti-Jewish to incessantly challenge the moral and ethical basis of Israel as a Jewish state. If the Timorese can have a country and if Eritrea and Kosovo can be carved out of Africa and Europe in the twenty-first century, then surely the Jewish people deserve the right to have a state of their own in a place where they have had a presence for more than three thousand years. Israel's demand for an end to the relentless threat to its very existence is valid and needs no justification or explanation. On the other hand, Israel needs to recognize that just as it has the right to a sovereign state with an internationally recognized and guaranteed border, so do the Palestinians. As long as Israel continues to occupy Palestinian territories, the rest of the world will deem it an occupying power.

The old David-and-Goliath metaphor of a tiny Israel surrounded by millions of hostile Arabs has now been turned on its head. Today, it is Israel that is seen as Goliath, while the slingshot is in the hands of the stone-throwing Palestinian youth of Ramallah and Nablus. Whereas during the cold war Israel could do no wrong in the eyes of the West, today, Israel's international isolation is such that it feels it can do no right unless it commits suicide.

Though it is true that many Muslim critics of Israel are motivated by Judeophobia, not all criticism – even the harshest – stems from anti-Semitism. Just as criticism of the abject mediocrity of the Palestinian leadership and the terrorist nature of Hamas should not automatically classify as anti-Arabism or Islamophobia, a critique of Israel's leadership and opposition to its occupation of Palestinian territories should not be seen as anti-Semitic.

It is in this context that I believe Israel and its policies have contributed to the rise of anti-Semitism in the Arab world, from where it is spreading to the rest of the Muslim world and today is finding resonance inside the radical Left of the West. To conclude that Muslim-Jewish distrust and hate is a one-way street with one party a victim and the other the perpetrator is inaccurate. If Muslim clerics and politicians throughout the world are guilty of spreading hatred against Jews, then some in the Jewish community in North America as well as in Israel are also guilty of unfairly portraying even the most liberal and progressive Arab leaders in a negative light.

The 2009 attacks on the American Task Force on Palestine, or ATFP, that associated the group with terror and crime is one such example. If even progressive and liberal leaders of the Arab-American community such as Dr. Ziad Asali, ATFP fellow Hussein Ibish, and Prof. Rashid Khalidi are depicted as extremists and a threat to the West, then who is next? Succumbing to a knee-jerk suspicion of all Muslims, particularly Arabs, is no different than the belief among many Muslims that all Jews are evil and devious people who are hated by Allah.

I too have been the target of such allegations. In March 2010, the American-Arab author Wafa Sultan, in a speech at a Toronto synagogue, accused Prophet Muhammad of committing rape. She said, "Muhammad raped Aisha" – his wife – "when she was nine, he was fifty-four."

I protested her hateful language in an op-ed piece in the *National Post*. I was not alone in finding fault with Sultan's logic or language; Mark Freiman, the president of the Canadian Jewish Congress, said, "It is ironic that it was in a Jewish synagogue a short while ago that an ex-Muslim made the sweeping allegation that Islam as a faith was intrinsically incapable of political moderation or respecting the norms of secular society. . . . I add my name and that of the Canadian Jewish Congress to the rejection of such irresponsible charges."

Nevertheless, I upset a lot of people. Dozens of anti-Muslim blog-gers were up in arms, calling me a wolf in sheep's clothing and accusing me of defending child rape. The Jewish Internet Defense Force, react-ing to my article, said:

> In reality, Islam is like a deadly, contagious disease. Once it invades the mind of its victim, it is capable of transforming him to a helpless pawn that has no choice but to execute what he is directed to do. Of the reported 1.3 billion Muslims in the world, millions are already trapped in the terminal stages of this affliction, while millions of others are rapidly joining them. The people enslaved with the extreme cases of Islamic mental disease are highly infectious. They actively work to transmit the disease to others, while they themselves engage in horrific acts of mayhem and violence to demonstrate their unconditional obedience to the dictates of the Islamic cult.

Another strident supporter of Israel and the Jewish community, Dr. Andrew Bostom, called me "a despicable taqiyya-mongering pile of excrement." Writing in Pajamas Media, Bostom accused me of "silenc-ing the Jews," claiming I was a bully, hateful, and disingenuous.[1]

Other pro-Israel blogs accused me of being a potential terrorist: "Tarek Fatah proves my point that there is no such thing as a moderate Muslim. . . . Every 'moderate' Muslim is a potential terrorist. The belief in Islam is like a tank of gasoline. It looks innocuous, until it meets the fire. For a 'moderate' Muslim to become a murderous jihadist, all it takes is a spark of faith."[2]

Of course this vitriol is not indicative of mainstream Jewish thought, but such attacks on Muslims, simply because we stand up and defend our Prophet, is a sobering reminder of the personal costs of battling hate. Countering such hatred against Muslims is primarily the responsibility of saner elements of the Jewish community and of other non-Muslims. I am glad many of them rose to the occasion and stood by me. An editorial in the *Calgary Herald* read: "Utterly unreasonable people are calling Fatah an anti-Semite for criticizing the speech for being held in a synagogue, just like he criticizes outrageous speech in mosques. Fatah . . . is no anti-Semite. On the contrary. The smears against this courageous, thoughtful man who has literally risked his well-being to push for moderation, are nothing short of disgraceful. Even Rabbis walked out of Sultan's speech. Are they anti-Semitic too?"[3]

Among the many mistakes Israel has made is its strategic error in how it played the divide-and-rule game with the Palestinians. There was a time when Israel considered Islamists the lesser of two evils and in fact encouraged them as a means of countering the secular and nationalist Palestinians. But Israel must recognize the mistake it made when it undermined the traditional leadership of its adversary by encouraging their religious and Islamist rivals, Hamas. Victor Ostrovsky, the former Mossad officer who wrote *The Other Side of Deception,* levels the charge that the Israeli Right had a hand in encouraging Islamic fundamentalism among Palestinians as a way to undermine the Palestine Liberation Organization. He wrote, "Supporting the radical elements of Muslim fundamentalism sat well with Mossad's general plan for the region. An Arab world run by fundamentalists would not be a party to any negotiations with the West, thus leaving Israel again as the only democratic, rational country in the region. And if the Mossad could arrange for Hamas . . . to take over the Palestinian streets from the PLO, then the picture would be complete."[4]

It is not just Ostrovsky who has made this claim. Ziad Abu Amr of Birzeit University, in his book *Islamic Fundamentalism in the West Bank and Gaza: Muslim Brotherhood and Islamic Jihad,* writes about the sudden appearance of Muslim Brotherhood and Hamas hoodlums on campuses trying to elbow out the PLO: "The Muslim Brotherhood leadership urged Fatah" – the dominant faction of the PLO – "to purge its ranks of Marxist elements, to be aware of the futility of secularism, and to cooperate closely with Islamic groups."[5] For his book *Devil's Game: How the United States Helped Unleash Fundamentalist Islam,* Robert Dreyfuss interviewed Philip Wilcox, the U.S. ambassador to Jerusalem in the mid-1980s. Wilcox told him that "there were persistent rumours that the Israel secret service gave covert support to Hamas, because they were seen as rivals to the PLO."[6]

The PLO and Fatah were aware of this nexus. The Palestinian leader Yasser Arafat accused Hamas and its leader, Sheikh Yassin, of acting "with the direct support of reactionary Arab regimes . . . in collusion with Israeli occupation." He told the Italian newspaper *Corriere della Sera* in 2001, "Hamas is a creation of Israel, which at the time of Prime Minister Shamir, gave them money and more than 700 institutions, among them schools, universities and mosques." According to Arafat, "Israeli Prime Minister Yitzhak Rabin admitted Israeli support for Hamas [to him], in the presence of Egyptian president Hosni Mubarak." Rabin, he said, described this support as a "fatal error."[7]

Not only did Israel have a hand in nurturing the budding crop of Islamists, it did everything possible to undermine the credibility of Palestine's secular and democratic leadership, which had reconciled itself with the state of Israel and was willing to build peace, if not friendship, with the Jewish state. When Israel complains that it has no peace partner, that is not entirely true. Israel had ten years to deliver on Oslo, but all it did was build additional settlements, restrict Arafat to his Ramallah compound, and put Marwan Barghouti in prison. Who did they expect would fill this vacuum? Gandhi?

Today, Israel holds all the cards in the Middle East dispute and thus carries a bigger responsibility to resolve the conflict. What happens inside Israel and the occupied territories causes ripples throughout the Muslim world. Every time Israel deals harshly with the Palestinians, anger at Israel grows. The road to anti-Semitism is short.

Take, for example, the publication in Israel in 2009 of the book *Torat Hamelech: Dinei Nefashot Bein Yisrael Le'Amim* (The King's Torah: Laws of Life and Death between Jews and the Nations), in which the authors, Rabbi Yitzhak Shapira and Rabbi Yosef Elite Elitzur, cite sources from the Bible, the Talmud, and later rabbinical literature to condone and justify the killing of non-Jews. Gentile non-combatants, they argue, including innocent children and babies, can be killed in situations in which their presence endangers, even indirectly, the lives of Jews. "Little children are often situated in this way," they write. "They block the rescue of Jews and they do this against their will. Even so, it is permitted to kill them because their very presence facilitates the killing [of Jews]."

According to the *Jerusalem Post,* the two rabbis also advocate the killing of young children if it is perceived that these children will grow up to be enemies of the Jews. "There is an argument for killing the very young if it is clear that they will grow up to hurt us [Jews]," write Shapira and Elitzur. "And in this situation the attack should be directed at them and not just indirectly while attacking adults."

In a chapter titled "Attacking the Innocent," the two rabbis argue that although the main brunt of a war effort should be against those with an intent to kill, even someone who merely belongs to the nation of the enemy should be considered an enemy. They assert that it is permitted to kill a civilian who helps combatants fighting against Jews. And as if they had not given their followers enough reasons to kill Muslims, Shapira and Elitzur also argue for vigilante freelance murder: "One does not need a decision by the nation to permit the spilling of blood of those from the evil empire. Even individuals attacked by the evil sovereignty can retaliate."[8]

The *Jerusalem Post* reported that the book, which was being sold at Mercaz Harav Yeshiva, the flagship educational institution of Orthodox Zionism, had sold out within a week of publication; the book's sales were soon news across the Islamic blogosphere. Critics of Israel fingered it as proof of Israel's anti-Islamic nature and used it to support their claim that Israel had deliberately killed children in their last incursion into Gaza. The book was released just a week after a Jewish settler was arrested for allegedly murdering two Palestinians and severely wounding a Christian.

While it is true that The King's Torah is an obscure book that most Jews do not take seriously, it does have the support of a vocal minority and it does fan the flames. The fact is, Islamists use such material to validate their portrayal of Jews as being fundamentally anti-Muslim.

Compared with the incessant slander of Jews in the Muslim world, though, expressions of hate towards Muslims such as The King's Torah are isolated. I have spent countless hours trying to locate explicit attacks on Islam by Jewish religious authorities, but have found little evidence of such literature, either in medieval history or in the modern era. Even in Maimonides' *Epistle to Yemen*, in which the medieval Jewish scholar bemoans the tribulations of Jews under a harsh Islamic ruler, the critique of the Muslim is mild. But the fact remains that even the rarest of attacks on Islam, Muslims, or Arabs validates the Islamist position that the Jews are the enemies of Muslims and that Israel is primarily a cancerous growth, placed in the heart of the Islamic world by the kuffar.

More than attacks on Islam or Muslims, the daily humiliation that a Palestinian experiences in his own town and neighbourhood is difficult to imagine for Muslims who may face occasional discrimination, but know very little about what it is like to live with restrictions placed on our movements and freedoms. An entire generation of Palestinians has known no other existence but occupation. One may fault the Palestinian leadership for avoiding every opportunity to resolve the conflict, but not the people who have no voice. The late Israeli foreign minister Abba Eban remarked soon after the Geneva peace talks in 1973 that "Arabs never miss an opportunity to miss an opportunity," but that is little consolation to the Palestinian who was born and died in a refugee camp.

If what Abba Eban said was true – and I believe it is – then is it not an acknowledgement of the legitimacy of the Palestinian grievance? Eban's remark may be seen as an indictment of the Palestinian leadership, but it is certainly an admission that in this dispute, the Palestinians have been wronged. And if successive Israeli governments, and most of Israel's political parties, agree that the Palestinian leadership, from the mufti to Arafat, is responsible for botching the peace process, it still does not address the central questions: Why cannot Israel withdraw unilaterally from territories it occupied in the Six Day War of 1967? What stops Israel from interpreting UN Security Resolution 242 the way it wishes to and pulling back so that a trip from Bethlehem to Ramallah ceases to be a nightmare for the residents of the two Palestinian cities? At the risk of sounding naive, have not the Israelis withdrawn unilaterally from South Lebanon and Gaza? Did they not walk away from the Sinai? And why not the West Bank and the parts of East Jerusalem that they are willing to vacate, which could then become the capital of a future Palestinian state?

For too long Israel has banked on the utter incompetence of the Arab leadership, while continuing its illegal and immoral occupation. There is a danger in overestimating the capacity of a people to suffer – the Jews should know that better than anyone else. Israelis may not be able to see themselves in that light, but increasingly they are viewed – rightly or wrongly, it does not matter – by the rest of the world as an arrogant, powerful nation that may be surrounded by enemies but is not making it easy for those enemies to come to terms with its existence. There was a time when support for Israel was almost unanimous in most Western countries, but not any more. Those in Europe who were once hesitant to display their anti-Semitism can today camouflage it by attacking Israel for its occupation of the West Bank. Israelis must reflect on how, within decades, the near-unanimous support in the West for their state has slowly dissipated.

Take the example of the New Democratic Party in Canada. *Toronto Star* reporter John Goddard has vivid memories of attending the annual convention of the federal NDP as a teenager shortly after the Six Day War. "The delegates were solidly behind Israel. I remember David Lewis" – the future leader of the party – "leading the discussion at the Royal York Hotel, the look of steely resolve on his face, and the sense of relief in the room over the defeat of the Arab armies."

Fast-forward to 2006 and the NDP convention in Quebec City, where 90 per cent of the delegates denounced Israel and praised the extremist group Hezbollah. When veteran Winnipeg M.P. Judy Wasylycia-Leis stood up to object, saying Hezbollah was a terrorist organization, she was roundly booed. The NDP has today become the bastion of anti-Israel sentiment. One New Democrat M.P. was quoted as fearing that the left-wing party was in danger of being hijacked by extremists. After seventeen years as a loyal NDPer, I too had to leave the party as I saw how it was being taken over by Islamists and apologists for the Iranian regime.

The Jewish narrative today faces a more vigorous challenge, one that appeals to the moral and ethical values the Jewish state claims as the basis of its existence.

The erosion of Israel's international standing is recognized in the country, but most people seem to be ignorant of the root cause of their isolation and blame it on the rise of the Left-Islamist network in the West. In February 2010, the Reut Institute, a security and socio-economic think tank based in Tel Aviv, issued a report stating that the

Jewish state was facing a global campaign of delegitimization. The government called on its ministers to treat the matter as a strategic threat.

The report cited anti-Israel demonstrations on campuses, protests when Israeli athletes competed abroad, moves in Europe to boycott Israeli products, and threats of arrest warrants for Israeli leaders visiting London. The report further stated that while most of the campaign activists were Palestinian, Arab, or Muslim, they were tightly linked to left-wing groups. It noted that the Western Left had changed its approach to Israel and now saw it as an occupation state.

Instead of seeing the writing on the wall, Israel is making cosmetic changes that will bear no fruit. In television commercials that are part of an initiative called "Making the Case for Israel," Israelis are being asked by their government to become "citizen diplomats." One government ad claims that people around the world believe Israelis use camels as a common form of transportation, while another spot suggests that they mistake Israeli Independence Day fireworks for military action. The commercials ask Israelis, "Are you fed up with the way we are portrayed around the world?" and urge them to teach non-Israelis that their country is modern, sophisticated, and peace loving. In February 2010, the *Globe and Mail* reported, "Brochures that provide helpful examples and statistics are being distributed by airlines."[9] The government of Israel, apparently, is blind to the reasons for ill will towards the Jewish state.

Even at the diplomatic level, the response to the negative image of Israel has failed to address the primary cause. Ron Prosor, Israel's ambassador to London, reacting to a spate of anti-Israel activity in Britain, concluded, "The combination of a large Muslim community, a radical left, influential, English-language media and an international university centre make London fertile ground for Israel's delegitimization."[10]

Long before there were any active Muslim groups in the West advocating the Palestinian cause, Israel's occupation of Arab lands was damaging its reputation around the world. After the 1973 Yom Kippur

War, when for a few days the very existence of Israel was threatened by the advancing Egyptian army, President Ephraim Katzir of Israel invited Jewish scholars and academics from around the world to a three-day seminar in Jerusalem for a "critical assessment" of Israel and its relations with the rest of the world. One of the speakers was Irwin Cotler, the respected Canadian human rights lawyer who later became the country's attorney general and justice minister.

Cotler's speech gave the first hints of how Canadian views of the Jewish state were changing for the worse because of Israel's occupation of Egyptian, Syrian, and Jordanian territories. He spoke of an initiative in Winnipeg in which Jews and non-Jews in academia, politics, business, and public service met to discuss the Yom Kippur War. From these meetings, which he described as "representing a microcosm of the general Canadian community," emerged a number of attitudes about Israel. Among them were three significant points:

- "The Yom Kippur War was seen as a continuation of the Six Day War. Accordingly, since Israel was the 'aggressor' in the Six Day War and unlawfully seized Arab territory, the Arabs had only gone to war to regain their lost territory."
- "The war was not unrelated to the 'intransigence' of Israeli policy. Israel should be less inflexible and more conciliatory – including the return of the occupied territories – if Israel genuinely wants peace."
- "The legitimacy – rather than the fact – of Israeli statehood was not understood. Palestinian 'homeland' was believed to have been 'usurped' in the creation of the state of Israel. A compensatory initiative – such as the creation of a Palestinian state – was now necessary."[11]

As early as 1973, Irwin Cotler had brought the message to Jerusalem – long before Camp David or Oslo – that Canadians felt the creation of a Palestinian state was crucial to justify the "legitimacy" of the Jewish state. Nearly forty years later, that Palestinian state seems as elusive as the mythical winged horse Buraq that is said to have transported Prophet Muhammad from Jerusalem to the heavens for a chat with Allah.

Many Israelis may think they have their Palestinian adversaries pinned down and crying for mercy, but I would suggest the opposite is true.

Palestine is to Israel what the Old Man of the Sea was to Sindbad the Sailor. During his fifth voyage, Sindbad was marooned after a shipwreck. He came across an old man, who asked Sindbad to carry him across a river. When Sindbad agreed, the old man jumped onto his back, riding on his shoulders with his legs twisted round Sindbad's neck, and refused to let go. Sindbad was trapped as the old man just would not let go, riding him both day and night.

If Israel is to survive as a nation state, not a pariah, it will have to get Palestine off its back; otherwise, the prognosis for the two is mutual annihilation. There is no other alternative but to end the occupation, with a complete separation of the two states. For too long, Israel has depended on cheap Palestinian labour to build the very settlements they hate. What is created by this bizarre interaction of profitability and hate is two dysfunctional societies that have put a gun to each other's heads.

If the most pro-Palestinian president in American history, Jimmy Carter, could not get the Palestinian leadership to drop their "all or nothing" doctrine, it is unlikely Barack Obama will succeed. In the days after 9/11, President Carter wrote an op-ed in the *New York Times* reminding Americans, as well as readers in the Arab world and Israel, about the Camp David Accords that he had negotiated between President Anwar Sadat and Prime Minister Menachem Begin:

"One of the basic elements of this accord was Israel's agreement to withdraw both political and military forces from the West Bank and

Gaza. The Palestinians were to have full autonomy under a self-govern-ing authority elected freely by the people in the West Bank and Gaza, and were to participate on an equal basis in future negotiations. . . . In addition, Begin agreed that Israel would cease putting settlements in the occupied territories until a final agreement was reached on how to fulfil the Camp David pledges."[12]

For signing the Camp David treaty in 1978 that would have given Palestinians full autonomy in all of the occupied territories of Gaza and the West Bank and put an end to the building of settlements, President Sadat was condemned in the Arab world as a sell-out and traitor, and later assassinated for the crime of bringing peace between Egypt and Israel.

The longer the Israelis wait for a Palestinian partner, the worse will be Israel's position in the international community. If the PLO rejected Camp David when there were far fewer settlements than there are today, it is unlikely that any Palestinian leader would be willing to appear weak and accept peace today. If Yasser Arafat rejected the peace deal offered by President Clinton and Ehud Barak in 2000 that would have given the Palestinians 95 per cent of the West Bank and all of Gaza, it is unlikely that Mahmoud Abbas would wish to be seen as the weakling in the long list of Palestinian leaders who want to be known as fighters, not statesmen. Few would wish to be labelled a quisling, as Anwar Sadat was made out to be.

Part of the problem Israel faces is that Palestinian leaders seem to be judged by their ability to stand up to Israel rather than by their capacity to make peace. Those who talk peace are considered "effemi-nate," while those who holler war and indulge in sloganeering end up respected and adored. Thus, when a few brave Palestinians and Israelis worked out the Geneva Accord in 2003, with the backing of Presidents Carter and Clinton, the former Palestinian information min-ister Yasser Abed Rabbo was ridiculed by his colleagues as irrelevant and a lightweight.

Both Abed Rabbo and Israeli justice minister Yossi Beilin, once official negotiators for their sides, continued to meet in an unofficial capacity after leaving their respective cabinets. The outcome was a detailed agreement that addressed the tough questions, including the acceptance of final borders, the issue of Jerusalem, and the question of Palestinian refugees.

The accord would force Israel to accept Palestinian sovereignty in East Jerusalem. It states that the Jewish neighbourhoods of Jerusalem would be under Israeli authority, and the Arab neighbourhoods of Jerusalem under Palestinian sovereignty. In addition, both sides agreed that Palestinian Jerusalemites who were permanent residents of Israel would lose this status upon the transfer of authority to Palestine of those areas in which they resided. The accord notes that Israel agreed to the renaming of the Temple Mount as the "Esplanade of the Mosques."

If the Israelis were willing to accept East Jerusalem as the capital of Palestine, what they would extract in return was an enormous concession from the Palestinians. The accord called for the Palestinians to renounce their right of return to Israel, restricting them to the territory of the new state of Palestine, and provided for adequate compensation.

The accord went beyond recognizing the simultaneous existence of a viable Palestinian state and an Israel with legitimate, secure borders. It traced, village to village, almost olive tree to olive tree, the line of partition. Although Israel was required to demolish most of the settlements along the border, it would retain some beyond the Green Line, as well as Jewish neighbourhoods in East Jerusalem, in exchange for an equal amount of territory.

As one commentator said, the Geneva Accord was not a plan by dreamers. It was a concrete plan, precisely negotiated, almost maniacally meticulous. Unfortunately, it was lost in the polemics of the dispute. A lesson in political pragmatism, handed out by the two civil societies to their leaders, was wasted, with hard-liners on both sides mocking Beilin and Rabbo rather than acknowledging the merits of their proposal.

In the absence of a Palestinian partner willing to negotiate, the challenge for Israel is complex. Conventional wisdom dictates that it take advantage of the situation, gloat over the impotence of its enemy, and keep building settlements. Such a path, which Israel has already embraced, may in the short term give it a stronger hand if the Palestinians return to the table, but it will not earn the Jewish state what it desires most: the security of its citizens and the recognition of its borders by the neighbouring Arab states.

Israel has another option. It can come to the realization that it does not need to prove its armed might and its ability to crush any attempt on its life by any state or terrorist organization. Notwithstanding the rhetorical flourishes of Arab leaders and clerics, the Egyptian dictator Nasser and his two thousand T-55 tanks and eight hundred MiG-21s are part of the scrap heap of history. The histrionics of Iranian president Ahmadinejad cause more panic in Jordan and Saudi Arabia than Israel would like to imagine. Now is the chance for Israel, as a victorious power, to live up to its Jewish heritage and prove the Islamists wrong. It is only Jerusalem that can afford, and has the ability to show, magnanimity. It must offer hope, justice, and dignity to its foes in the spirit of *Tikvah, Anavah*, and *Tikkun olam,* for that is the Jewish inheritance. When the prophet Amos said, "Let justice roll like water, and righteousness as a permanent torrent," I am sure he meant this justice not just for the Israelites, but also for us Ishmaelites.

Recent history shows us the difference between victors who have earned the friendship of the vanquished and those who have conquered and sown the seeds of hate. Israel still has a chance to choose. It can emulate the example of the United States, which in defeating Japan and Germany made them its allies, or that of Russia, which, even in liberating Poland and Hungary, created revulsion towards Moscow.

If as victors of many wars Israel still cannot facilitate the creation of a viable and sovereign Palestinian state with East Jerusalem as its capital, then it will always be known as a country that swallowed another state and people. The enmity this will generate will last for generations. At some time in the future, the Arabs are bound to regain their ability to stand up for themselves and take advantage of the strategic geopolitical position they command in the region.

It is not just the risk Israel faces from neighbouring Arab states, if ever they wake from their century-long malaise and slumber, but from its own Muslim citizenry, which makes up about 20 per cent of the population. Granted, these Muslims would rather live in Israel than any other country, and compared to the living conditions of minorities in Muslim states, Israel's Muslims have an enviable right to freedom of worship. However, even inside Israel, the Islamist forces are gaining in strength and influencing attitudes towards the state. If Israel chooses to remain an occupying power in the West Bank and blockades the Gaza Strip, it would be naive on the part of its leadership to assume this will have no effect on its Arab population.

In 2008 I visited Israel and spent time in Muslim towns and villages meeting clerics, politicians, and young Muslim men wearing distinctly Israel Defense Forces trousers. At every meeting I asked a blunt question: "As a Muslim, do you feel you live in an apartheid state?" Invariably, the answer was a firm no. As one man in his twenties, in the northern town of Shibli (where a sign reading *"Allahu Akbar"* graces the entrance), told me, *"Wallah al azeem"* – as God is my witness – "I will never wish to trade my Israeli citizenship for any of those wretched Arab countries who do not know how to treat their own citizens with dignity." I asked the same question of Imam Mohammad Odeh outside his spectacular mosque north of Haifa. He grinned before admitting, "We Muslims have difficulties, there is no doubt, and we feel Israel should end the occupation of the West Bank, but to say we Muslims are living in an apartheid state is a lie." After a tour of the mosque, where we prayed, he invited me to his home. What followed was a long, heartfelt story of a Palestinian living as an Israeli citizen, the imam of a mosque and leader of a community of two thousand. Hurt was written on his face, but his complaints were aimed not at Israel but towards the intellectual bankruptcy of the men who lead the Palestinians. I asked him if he truly, in his heart, felt Israeli, and without hesitating he said, "Yes."

It is Arabs like the young man in Shibli and the imam in Haifa that Israel risks alienating if it continues down its arrogant path of occupation. The humiliation experienced by their fellow Muslims while going through the ugly checkpoints that separate Israel from the West Bank is bound to affect the loyalties of Arab Israelis.

Within Israel itself the voices for an end to the occupation are no longer restricted to the fringe on the left. Authors such as Amos Oz and academics like Shlomo Avineri have long argued the positions taken up by the much-weakened Peace Now movement. But when its most decorated soldier, former prime minister Ehud Barak, joins these ranks and warns Israel of the risks of avoiding a peace settlement with the Palestinians, Israelis must pay attention. Labour leader Barak, who is defence minister in Prime Minister Netanyahu's coalition cabinet, shocked his audience when he told a conference on national security in early 2010 that if Israel failed to accomplish peace with the Palestinians, it would end up either as a state with no Jewish majority or an "apartheid" regime. Israelis who scoff at Barak do so at their own peril. The call for a just peace and the creation of a Palestinian state is not a favour to the Palestinians, but an absolute necessity for the survival of the Jewish state.

What was significant about Barak's unusually blunt warning to his compatriots was the fact that he shared the head table with Palestinian prime minister Salam Fayyad. This was a rare and public admission by a senior Israeli minister that the deadlocked peace process would hurt Israel, not the Palestinians. The Palestinians demanded an end to the construction of settlements before returning to the bargaining table, and Barak likely recognizes what other Israeli politicians are missing. They may see the absence of the Palestinians as an opportunity to expand their settlements, while he realizes that if the Palestinians stayed away, the West Bank would still cling to Israel.

Choosing his words carefully, Barak appealed to Israelis on both right and left by saying a peace agreement with the Palestinians was the only way to secure Israel's future as a "Zionist, Jewish, democratic state." "As long as in this territory west of the Jordan river there is only one political entity called Israel it is going to be either non-Jewish, or non-democratic. . . . If this bloc of millions of Palestinians cannot vote, that will be an apartheid state." Israel, he said, risked losing its very legitimacy if no peace deal were forthcoming. "The pendulum of legitimacy is going to move gradually towards the other pole."[13]

If my Israeli friends find the words of Ehud Barak jarring, then perhaps they should listen to another of their celebrated defence ministers, the legendary Moshe Dayan. Addressing Israelis who were angered by his invitation to the Palestinian poet Fadwa Toukan to his home soon after the 1967 Six Day War, Dayan told a radio show host, "If you, sir, living in Israel, don't want to hear what she [Toukan] is saying, this troubles me. I would have personally liked her to come to Tel Aviv and even if we should then bite our lips, we should listen to her, in order to understand what the public which she is representing is feeling. I don't think that if you would listen to her you would join Al Fatah. But you may perhaps understand why a youngster from one of the villages joins Al Fatah. And this is important not only so that you understand what is going on there now, in this period of warfare, but also so that we could understand which avenues to follow to reach a framework within which we could live together. For ultimately there is no choice, we shall have to live together."[14]

Moshe Dayan continued to pursue his campaign for accommodation with the Palestinians with respect and dignity. In 1969, he spoke to the students of Haifa University:

> I insist on saying that the problem of the State of Israel, after a hundred years of the return of Zion, is not how to expel Arabs, but how to live with them. We came here, to an area inhabited by Arabs, and we maintain here a Jewish state. In many instances we bought the land from the Arabs, and Jewish settlements were established on the sites of Arab villages. You, my student friends, may not even know the names of these villages as the geography books which described them have disappeared long ago; but so have the villages. Nahalal rose on the site of Mahlul. G'vat on the site of Jibta, Sarid on the site of Khneifes, and Kfar Yehoshua on the site of Tel Shaman.
>
> But now, after Israel has been in existence for twenty years, after there has been a war, and there is a Jewish population of two and a quarter million souls, living where it does, and there are about a million Arabs in Judea, Samaria, and the Gaza Strip – now we certainly should not say that we replace the Arabs and expel them across the bridges. In our present situation we have to seek avenues for living together with them. This is possible, and I will cite Hebron, and the Tomb of the Patriarchs, as an example.[15]

Moshe Dayan's closing remarks to the students in Haifa in 1969 echo what Ehud Barak told his audience in 2010. Forty years ago, Dayan – the man who, I was told as a teenager, was "the one-eyed Dajaal," or Antichrist – uttered words of wisdom that have gone unheeded.

"We have to supply the people [Palestinians] with employment and services, give them civil rights, and not treat them as enemies. The question is: What are we aiming for? Shall we be an occupying power, keeping the Arabs as an oppressed population of second- and third-class citizens and tell them: 'You won't do this, you won't do that, you won't study at the university, and if you protest, we shall impose curfew?' Or should we aim at a common life, with Jews learning to live together with Arabs? If so, we have to be neighbours, and not conquerors."[16]

Much water has flowed down the River Jordan since Dayan spoke those words in the wake of Israel's sweeping victory in the Six Day War. The Arabs and Israel clashed again in 1973, and blood soaked the Sinai before peace would dawn between Egypt and Israel, but not Palestine. Many opportunities have been lost, along with countless lives. It may very well be the fault of the Arab leadership for first promising the Palestinians a military victory, later usurping their land to expand their own territories, keeping them in refugee camps on a diet of fiery rhetoric, using their cause to further their own dictatorships and kingdoms, and in the end abandoning them as orphans of history in the lap of Iran and the ayatollahs. Today, these lost children of Ishmael have become helpless puppets in the hands of the world jihadi movement that forces young men and women to die while the dream of a Palestine recedes faster than ever. The idea of Palestine may well die in this game of deliberate tactics, yet the Palestinian will still be there, just like the Old Man of the Sea with his legs locked around Sindbad's neck.

Israel and the Jewish Diaspora must recognize that not all anti-Zionism or anti-Israelism necessarily reflects anti-Semitism or a hatred of Jews. As Bernard Lewis notes in *Semites and Anti-Semites,* "To determine whether opponents of Zionism or critics of Israel are inspired by honest or by dishonest (clandestine anti-Semitic) motives, one must examine each case – government, party, group, or individual – separately, and in doing so look for specific ascertainable criteria."[17]

Lewis admits this is a difficult task. However, he suggests that in trying to distinguish between honest and dishonest criticism of Israel, one should take into account the context and the culture from which this criticism emerges. In the Arab world, where tempers easily run high and the rhetoric is laced with religious zeal, for example, he says, "Fair comment may sometimes look like bigotry." He contrasts this with the West, where speech is restrained, and a comment that may appear fair and balanced could very well reflect bigotry. Lewis goes to the extent of suggesting that even when Arabs talk of "liquidating the Zionist entity," they are not necessarily expressing anti-Semitism. Because most Arabs consider the creation of the state of Israel an act of injustice and the continued occupation a standing aggression, he says, their language should be seen as an expression of their legitimate political objectives. He admits that Arab hostility towards Israel rests on a genuine grievance that has given rise to a prejudice, but adds that that prejudice was not the cause of opposition to Israel.

Having said that, Lewis does draw a firm line: "When Arab spokesmen, not content with denouncing the misdeeds of the Israelis, attribute these misdeeds to innate Jewish racial characteristics discernible throughout history . . . then no doubt remains that those Arabs who write and distribute these things are engaged in anti-Semitic activities."[18]

Today, more than at any time in the last hundred years, leading Palestinians have come to terms with the existence of Israel as a Jewish state and a fact of life. From President Abbas to Prime Minister Fayyad of the Palestinian Authority; from Prof. Rashid Khalidi of Columbia University to Ziad Asali of the American Task Force on Palestine, there is not a hint of anti-Semitism in their attitudes. Numerous ordinary Palestinians I have met in Toronto, New York, Bethlehem, and Jerusalem have issues with Hamas and reject the hysterical and religiously laced hatred spouted from the pulpit. These are men and women who see the future in a secular democratic Palestine that is sovereign and free from the diktat of either Iran or Saudi Arabia. However, if they too are attacked as anti-Semitic by U.S.-based Zionist groups and individuals, who at times cross the line and attack Islam as a threat to humanity, then the prospects are bleak indeed, not only for Palestine but for Israel as well.

In his 1991 documentary, *Deadly Currents,* about the first Palestinian intifada, Emmy Award–winning journalist Simcha Jacobovici interviews the eighty-eight-year-old Israeli philosopher Yeshayahu Leibowitz, the former editor of the *Encyclopaedia Hebraica.* Leibowitz predicts a gloomy future for Israel unless it ends the occupation. Calling for the establishment of a Palestinian state, he says, "There is no chance for a continuous existence of the state of Israel as an apparatus for violent domination of another people." When Jacobovici asks, "Do you mean Israel's survival is in danger if the occupation continues?" he responds, "Not only danger: doom is certain." Nudged to explain why, Leibowitz says: "Internally, the state of Israel will become a fascist state. Externally, we will have to face the entire Arab world from Morocco to Kuwait with the sympathy of the entire world on the side of the Arabs."

If the Palestinian state ends up as a stillborn child, then Israel will have to exist as a Jewish state with a Muslim majority population governed by race laws reminiscent of 1960s South Africa. At that stage, the words of Moshe Dayan in 1969, Yeshayahu Leibowitz in 1991, or Ehud Barak in 2010 will be meaningless. They will reverberate in the collective conscience of the Jews of Israel, reminding them that they could have avoided their dilemma but were too paranoid to see the opportunities and too overconfident to notice the minefield they were walking into.

Israel should grant freedom to the Palestinians by ending its occupation, not only because the occupation is illegal but because it is immoral. Helping to create an independent sovereign state of Palestine will be the right thing to do and would contribute immensely to the fight against Muslim anti-Semitism.

CHAPTER FIVE

Is the Quran Anti-Semitic?

In the spring of 2004, the leadership of the Muslim community in Montreal erupted in outrage. One of their own had dared to wash Muslim dirty linen in public by suggesting, "Anti-Semitism has become an entrenched tenet of Muslim theology, taught to 95 per cent of the religion's adherents in the Islamic world."[1]

The response was instant. Salam Elmenyawi, president of the Muslim Council of Montreal, exclaimed: "There is not an iota of evidence that this is correct." I doubt if Elmenyawi was unaware of the works of Sayyid Qutb, but like most Islamists, his reliance on rhetorical flourishes overshadowed the facts. As we saw in chapter 2, there is definitely more than an "iota of evidence" that anti-Semitism has become part and parcel of Islamic teachings. Any Muslim with a mustard seed of integrity would have considerable difficulty denying the contemporary narrative of jihad in the mosques of the world – and particularly in the West – which have become a breeding ground for anti-Semitism. How else can one explain the fact that many clerics conclude their Friday sermon with a prayer to Allah to defeat the kuffar – Jews and Christians?

The man who uttered the unmentionable was Khaleel Mohammed, a former Montreal imam who currently teaches Islamic law at San Diego State University in California. Professor Mohammed's credentials alone should have deterred his detractors from denouncing him, but respecting dissent among Muslims is a virtue that Islamists are not known for.

Mohammed was no run-of-the-mill Islamophobe. A former soldier in the Canadian army, he has a bachelor's degree in religion and psychology from Universidad Interamericana in Mexico City; an M.A. in religion, specializing in Judaism and Islam, from Concordia University; and a doctorate in Islamic law from McGill. And if his Western academic credentials in Islam were not sufficient, the good professor was also a graduate of the Islamic University in Riyadh, Saudi Arabia, where he studied sharia law.

However, responding with typical finger-waving umbrage and spewing allegations of racism and apostasy – histrionics that have become second nature to many fundamentalist imams – Montreal's Islamists immediately dismissed Khaleel Mohammed's comments as false and racist. They then added insult to injury by accusing him of "destroying efforts at building relationships between Jews and Muslims." Mohamed Elmasry, the president of the Canadian Islamic Congress who would later say that killing all Israeli civilians over eighteen years of age was justified, called the professor's remarks "outrageous."

However, Mohammed stood his ground, telling the Montreal *Gazette* that although the Quran preaches respect for Judaism, the Hadith, a collection of the Prophet Muhammad's oral proclamations written centuries after his death, contains anti-Semitic passages widely quoted by Muslim clerics. He said, "In Hadith literature . . . which Muslims have made to be part and parcel of Islamic teaching, you cannot respect the Jew, the Jew is God's enemy until the end of time. And that's ingrained."

This depiction of the Jew as evil, said Mohammed, "has become part of Islamic theology, so the average Muslim learns anti-Semitism in probably a subtler form, not overt anti-Semitism, but learns it as part of his theology."[2]

A deeply religious man with a dry sense of humour and a knack for naughtiness, Mohammed breaks every stereotype of an Islamic cleric one can imagine. With not a speck of facial hair and a complete absence of the guttural accent that has become the trademark of the mullah from Fiji to France, he is the type of imam who could salvage Muslims mired in the morass of ignorance and denial. But men like him have been chased from the mosque and excommunicated by their community. Still, he refuses to go away and continues to fight back the medieval madness that is creating monsters within the Muslim community.

The question that arises from the spat in Montreal is this: Is Khaleel Mohammed correct when he says the Quran preaches goodwill towards the Jews while the Hadith literature does the opposite? I wish to put his assertion to the test.

In the summer of 2009, the *National Post* asked me to write a piece on my experience with my holy book, the Quran, as part of a series about what Canadians read at the ages of four, fourteen, forty, and "forever," the dawn of my dusk. I had first read the Quran sitting beside my mother and had studied the complex book many times, but as I wrote about my relationship with it, I was taken aback by how the book was being read and explained to our youth, starting from the very first lines that every Muslim child memorizes – the Sura al-Fatiha (The Opening).

In the name of God, the beneficent, the merciful.
Praise be to God, Lord of the worlds,
The beneficent, the merciful, Master of the Day of Judgment.
You alone we worship, and You alone we ask for help.
Guide us on the right path,
The path of those upon whom You have bestowed your bounty,
Not of those who have earned Your wrath, nor of those who
go astray.

These words are beautiful and profound, the Islamic equivalent of the Lord's Prayer. But Muslims in the ninth century – that is, two hundred years after the words were revealed to Prophet Muhammad – inserted another meaning into the last verse that has unfortunately given divine validation to Muslim Judeophobia.

Until the day I wrote about this beautiful prayer, I had not probed beyond what I thought was the obvious meaning. This time I wondered who God was referring to when he talks about the people who have incurred his "wrath" or who have gone "astray." I read the commentaries on this verse in the many English translations of the Quran that grace my library. As well, I read the exegeses by medieval scholars like Ibn Kathir (1301–1373), whose words carry tremendous weight in the Arab world to this day.* What I discovered confirmed the premise of Khaleel Mohammed's thesis. While the Quran verse spoke in generalities about human nature, Ibn Kathir associated the two negative comments in the sura specifically with Jews and, to a lesser degree, Christians. For centuries, these hateful additions by a mere mortal have acquired the status of divine truth or revelation.

Ibn Kathir has no doubt the verse is referring to Jews and Christians. He does not explain why Allah would not mention the two religious

---

* Ibn Kathir was a fourteenth-century scholar in Damascus who wrote about the Quran and Islam in the aftermath of the destruction in 1258 of the Abbasid caliphate by the invading Mongols. He was a student of the Syrian theologian Ibn Taymiyya. Since that time, the two men have provided intellectual sustenance to most of the jihadi Islamists who even today are hell-bent on wreaking havoc on both the Muslim world and the West. Ibn Kathir's commentary on the Quran was the first to link the sayings of Prophet Muhammad and his companions to verses of the Quran. Today, his book, *Tafsir ibn Kathir*, is available all over the world, and its English translations are hugely popular among Muslim youth in North America and Europe. Though he died in 1373, his work has continued to instill radicalism in Muslim youth while making them view Jews and Christians as evil and as enemies of Islam.

communities by name or even by the reference "people of the book." Instead, he writes:

> Allah asserted that the two paths He described here are both misguided when He repeated the negation "not." These two paths are paths of the Christians and the Jews, a fact that the believer should be aware of so that he avoids them. The path of the believers [Muslims] is knowledge of the truth and abiding by it. In comparison, the Jews abandoned practising the religion, while the Christians lost their true knowledge. This is why "anger" descended upon the Jews, while being described as "led astray" is more appropriate of the Christians. . . . We should also mention that both the Christians and the Jews have earned the anger and are led astray, but the anger is one of the attributes more particular of the Jews. Allah said about the Jews, "Those (Jews) who incurred the curse of Allah and His wrath" (Quran 5:60).[3]

Ibn Kathir invokes another Quranic verse to back up his commentary identifying the Jews as the people who have incurred the wrath of God. However, in neither verse does the word *Jew* appear. Undeterred, Ibn Kathir deftly slips in the word *Jews* between parentheses.

Since Ibn Kathir is considered the foremost authority on the Quran, his commentary sometimes far supersedes the Quran itself. With few Muslims willing to challenge him, his words have acquired divine status simply because they were uttered in antiquity. However, within the Arab world, brave voices of pious and learned Muslims have begun to speak out.

—

Prof. Mahmoud Ayoub of Temple University, a Lebanese-Muslim scholar of Islamic history, states that the Quranic text in the Sura al-Fatiha is not a reference to any religious community, but rather addresses two attributes of people who may belong to any racial or religious group. Prof. Khaleel Mohammed in his commentary quotes the scholar al-Nisaburi (d. 1327), who he says rendered the obvious interpretation: "Those who have incurred God's wrath are the people of negligence, and those who have gone astray are the people of immoderation."[4]

Notwithstanding the few scholars who have rejected the notion that the opening chapter of the Quran has an anti-Jewish tone, the fact is that an overwhelming majority of exegetical works on the Quran have embraced this hostility towards Jews. After the copious Hadith was compiled, peppered with anti-Jewish content, this contempt for the Jew was superimposed on the Quran, literally putting words in God's mouth. What the Creator did not say in the Quran, Muslim anti-Semites made sure he was made to.

From a young age, Muslim children read the Quran and are exposed to the negative depiction of Jews and Christians, but no one ever tells them that the Muslim holy book, which we believe is the very word of God, does not support this view.

Since most Muslim children do not understand or speak Arabic, one would have hoped they would escape this hate. However, the opposite is true. While Arab children can see that the opening verse of the Quran does not depict Jews negatively, the non-Arab child is at the mercy of his teacher at the madrassah, who may not know Arabic, but can sound as if he does, and tells the children the translation of the words in question is "Jews." It is little wonder that the madrassahs of non-Arab Pakistan produce far more jihadis than the ones in Arab Egypt.

The imams who incorporate anti-Semitism into Islamic teachings do not act alone. They have the backing of the Kingdom of Saudi Arabia, which pumps billions of dollars into its worldwide Islamist enterprise by publishing anti-Semitic Islamic propaganda, at times through publishers based inside the United States.

In July 2006, NBC News reported on how Saudi textbooks preached intolerance and hate, despite a promised post-9/11 policy change. Schoolchildren were being taught from textbooks that equated Jews with "apes." A study by the Hudson Institute's Center for Religious Freedom found examples of intolerance, even hate, in numerous Saudi textbooks used in grades one through twelve. Some of the books, which are distributed not just inside the Saudi kingdom but also in North America, include the following:

- Jews and Christians are "enemies" of Muslims.
- Every religion other than Islam is "false."
- "The hour [of Judgment] will not come until the Muslims fight the Jews and kill them."

Nina Shea of the Center for Religious Freedom said the Saudi textbooks "taught that Christians and Jews are the enemy of the Muslim, and that the Muslim must wage jihad in order to spread the faith in battle against the infidel." What's more, she said, "an eighth-grade text equates Jews with 'apes' and Christian infidels with 'swine.' This is the ideological foundation for building tomorrow's terrorists."

The Saudi hate machine is not restricted to describing Jews as apes in school textbooks. The Saudis have exported a version of the Quran to Canada and the United States that plugs the word *Jews* into the English translation of verses. Where the Quran refers to "people" who have "strayed from God's laws," the Saudis insert the word *Jews* in parentheses.[5] It is no coincidence that the Quran found in the home of the convicted New York Times Square bomber, Sohail Shahzad, was the same version distributed by Saudi Arabia in the United States.

This Saudi translation of the Quran can be obtained from any Saudi embassy and is distributed to almost every Sunni mosque throughout the world. In their plentiful footnotes, the translators supply the same information that is provided in the works of Ibn Kathir, but they also insert references to Jews and Christians straight into the translation itself. Here is how they translate the last verse of Sura al-Fatiha: "Not the way of those who have earned Your anger (such as the Jews), nor of those who went astray (such as the Christians)."

The Saudi translators have dragged Judeophobia from the footnotes straight into the opening verse of the Quran. What was before a reference saved for the commentary is now right there, smack on the seventh line of the first page of Islam's holy book. In addition, if there was any doubt left in the mind of the innocent child reading the Quran for the first time, or the adult rereading it, the translators write in the preface: "Some additions, corrections, and alterations have been made to improve the English translation and to bring the English interpretation very close to the correct and exact meanings of the Arabic text."

Although references to Jews in Hadith literature can be seen as hostile to Jews as a people, a study of the Quran reveals a much more positive image. In fact, the Quran, when read without being filtered through the prism of Hadith, is unlikely to trigger any of the virulent anti-Semitism that is so endemic in the Muslim world. Take, for instance, verses 5:20 and 5:21. The two are rarely discussed, but if read on their own merit, they would shock Muslims in how they authenticate the Jewish claim to their rightful presence in Palestine and Jerusalem.

5:20: Call to mind when Moses said to his people: "O my people! Remember the favour which Allah bestowed upon you; He raised up prophets from among you and made you rulers and gave you that which had not been given to anyone in the world.

5:21: "O my people. Enter the Holy Land, that Allah has destined for you, and do not turn your backs or you will turn about losers."

The Hadith, on the other hand, delivers the opposite message – all of the land of Israel is Muslim territory, and it needs to be wrested from the evil Jews in a bloody battle to end all battles.

Until the twentieth century, most Islamic scholars read these verses as benign words about a people whom they had vanquished more than a millennium ago and who posed no threat to the Muslim world. Before the Zionist enterprise, the two verses in which Allah himself says the Holy Land has been "destined" for the Jews were interpreted as little more than a symbolic gesture. After all, Jerusalem and the Holy Land were under the governance of the Ottoman caliphate that ruled from Istanbul. Jerusalem was a sleepy backwater, where Muslim Arabs were the dominant population, living in relative peace alongside enclaves of Jews, Armenians, and other Christian groups. So what if God had promised the land to Jews under Moses? we Muslims could argue. Most Muslims viewed these verses with a historical detachment that is today conspicuous by its absence. In fact we argued that the sorry state of Jews before the twentieth century was because they had "turned their backs" on the Holy Land against the wishes of Allah even though he had "destined" the land to them.

However, the centuries-old status quo was about to change. After the First Zionist Congress met in Switzerland in 1897 with the aim of establishing a Jewish state – and the resulting Balfour Declaration made such a state possible – the same verses of the Quran would take on a whole new meaning. Was the Jewish state of Israel a reflection of Allah's promise in the Quran? And if that was the case, what about the Muslims who had lived for centuries on that land, ever since the Arabs sprang out of the deserts of Arabia to conquer what were then Byzantine Christian lands?

The two verses were hotly debated by Sheikh Abdullah Nimr Darwish, the founder of the Islamic Movement in Israel, and Khaleel Mohammed at a conference in Jerusalem in 2004 – an exchange that unfortunately can take place only outside the domain of Islamic institutions or countries. Mohammed told the audience attending the panel discussion, "Focusing on Elements of Tolerance and Openness in the Koran," that verses 5:20 and 5:21 were not the only passages in the Quran that validated a Jewish presence in the Holy Land. He listed several others, among them verse 10:93, which is even more explicit than 5:20 in endorsing a Jewish presence in the Holy Land.

> We settled the Children of Israel
> in a beautiful dwelling place
> And provided them sustenance of the best;
> It was after knowledge had been granted to them
> That they fell into schisms.
> Verily, Allah will judge between them
> As to the schisms amongst them
> On the Day of Judgment.

There is little agreement among past or contemporary Islamic scholars and Muslim academics about the exact location of the "beautiful dwelling place" that Allah gave to the Jews. While al-Tabari's medieval commentary on this verse mentions Palestine and Jerusalem as the land God assigned to the Jews, it also lists other possibilities, such as Mount Sinai "and that which is around it," Syria, Jericho, Damascus, and Jordan. Others like Taj Hashmi, previously a professor of Islamic and Asian history at the University of British Columbia, however suggest this Holy Land is not in historical Palestine, but in the Sinai. He wrote to me, "As I see it, God wanted Jews of eastern Egypt to enter the 'Holy Land,' which seems to be the Sinai peninsula rather than Jerusalem." Sheikh Muhammad al-Husseini, a British imam who teaches a course on the Quran at the Leo Baeck College in London, says: "They are pointing to the same area – it is not Egypt,

Saudi or Iraq." According to al-Husseini, "the traditional commentators from the eighth and ninth century onwards have uniformly interpreted the Koran to say explicitly that Eretz Yisrael has been given by God to the Jewish people as a perpetual covenant. There is no Islamic counterclaim to the Land anywhere in the traditional corpus of commentary."[6]

Khaleel Mohammed says that among the verses of the Quran that are pertinent to the issue of the Holy Land, 5:21 is the most significant, not because of what it says, but because of the manner in which medieval Muslim exegetes explained it. To elucidate his point, he rendered verse 5:21 in as literal a manner as possible, translating the Arabic word *kataba* as "written." Mohammed says the word *kataba* "has definite theological connotations: in Islam, as in Jewish belief, it conveys the idea of decisiveness and finality, e.g. in 'written Torah' as opposed to 'oral Torah.' In some twenty-two instances in the Quran where this action is attributed to God (directly *kataba* or indirectly, *kutiba*), it likewise conveys the idea of decisiveness, finality, and immutability. One such example is the verse (2:183) used by Muslims to indicate that the Ramadan fast is compulsory: Kutiba alaykum al-siyaam . . . literally, 'written upon you is the fast' – but understood to mean, 'Obligatory upon you is the fast.'"[7*]

---

* To support his point about the significance of the word *kataba,* Mohammed quoted from the works of Islam's most prominent exegetes of the Quran, Abu Ja'far al-Tabari (d. 922); Abu Ali al-Tabarsi (d. 1153), the Shi'ite commentator who repeated al-Tabari's statement without any change; and Ibn Kathir (d. 1373), who explained *kataba* in terms that would have pleased the most ardent Zionists: "'That which God has written for you' – i.e., that which God has promised to you by the words of your father Israel as the inheritance of those among you who believe," wrote Ibn Kathir.

One of the earliest commentaries on the Quran was made by the eighth-century scholar Muqatil ibn Sulayman. According to Sulayman, the word *kataba* in verse 5:21 means "ordered." Thus, Moses was saying to the Israelites: Enter the Holy Land as God has ordered you to do. (Muqatil even specifies the Holy Land as Palestine.) But what he states next is bound to shock many Muslims unaccustomed to reading the early commentaries on the Quran. According to Sulayman, Allah instructs Moses to order the Jews: "Do not retreat from that land, or you will be losers. This is because God said to Abraham, when he was in the Holy Land, 'Verily, this land in which you now stand will be an inheritance for your son after you.'" No wonder Sulayman's works are banned in present-day Egypt.

Khaleel Mohammed's position did not sit well with Sheikh Darwish. The cleric dismissed the American professor's premise, claiming since he was an Arab, he was more familiar with the relevant verse than an American academic of Indian ancestry and Guyanese birth. Sheikh Darwish told the audience that verse 5:21 of the Quran does not prove any ownership of the land. "The verse says that Musa's people must enter the Holy Land. Does ownership derive from this? When I invite someone to enter my office, does the office become his? Definitely not."

In Darwish's opinion, the fact that Abraham and Jacob paid for their burial site in present-day Hebron with money is evidence enough that the land did not belong to the children of Israel. "If we're talking about religion, then according to Islam only the prophets inherit from one another. Mohammed succeeded all the prophets who came before him, including Musa, who is Moses, and he brought the word to all human beings. This does not mean that the Muslims are claiming the lands of others if they do not have certification of ownership in the land registry, and the use of the world 'kataba' does not justify anything."[8]

Sheikh Darwish not only ignored the American professor's argument by making a horribly skewed analogy; he chose to go against every classical exegete by denying the significance of the word *kataba*. What was until the nineteenth century a purely academic argument about the meaning of a word in the Quran is now staring Muslims in the face, yet our clerics respond with little more than clichés and pamphleteering rhetoric.

According to Darwish, the conflict between the Israelis and the Palestinians is national and political, not religious. "The Palestinians are fighting against the occupation, not against Judaism, and therefore it is necessary to reach a political compromise with them, not a religious compromise," he explains. Here he is right, but did he not see the irony that in dismissing Mohammed's position, he too invoked biblical references, to Abraham's paying for his own burial site? And so the question that confounds Muslims is this: If, as Sheikh Darwish says, this a political dispute, not a religious one, then why do he and Hamas rely on divine texts to make their case against Israel? If the eminent Islamic scholar genuinely believes the Israeli-Palestinian dispute is one of politics, then he must agree that the religious incitements to violence, exemplified by calls to jihad, and talk of ethereal virgins are wrong and must cease.

We Muslims cannot have it both ways. If we choose to refer to the Hebrew Bible on one aspect of the argument – using Abraham's purchase of his place of burial as evidence that he did not own the land – then why not use the Hebrew Bible to resolve the matter? Or, as Khaleel Mohammed asks: "Are we to assume somehow that when Jews claim biblical sanctity for their views, they are somehow misinformed regarding the interpretation of their own book, and need a Muslim . . . to advise them?"[9]

—

It would be disingenuous of me not to acknowledge that the Quran does contain some pretty harsh language about Jews and, to a lesser degree, Christians. The voluminous book *The Legacy of Islamic Anti-Semitism,* edited by Andrew Bostom, dedicates an entire chapter to highlighting no fewer than fifty-two verses that are said to depict Jews negatively. However, most of these verses do not contain the words *Jew* or *Banu Israel* in the original text. The mention of Jews, as we have seen, has been added by Muslim scribes in the commentary.

Still, there is no question that the Quran does contain verses that curse the Jews. As a Muslim, some have left me deeply troubled. For instance, God has this to say about the Jews:

> Curses were pronounced on those among
> The Children of Israel who rejected Faith
> By the tongue of David
> And of Jesus, the son of Mary
> Because they disobeyed and persisted in Excesses. (5:78)

And if the curses were not sufficient, Allah ratchets up his wrath against the Jews by promising his "anger" on the children of Israel:

> Degraded they shall live wheresoever they be
> Unless they make an alliance with God and alliance with men,
> For they have incurred the anger of God,
> And misery overhangs them.
> That is because they denied the signs of God
> and killed the prophets unjustly,
> and rebelled, and went beyond the limit. (3:112)

If God Almighty curses all Jews for the actions of the few that disobeyed Moses three thousand years ago, then how does he feel about all of us Muslims because of the few who not only disobeyed Prophet Muhammad but massacred his entire family? Could God be talking about us Muslims in the above verse, and not the Jews? After all, God does say that his promised wrath on the Jews would cease if "they make an alliance with God and alliance with men." What if the Jews did make an alliance with God, thus ending the wrath? What if, instead of the Jews, the wrath of God is now on us Muslims? Is the joke on us?

Sadly, too many Muslims use their holy book not for reflection and wisdom, but as an idol of worship or as a guide for political action. Scores of books using Quranic verses to generate hate and anger are sold throughout the Muslim world. And it is not just in the Muslim world that this literature is being circulated. For instance, as early as 1963, one Akbar Ali in the U.K. published *Israel and the Prophecies of the Holy Quran,* in which the author uses the Quran to launch a hate campaign against Jews. He writes:

> The history of the "scattered tribe" of Jews has been a history
> of fraud and deceit, criminality and cunning, sabotage and
> destruction. For the last 2,000 years they have been engaged
> in all sorts of crimes against humanity and the worst suffer-
> ers have always been those nations who committed the blun-
> der of opening their doors to this highly insidious cabal. If we
> just look at the history of only the recent past the truth of the
> statement would be quite manifest. I think a brief survey will
> be useful: They were turned out of Portugal and Spain. They
> were driven out of England in 1290. They were twice pushed
> away from France, once in 1306 and again in 1934. They were
> exiled in Belgium in 1370 and from Czechoslovakia in 1380. . . .
> Indeed exilement has been their lot since the beginning; and if
> we look at the earlier history too we will find that they have
> met the same fate all along. It is a punishment and a curse over
> them although they like to remain under the self-deception of
> being "God's Chosen People."[10]

The author then asks the rhetorical question about Jews: "Why has so much degradation and humiliation become part of their destiny? After all what is wrong with them." I wish he had posed this question to the Muslims of the world today, because it is we who find ourselves in so much "degradation" and "humiliation" that he pins on the Jews.

The challenge of reconciling the Quran and Islam with modernity, the nation state, and universal human rights falls at the feet of individual Muslim reformers, scattered across the globe. Despite being starved of resources and lacking the organizational skills of their Islamofascist adversaries, these Muslim reformers are getting their voices heard.

Women such as Amina Wadud of the United States, Fatema Mernissi in Morocco, Farzana Hassan and Raheel Raza in Canada, and Yasmin Alibhai-Brown in Britain are posing serious challenges to the men in cloaks and beards. Standing alongside them are men such as Dr. Zuhdi Jasser in Arizona, Imam Muhammad al-Husseini of Britain, Professors Khaleel Mohammed and Abdullahi Amed An-Na'im in the United States, Sa'd al-Din Ibrahim of the Ibn Khaldun Center for Development Studies in Cairo, former president Abdurrahman Wahid of Indonesia, and Pakistan's Javed Ahmad Ghamidi. They are joined by Muslim politicians like the French parliamentarians Fadela Amara and Rachida Dati, Danish M.P. Naser Khedar, and British minister Baroness Sayeeda Warsi in marking new territory for Muslims who believe in liberal democracy and the separation of religion and state. Some have paid dearly for standing up against the Islamists. The former prime minister of Pakistan Benazir Bhutto was assassinated by the Taliban in 2008, and the killing of Iranian teenager Neda Agha-Soltan probably became the most widely witnessed death in human history when she was shot dead by police on June 20, 2009, as she demonstrated against the ruling ayatollahs of Iran.

The task of these Muslim reformers is obstructed not just by the Islamists and the jihadis but also by non-Muslims who would rather these reformers fail so that Muslims continue to be seen as a people devoid of reason and consumed by hate.

For instance, the scholar Robert Spencer has written a number of books analyzing Islam and the Islamist movement. Since any attempt by Muslims to end Muslim hate for the Jews is a serious impediment to Spencer's thesis that Islam itself is the problem, he does his best to undermine the work of Muslim reformers. In a piece for the *Middle East Quarterly,* Spencer dismisses the position of Imam al-Husseini, saying that although the imam's position is "an extremely comforting message to supporters of Israel, it is not true and is based on a partial and inaccurate reading of the Qur'an." He makes the argument that "if this exegesis [of al-Husseini] is correct, why does the Islamic world from Morocco to Indonesia manifest such hostility to Israel? Why have so few Muslims noticed that God wants the Jews to possess the Holy Land?"

Spencer relies on the Islamic extremists' perspective. He writes, "This is simply not a mainstream view or one that most of those who are familiar with the totality of the Qur'an would ever advance. It gives Jews and all supporters of Israel hope, yes, but only a false hope."[11]

Other critics of Islam such as Andrew Bostom similarly dismiss the work of Muslim reformists, arguing that the only way Muslims can bring about an enlightenment in their faith is by rejecting Islam itself. In an interview with the online magazine Jewcy.com, Bostom said, "I think Islam needs to undergo such a process [enlightenment]. And we see its possibilities in a person like Ayaan Hirsi Ali. A mass movement of enlightenment amongst Muslims is required. Ibn Warraq's book, *Leaving Islam,* had a very interesting concise history of the real freethinkers within Islam."[12] Ayaan Hirsi Ali is a fascinating writer who has rejected Islam. Ibn Warraq is a brilliant scholar who has contributed much to the continuing debate about Islam. However, because they have left Islam, the two would be the last people on earth who could bring about any reform in Islam or an era of enlightenment among the Muslims. One billion plus Muslims on this planet are not going to give up their faith, no matter how hard Hirsi Ali or Ibn Warraq may try to make them.

On one hand, we have well-intentioned former Muslims who have walked away from Islam, either becoming atheists or converting to another religion. On the other, we have Islamic extremists who would rest only when these former Muslims were killed. In between these two extremes are the vast majority of Muslims, ranging from the liberal who barely ever visits the mosque to the orthodox conservative who prays five times a day. All these Muslims live with varying degrees of suspicion of the Jews. We have a choice. Either we allow ourselves to be consumed by hatred, or we approach Jews as fellow human beings, at worst as adversaries in a political dispute, not as monsters destined to be our enemy for all time. God makes it explicit in the Quran that he is referring not to all Jews but only to a specific group, at a specific time. Here is the Quran on the subject of Christians and Jews:

> Yet, all of them are not alike.
> Among the people of the Book is a section upright, who recite
> The scriptures in the hours of the night
> And bow in adoration and pray,
> And believe in God and the Last day,
> And enjoin what is good
> And forbid what is wrong,
> And who hasten to give in charity:
> They are among the upright and the doers of good.
> And the good they do will not go unaccented;
> For God is aware of those who keep away from evil. (3:113)

As mere mortals, we need to dig deeper into our souls and search for the humility that is required of us as Muslims. We need to be scared of ourselves, not of God, for it is we who are the instruments of our own destruction, not him. Hating Jews is no cure for the scars we have inflicted on ourselves – we who massacred the family of Prophet Muhammad, yet have the audacity to lecture Jews that they disobeyed Moses.

Whereas Islamists and radical jihadis have had to use some fancy semantic footwork to incorporate anti-Semitism into the Quran, there is no such need where the Hadith literature is concerned.

A number of scholars have written about the negative portrayal of Jews in the Hadith. One article that stands out for me is "Demonizing the Jews," by Kadir Baksh.[13] The author cites several traditions from the Hadith collections, including two quotes attributed to Prophet Muhammad that are used today by many Islamic clerics to portray Jews in negative light:

- God's Messenger said: the Hour will not be established until you fight with the Jews, and the stone behind which a Jew will be hiding will say, "O Muslim! There is a Jew hiding behind me, so kill him!"
- God's Messenger said: the Antichrist will be followed by seventy thousand Jews, all of them wearing prayer shawls.

The sad significance of both Hadith is that they do not foster any hope for peace until the end of times. In the first, the Jew is the enemy against whom the final battle of good against evil must be fought. In the second, the Jew is presented as the Antichrist – that virulent Judeophobic concept imported from a medieval Christian misunderstanding of the epistles of John. Imams who agitate against lasting peace with Israel rely extensively on these two supposed sayings of Prophet Muhammad to justify anti-Jewish rhetoric. Is it any wonder that despite the Oslo and Madrid agreements, despite the Road Map and talks between the Palestinian Authority and Israel, the Muslim Brotherhood–inspired Hamas refuses to accept any peace with the Jews?

For Muslims, the two Hadith stories concerning Jews present a challenge. If they are accurate – as most Muslims are taught by clerics to believe they are – then there is no point in making peace with Israel. In which case, Hamas is on the path of righteousness while the rest of us who call for an end to the occupation and the creation of a sovereign state of Palestine are wrong. Could we, who believe in peace with the Jews, be going against the very wishes of Prophet Muhammad? Where does this leave the leaders of Egypt and Jordan who have signed peace treaties with Israel? What about Israel's own substantial Muslim population, let alone Muslims who serve in the Israeli army? Should they view the Jews around them as enemies because a ninth-century text claims the Prophet of Islam said so?

(For the non-Muslim reader accustomed to discussing religious texts with some degree of objectivity, these questions may sound quaint. Unfortunately, few Muslims are willing to study their religious texts with historical detachment. The vast majority of insular Islamic clerics and their students consider such a detached approach an act of apostasy, making it extremely difficult to have a discussion of the kind I am doing in this book. Most Muslims have a deep emotional intimacy with their religious texts, making any discussion of the subject a potential cause of unintended hurt or insult.)

While the Hadith talks of an endless conflict with the Jews, it contradicts the Quran, which Muslims believe is the very word of God. The Quran commands explicitly: "To you your religion and to me mine." Elsewhere in the Quran, God says, "Let there be no compulsion in matters of faith." How do we reconcile these words of God with the Hadith literature written by oridnary men who demand we continue fighting the Jews until the end of time?

For some Islamic scholars the answer is simple: the Hadith are spurious, man-made texts, written two hundred years after the death of the Prophet, and should therefore be read not as divine texts, but merely as the observations or opinions of its contributors. There is much in the Hadith that makes sense and is a source of piety, but there is a lot that is outrageous and embarrassing and stands in contradiction to the Quran.

In addition, there is no requirement in the Quran for Muslims to obey or pay heed to instructions written by anyone other than Allah or his Messenger. In fact, one verse unambiguously describes the Quran itself as the Hadith: "God has revealed the best Hadith, a book that is consistent with itself, yet repeating (its teachings)" (39:23). Elsewhere, the Quran states: "These are God's signs that We recite to you with truth. So, in which Hadith, after God and his signs do they acknowledge?" (45:6).

With such clear direction in the Quran, why pay reverence to man-made Hadith texts that can best be described as hate literature, when Muslims know we have no obligation to embrace them?

The eminent Muslim scholar and modernist Fazlur Rahman has written about how the Quran became overshadowed by interpretations that sometimes differed markedly from the obvious meaning of the text. According to Rahman, it is indeed true that "whatever views Muslims have wanted to project and advocate have taken the form of Quranic commentaries."[14] Thus, if a certain individual or group had a specific political agenda, they had a choice. They could convince the congregation or the community of the merits of their case by a rational method, or they could take a supposed saying of the Prophet from the Hadith, blend it with the commentary of the Quran, and then present this dubious combination as a confirmation of their ideology. This latter method, ensuring that any opposition to their doctrine would be labelled opposition to Islam itself, has been used by Islamists throughout history.

The two texts from Hadith quoted above are not the only ones that suggest Prophet Muhammad framed Jews in a negative light. The Muslim Students' Association, a U.S.-based Islamist organization that is accused of deriving its inspiration from Egypt's Muslim Brotherhood and Jamaat-e-Islami, its Indo-Pakistani-Bangladeshi manifestation, has posted on its website English translations of what it calls the three "most authentic" Hadith books, Sahih Bukhari, Sahih Muslim, and Sunan Abu Dawud. Here is a selection that is available to all Muslim students around the world.

- Narrated Ibn Abbas: Once [Caliph] Umar was informed that a certain man sold alcohol. Umar said: "May Allah curse him! Doesn't he know that Allah's Apostle said, 'May Allah curse the Jews, for Allah had forbidden them to eat the fat of animals, but they melted it and sold it.'"
- It is narrated on the authority of Abu Hurraira that the Messenger of Allah (may peace be upon him) observed: By Him in Whose hand is the life of Muhammad, he who among the community of the Jews or Christians hears about me, but does not affirm his belief in that with which I have been sent and dies in this state (of disbelief), he shall be but one of the denizens of Hell-Fire.
- This Hadith has been narrated on the authority of Abu Ayoub through some other chains of transmitters (and the words are): "Allah's Messenger (may peace be upon him) went out after the sun had set and heard some sound and said: "It is the Jews who are being tormented in their graves."
- Narrated Muhayyisah: The Apostle of Allah (may peace be upon him) said: If you gain a victory over men of Jews, kill them. So, Muhayyisah jumped over Shubaybah, a man of the

Jewish merchants. He had close relations with them. He then killed him.

- Narrated Ali ibn Abu Talib: A Jewess used to abuse [i.e., write satirical verses about] the Prophet (may peace be upon him) and disparage him. A man strangled her until she died. The Apostle of Allah (peace be upon him) declared that no recompense was payable for her blood.

- Narrated Abu Hurraira: Suhayl ibn Abu Salih said: I went out with my father to Syria. The people passed by the cloisters in which there were Christians and began to salute them. My father said: Do not give them salutations first, for Abu Hurraira reported the Apostle of Allah (peace be upon him) as saying: Do not salute them (Jews and Christians) first, and when you meet them on the road, force them to go to the narrowest part of it.[15]

From labelling Christians and Jews pigs and apes to prohibiting Muslims from playing chess, Hadith literature has been a source of much embarrassment to Muslims. If we Muslims continue to study these Hadith texts as if they were divinely ordained, and believe that they should shape our lives in this day and age, then we will have considerable difficulty convincing anyone that Islam is a pluralistic religion that promotes peace and harmony among peoples. Eventually, any student of Islam will pick up these Judeophobic Hadith and literally throw the book at us. We will lose credibility among the nations of this world and be remembered as a people who are anti-Jewish above all.

This is precisely why Muslim reformers like Sa'd al-Din Ibrahim have called for a re-evaluation of how Muslims relate to their faith in contemporary times. Ibrahim and other Muslim thinkers issued a statement in 2004 that called for "confronting all institutions – whether composed of clerics or lay persons – that claim a monopoly over religion

[Islam] and the proper interpretation of its holy text. Instead, a new spirit should seek to establish the right of ijtihad for all, under the banner of an Islamic reformation relevant to the current century." In addition, these scholars called on the world's Muslims to rely exclusively on "the Quranic text as the sole authentic source to be utilized for reviewing the entire Islamic heritage."[16]

The controversy about the Hadith's authenticity as a religious text goes back to the seventh century. In medieval times, discussing the validity of Hadith texts was the domain of political and religious leaders who would proclaim edicts that the ordinary citizen simply had to follow without question. Beginning in the eighteenth century, this changed dramatically. The political leadership in Islamdom was replaced by the colonial authorities, while the clergy lost the patronage of the caliphs to enforce religious discipline and conformity. In addition, with the advent of the printing press, this debate was no longer controlled by the clergy or the calligraphists who controlled the written word. The doors were flung open to the emerging educated middle classes in the early twentieth century in Turkey, India, and Egypt.

Dale Eickelman, who teaches anthropology at Dartmouth College, says, "Today, the major impetus for change in religious and political values comes from below."[17] Many of today's Muslims, Eickelman says, have bypassed the clergy and are engaged in what he refers to as the "reconstruction" of their religion, community, and society. This democratization of religious debate could not have been possible at any time in the era before mass communications allowed the free flow of ideas and the right to free speech without fear for one's life. Nevertheless, the obstacles remain formidable. The Egyptian group Ahl al-Quran, or People of the Quran, has been brutally suppressed by the Egyptian authorities as well as the traditional orthodoxy.

Among the key figures of the Muslim world who challenged the use of Hadith as a source of Islamic law was the Egyptian Rashad

Khalifa. Khalifa immigrated to the United States in 1959, earned a Ph.D. in biochemistry, and settled in Tucson, Arizona. By the mid-1970s, he was objecting to the available English translations of the Quran and set about creating his own. At the same time, he announced his rejection of the traditional Hadith, calling it fabrications and lies attributed to Prophet Muhammad. Among the objections Khalifa raised about the Hadith was its references to Jews and Christians as apes and pigs. Because Khalifa rejected the Hadith – and because he claimed prophethood – he alienated the overwhelming majority of Muslims. His rejection of all Hadith as spurious was seen as a rejection of Islam, not a reformation of it. In 1990, Khalifa was murdered at the mosque in Tucson where he had regularly worshipped.

Other critics of the traditional medieval understanding of Islam were equally emphatic about the doubtful nature of the Hadith. Prominent among them was Ghulam Ahmed Pervez of Pakistan and Turkey's Edip Yuksel, who has recently partnered with others to publish the brilliant *Quran: A Reformist Translation*.

Pervez, who was born in British India and rose through the ranks of the civil service before migrating to Pakistan in 1947, has emerged as the country's foremost reformist Muslim scholar. (He died in 1980.) After extensive study of Islam and Islamic history, Pervez came to the conclusion that the Hadith was spurious at best and had to be rejected if Muslims were to awaken from their centuries-old slumber. He claimed that Islam had been treacherously perverted by caliphs and the clergy who had created the Hadith literature for their own interests. He called Hadith literature a fabrication, arguing that it was not God who had vouchsafed their transmission as was the case with the Quran.

Pervez's lectures were published as a series of "Letters to Saleem." In one, titled "The Fundamental Principles of the Islamic System," he critiques the Hadith in these words:

Now, if there was more revelation (i.e., Hadith), then the Prophet's duty should have been to transmit that as well, in a fashion similar to that of the Quran. But neither did he order it to be written down anywhere, nor did he oversee its memorization, nor did he compile some sort of collection of it, nor did he make any sort of accommodation whatsoever for its preservation. Rather even if someone, out of good will, attempted to record anything on his own, he stopped them saying "Don't record anything of me other than the Quran," – Sahih Muslim (Hadith scholars claim that shortly before his death, the Prophet allowed some Hadith writing. But still, he neither commanded it nor double-checked it to ensure its quality as he did for the Quran).[18]

Like Rashad Khalifa, Pervez too was declared an apostate by traditional Muslim scholars, worthy of death for denying the authority and authenticity of the Hadith. However, such was the secular climate in the Pakistan of the 1960s and '70s that the Islamists dared not muster the courage to assassinate the respected scholar. (In today's Pakistan, Pervez would not have lasted a day.) The scholar of the Quran was adamant and spoke fearlessly every Friday in Karachi, drawing large crowds, including many of the young leftist activists of the city who found in his message a sense of reformation and renaissance.

Pervez claimed that "even Quranic orders were not safe" from the Hadith. "The Hadith (unrecited revelation) not only specified those things Allah left unspecified in the Quran, it even changed and abrogated those things Allah specified in the Quran! For example, the Quran gives the crime of zina [adultery] the punishment of 100 lashes. But according to Hadith, this punishment is only for fornicators (unmarried), whereas the punishment for adulterers (married but unfaithful) is stoning to death (a punishment which has no basis in the Quran). . . .

The scholars of Hadith are witnesses to the fact that fabricated Hadith number in the thousands."[19]

The debate about the authenticity and authority of the Hadith is not exclusive to our own time. We know that Muslims have been wrangling with the issue since long before the first Hadith collections were compiled in the ninth century. The second caliph of Islam, Umar bin Khattab, who is credited with laying the foundations of the Islamic empire, was a close companion of Prophet Muhammad. The fact that Umar is quoted as saying that he was against the writing and recording of the Prophet's sayings in book form – what we now know as the Hadith – is significant. In the third century of Islam, the narrator Ibn Saad wrote how Umar called on the people to bring him all the Hadith they had collected, and then he ordered the entire lot to be burned. Afterwards, Umar is quoted by Ibn Saad as forbidding the writing of any more Hadith.

It was not only Umar who prohibited the Hadith. Hadith literature itself reports that Prophet Muhammad himself ordered his followers not to write down anything he said, other than the Quranic verses revealed to him. The concern was that people would use spurious quotations attributed to him and give those words the same weight as the divine Quran.

Today, Muslims have a chance to dwell once more on this subject. It is not necessary to reject the Hadith altogether. Rather, we can look at the medieval texts and employ twenty-first-century rationalism and reasoning to make sure we lift the prohibition against chess.

And while we are at it, can we Muslims not be brave enough to say that the hatred against Jews that permeates the texts be set aside as inapplicable in societies where the universality of human rights and the equality of races and religions is the cornerstone of civilization? Surely this will be the first step to bringing about an end to the systemic and institutional contempt for Jews that is embedded in the Hadith.

CHAPTER SIX

The Jews of Banu Qurayza

It is not just Hadith literature that nourishes Muslim anti-Semitism. At the core of Jew hatred among the Arabs and Pakistanis (more than any other Muslim community) is a legend written in the ninth century that records how in 627, in the city of Medina, the Prophet of Islam participated in the slaughter of between six hundred and nine hundred Jews.

This dramatic account, which reads like a screenplay, vividly details the historic Battle of the Trench (Ghazwah al-Khandaq) – also known as the Battle of the Confederates (Ghazwah al-Ahzab) – where Prophet Muhammad and his Muslim followers in Medina successfully defended themselves against a much larger invading Meccan army. After the battle, we are told, the Muslim army laid siege to a Jewish fortress, culminating in the cold-blooded murder of hundreds of Jewish men who had remained neutral in the battle. This slaughter has weighed heavily on the Muslim mind ever since, and to this day it determines how we view our Jewish cousins.

Written two centuries after the massacre, the account has acquired the status of divine truth in the minds of Muslims. With each passing generation and century, blind belief in this myth has grown. As the Muslim world declined in all aspects of human development, our failures could always be blamed on the "treacherous and untrustworthy" nature of the Jew.

Even though the Quran makes no mention of such a mass murder, Muslims have been conditioned to believe that this fiction is historical truth, and that it should define our attitude and behaviour towards the Jew of today. The present-day Jew-hater in the Muslim world finds solace in the belief that he or she is not going against the teachings of Prophet Muhammad, but rather is following his example.

One would expect Muslims to denounce the depiction of their Prophet as a mass murderer. On the contrary, any Muslim who questions or denies the reliability of this legend is labelled anti-Islamic and a traitor to the faith. In the absence of any physical evidence, one would expect Muslim historians, archaeologists, and academics to question this fable. However, in a reflection of the sorry state of Muslim wisdom today, most clerics and scholars not only insist this legend is true but cite it as a source of pride. Islamists, who riot at any negative portrayal of the Prophet in cartoons, are apparently quite comfortable with the apostle's depiction as a mass murderer. (I will discuss the lack of evidence to support this mass murder in chapter 7.)

Thus, believing that Prophet Muhammad was involved in the murder of hundreds of Jews, the Muslim Jew-hater feels no guilt as he or she boasts about the glory we once enjoyed, and transmits this hatred to the next generation. For both medieval and contemporary Islamists, the Quran's silence on this murder is dismissed as irrelevant. We are told simply that if the story exists in the Hadith literature and the *Sira* – the biography of the Prophet – then it must be true.

Medieval fiction cannot withstand the scrutiny of analysis, but why let facts get in the way of a juicy mass-murder chronicle – even when it brings shame on the very man Muslims believe to be our leader and the favoured Messenger of God? With friends like these, do Muslims need enemies?

—

In 622, Prophet Muhammad and the small band of companions who had answered his call to Islam escaped from Mecca to seek refuge in Yathrib, the city we know today as Medina. Within two years, Muhammad had gained the trust of the various tribes in the city, including several Jewish and pagan groups, and led them in a coalition bound by the Compact of Medina, a treaty that outlined the responsibilities of each group. After consolidating his position in Medina, Muhammad led the Muslims into a decisive victory over his Meccan enemies at the Battle of Badr, only to lose the next encounter, at the Battle of Uhud, in 625.

By 627, Muhammad had gained considerable strength in Medina. His ranks had grown from fewer than a hundred men into an army of thousands. The tribes of Mecca, worried by his growing influence, which threatened their trade monopolies as well as their pagan gods, regrouped in an alliance with other Arabs in the hinterland. The alliance included two Jewish tribes that the Muslims had expelled from Medina for what they claimed was a breach of the treaty they had signed with Muhammad. An army marched out of Mecca to strike a final blow against Muhammad.

However, the Prophet's spies in Mecca alerted him to this new alliance and the advancing army. Instead of adopting the Arab tradition of meeting his enemy in an open field, Muhammad ordered a trench to be dug to block the northern entrance to the city. This tactic rendered the enemy cavalry ineffective, forcing the Meccans to camp out in the open desert for a siege they had least expected.

The siege lasted twenty days. Historians estimate that around ten thousand men with six hundred horses and some camels besieged Medina, while the defending Muslims numbered barely three thousand fighters.

While two of the more than a dozen Jewish tribes in Medina openly aligned with the Meccan forces, other Jews, both inside and outside the city, remained neutral. The pagan Meccans tried to persuade the neutral Jewish tribe of Banu Qurayza to join them in attacking the Muslims from the rear, but the Jews refused. In the end, the well-organized defence line behind the trench and a severe sandstorm forced the attackers to break camp, lift the siege, and return to Mecca.

The massacre of the Banu Qurayza Jews does not figure in the Muslim narrative until after the eighth century, when Muhammad's first biography, *Sirat Rasul Allah,* or just the *Sira,* The Life of God's Messenger, is penned by Ibn Ishaq almost a hundred years after the Prophet's death in 632. No copy of Ibn Ishaq's original *Sira* survives, although we do have one recreated by the ninth-century historian Ibn Hisham.[1]

The copious biography is based partly on the stories of many wars fought by Muhammad and later his companions and the caliphs. In introducing the alleged massacre of the Jews, Ibn Ishaq sets the scene by taking us to the fifth year of Muhammad's stay in Medina. By now the Muslims have consolidated their presence in the city, but their opponents in Mecca are building an alliance, known as the confederacy, with the intention of delivering a final blow to the rise of Islam. Right up front, the narrator accuses the Jews of scheming, of manipulating the Meccan pagans and being responsible for this anti-Islamic coalition.

> A number of Jews went to the Quraysh [tribe] in Mecca and invited them to wage war against the apostle of Allah, saying, "We shall aid you against him until we wipe out him and his followers." The Quraysh replied, "You are the possessors of the first scripture; tell us whether our religion is better than his?" They said, "Your religion is better than his, and you are nearer to the truth than he." Then the Quraysh were encouraged to accept the invitation to fight against the apostle of Allah, and the Jews went to the Ghatafan [tribe] and invited them to wage war against the apostle of Allah, saying they

would aid them, and that the Quraysh had already consented to fight. So the Quraysh marched out under the command of Abu Sufyan [head of the Meccan pagans], and the Ghatafan under the command of Uyayna.

What is interesting in this rendering is how the sworn enemies of the Prophet are depicted as victims of Jewish manipulation and not as the primary adversaries. This is significant because at the time the *Sira* was being pieced together, the great-grandsons of the pagan Meccans who had fought Muhammad had by now taken over the reins of Islam and were the ruling caliphs. It was in their interest to show their own forefathers as having been victims of Jewish scheming and conspiracy, thus allowing the Umayyads to assuage some of the guilt associated with their reputation as kings who had stolen Islam from under the very noses of the Prophet's family.

Ibn Ishaq writes that on learning about the impending attack, Muhammad, on the advice of his Persian companion Salman, had a ditch dug outside the northern approaches to Medina. From the *Sira* we learn that some Muslims made excuses to avoid the task of digging the trench. According to Ibn Ishaq, this is when God sent a revelation to Muhammad, warning Muhammad's followers of serious consequences if they did not report for duty. He writes, "Allah, the most high and glorious, revealed the verse:

"When Believers [Muslims] are engaged with the apostle in public business, they do not depart without asking his permission. For those who ask permission are those who believe in Allah and in His apostle. . . . But Allah knoweth those who steal away privately; let those who resist His command take heed, lest some calamity befall them, or grievous punishment."

It is obvious from this Quranic verse that God was keenly involved in the micromanagement of the war effort, sending revelations to the

Prophet through the Archangel Gabriel to stem a loss of morale and maintain discipline among the troops. However, I wonder why, if the Jews of Banu Qurayza were plotting secretly against Muhammad, did Allah not send a revelation to his apostle warning him of the danger lurking behind the Jewish fortress? Had such a revelation come to Muhammad through Gabriel, it would have been part of the Quran – but it is not.

It is also during the lead-up to the Medina siege and the digging of the trench that some of the miracles attributed to Prophet Muhammad are said to have happened. The terrain was rugged, and without the right tools, the Muslims were finding it difficult to dig through stones and rocks. This is when Ibn Ishaq talks about the miracle performed by Muhammad.

"While the ditch was being excavated, Allah caused certain things to happen to display the truth of His apostle and confirm his prophetic dignity. The hard soil which they met with in some parts of the trench distressed the Muslims, and they complained to the apostle, who asked for a vessel of water. He spat into it, prayed for a while according to the will of Allah, and then poured the water on the hard soil. Those who were present said, 'the soil softened till it became like a sand heap, and resisted neither pickaxe nor hoe.'"

The Prophet's miracle may have turned hard rock into soft soil, but it was the pickaxes and hoes that played a crucial role in ensuring the trench was completed before the pagan armies arrived. And the very text that Muslims cite to portray the Jews of Medina as untrustworthy treaty breakers also reveals that those very pickaxes were donated by none other than the Banu Qurayza Jews. Few scholars are willing to address this fact. Had the Jews wanted to betray the Muslims, why would they donate the pickaxes and help dig the trench? I can hear the cynic argue that the Jews were simply hedging their bets in case the Muslims came out as winners.

At other places in the *Sira* there is clear indication the author is rewriting history to defend myths created later. Parts of the tale are crafted in a way that would make the reader believe historical events had been prophesied much earlier than they actually were. For example, here is a passage suggesting that the Prophet foretold future Muslim victories over Spain in the west, Yemen in the south, and India and Persia to the east.

> Salman the Persian told how, "I was digging in a portion of the Ditch and found it hard. The apostle was near me, and when he saw how troublesome the spot was, he came down, took the pickaxe from my hand, and struck the soil thrice. And each stroke brought forth a spark. Then I said, 'Thou art to me as my father and mother, O apostle of Allah! What was this lightning I saw under the pickaxe when thou struck the soil?' He asked, 'Didst thou really see it, Salman?' and I said, 'Yes.' He told me, 'The first spark means that Allah has promised me the conquest of Yemen; the second that Allah has granted me the conquest of Syria and the West; and the third that Allah has bestowed upon me victory over the East.'"

At the time Ibn Ishaq was writing these words, Muslim armies had already conquered Spain in the west and Yemen in the south and had reached India in the east after routing the Persians. It seems the *Sira* permitted each conquering caliph to sanction his accomplishment as the actualization of Muhammad's prophecy, thus adding to the caliphs' claim of having divine authority to rule and allowing them to position themselves as instruments of Allah's will.

Soon after the trench was completed, the army of the Quraysh tribe arrived and set up camp at the confluence of two dried-up torrents. Finding the Muslim army in a defensive position behind the trench, the Meccan pagans attempted to encircle Muhammad. The only way this was possible was to entice the Jewish tribe of Banu Qurayza, who were bound by treaty with the Muslims, to switch sides and attack the unsuspecting Muslims from their exposed positions on the city's southern access.

According to the *Sira*, the leader of the pagans, Abu Sufyan, sent one of his Jewish allies, Huyayy Ibn Akhtab, to the fort of the Banu Qurayza asking them to betray the Prophet. Ibn Ishaq reports that the Jews of Banu Qurayza were unwilling to break their treaty with Muhammad: "When Ka'b [the head of the Banu Qurayza tribe] heard of Huyayy's coming he shut the door of his fort in his face, and when he asked permission to enter, he refused to see him. Saying he [Huyayy] was a man of ill omen. And that he himself [Ka'b] was in treaty with Muhammad and did not intend to go back on his word because he had always found him [Muhammad] loyal and faithful."

The *Sira* then records an argument between the two Jews, with the emissary of the pagans taunting Muhammad's ally for being inhospitable and "not letting him eat his corn." After a while, the pagan emissary is allowed to enter the fort, where he makes the case for betrayal. The very *Sira* that subsequently accused Ka'b the Jew of betraying the Muslims records the man rejecting all overtures to change sides. The chief of the Banu Qurayza Jews says angrily: "By God, you [the pagan emissary] have brought me immortal shame and empty cloud which has shed its water while it thunders and lightens with nothing in it. Woe to you Huyayy leave me as I am, for I have always found him [Muhammad] loyal and faithful."

According to the *Sira*, the emissary kept on "wheedling Ka'b" until the tribal chief "gave way in giving him a solemn promise that if the Quraish returned without having killed Muhammad, he [Huyayy] would enter his fort with him and await his fate." It is unclear in the *Sira* what is meant by this promise, but it is enough for Ibn Ishaq to pass judgment: "Thus Ka'b broke his promise and cut loose from the bond that was between him and the apostle." This despite the fact that, by his own account, Ka'b clearly intended to honour his treaty with the Prophet.

By this time, rumours had reached the Muslim camp that their enemies had managed to persuade the Banu Qurayza Jews to break their treaty with Muhammad. This led some Muslims to start questioning the wisdom of Muhammad. Ibn Ishaq writes, "The Hypocrisy of some became manifest, and one man even declared, 'Muhammad used to promise us that he would swallow the treasures of Croesus and of Caesar; but at this moment, no one of us can even feel safe when he goes to relieve himself.'"

The siege continued, without any hostilities taking place save for the shooting of arrows and one brief skirmish. Tired after almost three weeks in the cold and with supplies running out, Abu Sufyan addressed his army: "'This is not our home. Our cattle and camels have perished, the Banu Quraiza have abandoned us and their attitude is disquieting. We suffer from this violent gale; not a cooking-pot is safe, nor a fire burning, nor a tent standing! Go, as I am going!' Then he went to his camel and mounted, and whipped it upright."

The next morning, the Muslims woke to find the Meccan army had vanished along with their Ghatafan allies. It was now time to go home. A great threat had receded, and the Jews of Banu Qurayza, despite rumours, had not attacked the Muslims from the rear. If the Jews had broken their word in any way, it was to their supposed alliance with the pagans, not the Muslims. The *Sira* records that "the apostle of Allah and his army left the Ditch and returned to Medina and put away their arms."

There is no mention of any bitterness or anger among the Muslim army against the Banu Qurayza at this stage. If the lifting of the siege was noticed at the break of dawn, it would not have taken long for the

Muslims to make the one-mile trek back to the city and "put away their arms." The Muslims must have already been back in the city for a few hours upon the arrival of Archangel Gabriel, as reported in the *Sira*.

Apparently, Gabriel appeared to the apostle of Allah dressed in a turban of silk embroidered with gold that covered his face. He rode a mule with a velvet brocade saddle and asked Muhammad: "Have you already put aside your arms, O Apostle of Allah?" When the Prophet answered that yes, he had, Gabriel taunted him that the angels had not yet put aside theirs, and that he had just returned after pursuing the enemy. He is then said to have instructed the Prophet: "God commands you, O Muhammad, to march against the Banu Qurayza. Indeed, I am on my way to them to shake their strongholds."

On reaching the Banu Qurayza fort, the *Sira* quotes Muhammad as saying: "You brothers of monkeys, has God disgraced you and brought his vengeance upon you?" Surprisingly, the response from the fortress was rather complimentary: "O Abul-Qasim," the Jews called back, "you have never been a barbarian."

According to the *Sira*, "The Apostle of Allah – may Allah bless him and grant him peace – besieged them twenty-five days until his siege exhausted them and Allah cast terror into their hearts." The siege by the Muslims left the Jews and their chief, Ka'b bin Asad, trapped inside the fort, along with Huyayy, the Jewish emissary of the pagans.

With no end in sight, the Jews asked the Prophet to send one Abu Lubaba, a Muslim whom they trust. When he arrived at the fort, they asked him whether they should surrender to Muhammad's judgment. Abu Lubaba said they should, but then made a sign with his hand towards his throat indicating that if they surrendered, they would all be killed.

Abu Lubaba immediately realized he had made a mistake in revealing to the Jews that their fate had already been determined. He said, "I realized I had betrayed Allah and His Apostle." It is said that Abu

Lubaba was so remorseful that he tied himself to one of the pillars in the mosque, saying, "I shall not leave this place until Allah pardons me for what I have done." Then he promised Allah, "I shall not come to the Banu Qurayza ever again, nor shall I ever again be seen in a city in which I betrayed Allah and His Apostle." The next morning, the Prophet ordered Abu Lubaba set free and forgave him his indiscretion.

The *Sira* has a detailed account of the discussions among the Jews trapped inside the fort as they examined their options. Conversion to Islam, mass suicide, and all-out battle were discussed, but they were all ruled out. There was talk of a new Masada. It is likely that Ibn Ishaq obtained details of the discussions from the recollections of the young Jewish boys who were spared death and who later converted to Islam. There is no other way the biographer could have obtained these details. It is also possible that the children and grandchildren of the Jewish converts introduced some of the anti-Jewish twists in the *Sira*.

The closest Muslim allies of the Jews in Medina were the tribe of the Aws, who pleaded their case with the Prophet, asking him to show mercy and, instead of killing them, expel them from the city. According to the *Sira*, Muhammad asked the Aws, "Would you be satisfied, O People of Aws, if one of your own men were to pass judgement on them?" "Certainly," they replied.

The Prophet appointed one Saad bin Mu'adh arbiter of the fate of the Banu Qurayza and asked that he be taken to the Jews before passing judgment. However, if Abu Lubaba is to be believed, the decision had already been made, and only a show trial awaited the Jews.

The *Sira* claims that Saad obtained agreement from both the Aws tribe representing the Jews and the Prophet that his decision would be binding on both parties. No one bothered to ask the Jews for their opinion.

The Sira says that, on getting the nod of approval, Saad passed judgment without any hesitation, questions, or investigation, proclaiming,

"My judgement is that the men be executed, their property divided, and the women and children made captives."

The Jews were let out from their fort and marched to Medina, where they were locked in the house of a woman named Bint al-Harith. According to Ibn Ishaq, the apostle went to the market of Medina and had trenches dug. After that, he sent for the Jews in small groups and had them decapitated and thrown into those trenches.

As the slaughter continued, the *Sira* records an interesting exchange between the chief of the Jewish tribe and his fellow prisoners. As the nine hundred were slowly led out, those who were waiting asked the chief: "O Ka'b, what do you think he [Muhammad] will do with us?" To which the chief replied: "Will you never understand? Can't you see that the summoner does not cease, and those who are led away from you do not return? By God, it is death!"

The *Sira* concludes rather coldly: "These proceedings continued until the Apostle of Allah – may Allah bless him and grant him peace – had finished them off."

After the mass slaughter ends, the biographer of the Prophet paints a picture of Muhammad as a conqueror, not the Messenger of God.

> The Apostle of Allah – may Allah bless him and grant him peace – divided the property of the Banu Qurayza along with their wives and their children among the Muslims. On that day, he announced the shares for both horses and men, and he took out the fifth for himself. Each cavalryman got three shares – two for the horse and one for its rider. Each infantryman, having no horse, got a single share. There were thirty-six horses taken on the Day of the Banu Qurayza. They constituted the first spoils for which lots were cast and from which the fifth was taken. The allotments were made in accordance

with established practice and what the Apostle had done, and this became the customary practice for raids.[2]

Muslims today have a choice. We can reject this story, since there is no historical evidence to support it, and because there is no requirement for us to cling to this sordid tale of mass murder. Or we can choose to cling to this medieval myth. If that is the case, then we will need to reconcile the contradiction that arises from our belief in this tale.

We will need to reconcile ourselves to the fact that while we claim our Prophet was an embodiment of mercy and compassion, we believe in a document that portrays him as someone who supervised and participated in the murder and collective punishment of an entire community for the supposed "crime" of one man.

Even if it were true that the leader of the Jewish tribe had committed an act of treachery – there is ample evidence to the contrary – should the rest of the tribe have been slaughtered or enslaved? Those who suggest that this punishment was justified because it was based on biblical laws add insult to injury. We cannot first claim that the Jews have corrupted the Torah, rendering it suspect, and then when it suits us, use the same "corrupted text" as a source of divine law to justify mass murder. If we claim that all Muslims need to emulate the life, work, and everyday actions and decisions of Prophet Muhammad, then are we willing to repeat the slaughter of the Jews of Banu Qurayza?

The Sira describes how, after the slaughter, Prophet Muhammad "divided the property of the Banu Qurayza along with their wives and their children among the Muslims." As if this act of plunder ascribed to the name of the noble apostle were not enough, Ibn Hisham writes that the Prophet then sent "some of the female captives from the Banu Qurayza to Nejd, where he sold them for horses and arms."

This is not some anti-Muslim Islamophobe in Denmark slandering the Prophet by saying Muhammad sold women for horses; it is we

Muslims who are saying it. Shamelessly and without guilt or hesitation, for generations we have attributed a serious act of mass murder to our very own leader, our role model, the one we refer to as the Last Messenger of God, the man who we say introduced the Religion of Peace on earth. If we ourselves say Muhammad was indulging in the selling of human beings, then why do we react in indignation when our "enemies" slander the Prophet?

Contemporary Islamists and clerics evoke the story of the slaughter at Medina to recruit young Muslims into the hatefest targeted at the Jew.

The Egyptian televangelist Amr Khaled is a leading Islamic preacher with a huge international following. The charismatic cleric is a regular feature on the European and North American "Islamic Fest" speaking circuit, with tens of thousands of young Islamist followers hanging on his every word. In his rendering of the Battle of the Trench, Amr Khaled goes into details that escaped the attention of even the ninth-century scribes. Extolling the virtues of the battle, the Egyptian firebrand uses the opportunity to take a swipe at every Islamist's favourite whipping horse – the West.

"Let's learn from this [battle] that our resources are valuable and that we must not sacrifice them easily. The West and imperialism wronged us greatly when they took our raw material and returned it as products. They became wealthy and our youth stayed unemployed. This right should return and there should be justice in production worldwide."[3]

Using a battle that took place almost fifteen hundred years ago to attack the West reflects the intellectual bankruptcy that is so ubiquitous among Islam's clergy. Amr Khaled, who champions himself as a moderate, could have said that the battle and its outcome do not apply in this day and age. He could have said that in the era of international law, disputes between peoples and states are resolved not through sieges and mass slaughter, but through negotiations and the United Nations. Instead, Amr Khaled equates the seventh-century Banu Qurayza Jews with the "West and imperialism."

He goes on: "Dear brothers, victory is not offered as a piece of cake for anybody. Victory is bestowed on those courageous faithful believers who exert all their effort to vindicate Allah. . . . In our Arab world, we are in a stage that says a new history is being written for us. There is the possibility of a revival, but people have to be positive, serious, and ready to sacrifice."

With regard to the slaughter of the Jews, Amr Khaled dismisses the entire episode in a single paragraph. He writes that the Muslim army "reached Bani Qurayza and besieged them for fifteen days. Bani Qurayza offered to leave their weapons and get out of Medina, but the Prophet totally refused. He wanted them to obey his ruling, but they accepted the ruling of Saad ibn Moaz only. Saad said that they committed high treason, and accordingly all men should be killed, women captured, and money confiscated. The Prophet approved this judgment. Islam is a great mercy, but betrayal and corruption are not acceptable."

If a latter-day Islamic televangelist like Amr Khaled is comfortable with a judgment that "all men should be killed" and "women captured," then imagine what the hardcore jihadi Islamists have to say on the subject.

Another Islamist who presents himself as a reformist Muslim scholar, Tariq Ramadan, the grandson of the founder of the Muslim Brotherhood, refers to the slaughter of the Banu Qurayza Jews as a "twofold victory." Defending the doctrine of collective punishment and mass executions, Ramadan writes, "The fate meted out to the Banu Quraiza men delivered a powerful message to all neighbouring tribes that betrayals and aggressions would henceforth be severely punished."[4]

Both the Egyptian televangelist and the academic demonstrate the blind faith Islamists have in the written word of Ibn Hisham. They do not stop to consider even for a moment the possibility that the entire story is a fabrication. There is not even a hint of doubt in their celebratory rationale of the *Sira* story. And they are far from alone. The root of the problem – how we Muslims have started accepting the commentaries of the Quran as the Quran itself – goes back to the fourteenth century, when the most popular commentary on the Quran was written. Damascene scholar Ibn Kathir wrote the *Tafsir al-Quran al-Azim*, popularly known as *Tafsir ibn Kathir*, and it has become a classic commentary, popular around the Muslim world as well as with Muslims living in the West. Ibn Kathir is said to be the first commentator of the Quran who started linking the sayings of Prophet Muhammad, the Hadith, and the ninth-century biography of the Prophet to his explanation and commentary on the holy book.

Ibn Kathir claims, for instance, that it was God, through the Archangel Gabriel, who asked Prophet Muhammad to attack the Jews of Banu Qurayza. Quoting from the Hadith, Ibn Kathir writes: "Then he [Gabriel] said, 'Allah, may He be blessed and exalted, commands you to get up and go to Banu Qurayza.' . . . So the Messenger of Allah got up immediately and commanded the people to march towards Banu Qurayza."[5]

Ibn Kathir claims, too, that Saad bin Mu'adh was in fact appointed by God himself, not by Muhammad: "Allah . . . decreed that they [the Jews] would agree to be referred to him [Saad] for judgement, and this was their own free will." And according to Ibn Kathir, God caused the Jews to be convinced that Saad would be fair or lenient in his judgment and thus they accepted him as a neutral arbiter. In other words, Muslims insist that the punishment of mass slaughter was made by someone chosen by the Jews themselves.

The mythology that Ibn Kathir introduced into the Quran in the fourteenth century persists to this day among contemporary Islamic scholars. Syed Abul Ala Maududi, founder of the Jamaat-e-Islami, a prolific writer, and a significant player in the political arena of South Asia, is considered one of the dons of the world jihadi movement. He is also respected as one of the most credible interpreters of the Quran. Yet Maududi too buys into the legend of the Banu Qurayza slaughter without any hesitation. In his multivolume commentary, *Tafheem al Quran,* The Meaning of the Quran, he repeats Ibn Kathir's claim that it was God who ordered the attack, not Muhammad, and repeats the legend about how the Jews brought upon themselves their own slaughter.

My understanding of Islamic history and the Islamist teachings of Syed Qutb, Hasan al-Banna of the Muslim Brotherhood, and Syed Maududi of the Jamaat-e-Islami confirms that hatred of the Jew in Islamdom today is rooted in the narrative of this supposed slaughter of Jews by Prophet Muhammad, which makes it acceptable for a fanatic Muslim to kill a Jew. After all, he or she could argue, if it was okay for the Prophet to kill Jews on the instructions of the Archangel Gabriel, why not continue with that task in order to please Allah? Perhaps this is why otherwise intelligent Muslims, some in the corridors of academia, consider every Jewish citizen of Israel a legitimate military target. Perhaps this is why, in 2002, a student of the London School of Economics slaughtered American journalist Daniel Pearl like a goat, just because Pearl was a Jew.

Hatred of the Jew amongst us Muslims is not of the same nature as the more robust and violent Christian anti-Semitism of Europe. While medieval Christianity invoked the love of Jesus as the source of hating the Jew, Muslims were left with an uncorroborated fable outside the Quran as the source of this repugnant behaviour in so many of us.

In the almost fifteen-hundred-year checkered history of Islam, Muslims have seen themselves rise as the world's premier superpower, from the eighth to the twelfth centuries, and then sink to a low where almost all of us became subjects of Europe's expansionist colonial powers. Through all of the upheavals of our rich history, we have faced adversaries.

And when we sank to the depths of impotence, we were defeated and conquered by the Mongols in 1258, expelled from Andalusia by Catholic Spanish monarchs in 1492, lost Muslim India to the British and Indonesia to the Dutch. Why, then, do we not harbour any hatred towards Britain or the Netherlands or Spain? Why no ill will against Catholics or Zoroastrians or Buddhists? Why do we save our most contemptible sentiments for the Jews?

If we can forgive the Dutch for occupying Indonesia for two hundred years, if we can embrace the language and culture of the British that toppled the last Muslim emperor of India, if we can befriend the French and make France our home despite the memories of the Algerian uprising, then why do we continue the centuries-old hatred of the Jews?

The story of the massacre of the Jews of Banu Qurayza feeds our hatred and gives us moral and religious validation for that hate. I have been to the battlefields of Medina and have seen for myself that the myth is not borne out by the reality on the ground. In the next chapter, I will scrutinize the story in the *Sira* against the evidence on the ground and demonstrate why we Muslims need to abandon the tale as one more medieval myth.

CHAPTER SEVEN

Muhammad Comes to the City of Jews

The city of Medina defies all the stereotypes associated with the desert kingdom of Saudi Arabia. Yathrib, as Medina was known in pre-Islamic times, lies at the heart of a fertile oasis surrounded by Mount Sala to the northwest and the wall-like Mount Ayre, which stretches east–west, cradling the valley of Aqeeq to the south, through which lay the historical caravan route to Mecca, five hundred kilometres farther on.

To the north, Medina is shielded by another east–west mountain called Jabal Ohud. This is where Muslims under Prophet Muhammad suffered a near-fatal defeat at the hands of their Meccan enemies, but lived to fight another day. Mount Ohud is also the site of the grave of Hamza, the Prophet's uncle, who was killed in that battle and whose body is said to have been mutilated by the pagans.*

According to legend, the first inhabitants arrived in the area just after the Great Flood. Residents of Medina who trace their history through many generations even carry the name of the first Medinan – Gayna ibn Mahla ibn Obail – who, they claim, was a descendant of prophet Noah.

Ali Hafiz, the Saudi historian and founder of the newspaper *Al-Madina*, writes in his book *Chapters from the History of Madina* that the

---

* Anthony Quinn immortalized the role of Hamza in *The Message,* the Libyan-financed 1976 Hollywood classic on early Islam.

city owes its existence to two historic events. He quotes medieval historians who claim that Moses passed through the area on a pilgrimage and that many of his followers remained in Medina, as they "found in it a resemblance to a city where a Prophet would emerge, as described in the Tawrat [Torah]."[1]

The other major movement of people to Medina occurred in the wake of the great flood in Yemen in 450, when the Ma'rib Dam is said to have burst, forcing about fifty thousand people to flee north. The tribes of Aws and Khazraj in the Medina of Muhammad's time are said to be the descendants of these refugees, and are known collectively as the Ansar (literally, helpers).

Thus, at the time Prophet Muhammad sought refuge in the city to escape persecution at the hands of Meccan pagans, Medina was populated primarily by two groups – monotheistic Jews and pagan Arabs. The day the Prophet rode into town on his camel, the city had a population of ten thousand, equally divided between Jews and pagans, with fewer than a hundred Muslims. A decade later, Muhammad had changed the very character of Medina from a pagan-Jewish city to one that was overwhelmingly Muslim and Islam's capital.

I first visited Medina, the City of Light – Medina al Munawarah – in the winter of 1978. Since my childhood, I had dreamed of being on the historic battlefields that proved so crucial to the birth of my faith and are the last resting place of its founder, the Prophet Muhammad.

My friend Rizwan Pasha drove me to Medina from Jeddah, a five-hour journey that was taking much longer because of the busloads of pilgrims headed in the same direction. The full moon glistened in the desert sky on that November night. As swirling sand from the dunes eddied across the precarious two-lane highway and performed a shimmering dance in the Honda Civic's headlights, we raced towards Medina. I had just performed the pilgrimage of hajj in Mecca and wanted to complete the rites by paying my respects at the grave of the Prophet.

The chill of the night air surprised me. Notwithstanding my bald head – shaved as part of the rites of hajj – I had expected Saudi Arabia to be a hot place and was unprepared for the bone-chilling cold of the Medina night. Centuries earlier, it was this same bone-chilling cold that had forced the Meccans to end their siege, saving the nascent Muslim community of the Prophet from being annihilated.

Oil wealth had started pouring into Saudi Arabia in 1978, but had not made its way to the shack-like roadside food stalls, restaurants, and gas stations that dotted the route of the hajj caravans, traversed by thousands of white Iranian-made automobiles heading back to the Shah's Iran. Hulks of burnt-out cars, involved in sure-death head-on collisions, littered both sides of the road. The dead hajjis had perished in the Holy Land, the ultimate dream of many a Muslim.

We refuelled at one of the "benzene stations" before the last leg to Medina. As we sat and sipped translucent shai from what looked like miniature beer mugs, a couplet from a devotional song of my childhood came to my lips.

> The streets of Medina breathe fragrance into the air.
> If this be not Paradise, then pray tell me what is?

Pasha rolled his eyes. "One week in the kingdom and now I have to put up with your religious side," he quipped. He had known me since our university days as a hard-nosed leftist secularist with little respect for mullahs, and had warned me on the day I arrived at Jeddah airport: "You want to survive here, you better keep your big mouth shut, or you'll end up being deported or, worse, jailed."

As a child, I had grown up listening to devotional songs written in praise of the Prophet Muhammad. An entire genre of poetry, the Na'at, is dedicated to praising the Prophet. As a little boy I had memorized many of the verses and can still sing a few. Mom had inculcated in us a devotion to the apostle that was much more than religious; he was a family member. Prophet Muhammad was our uncle, the one we could turn to when help was needed and the one who, we were told, would intercede on our behalf on the Day of Judgment. Every month Mom would invite her friends over, and they would read the Quran and later stand up together and sing the praises of the Prophet. I usually waited until the last of the guests had gone to grab at the leftover sweetmeats and the succulent dates that were holy simply because our beloved Prophet liked them.

Whereas I had approached Mecca in 1978 with some trepidation, uncertain what to expect, my trip to Medina was very different. I was going to see the man who had dominated my life as a child, a man I had talked to as if he were right there standing next to me when I played cricket with a tennis ball or lost my marbles to the street bullies. While Mecca was the city of God, the divine power we were all conditioned to fear and submit to, Medina was the city of Muhammad, the man we had grown to love and adore.

We arrived in Medina just before the crack of dawn and headed straight to the Masjid-e-Nabawi, the Mosque of the Prophet. After the Fajr prayers, we stayed inside the mosque until the noon Zuhr congregation, amidst the cacophony of a polyglot crowd: Turks jostling with Nigerians; the overzealous Pakistanis elbowing out Yemenis; groups of tearful Shia Persians huddling together matched in their devotion only by the Indonesians; loud Egyptians in tent-like attire walking around with a sense of entitlement that was in stark contrast to the prim and proper North Americans, who politely found their right-of-way. A hundred different guttural Arabic accents rained down like flower petals in the mosque of the man these men revered so much.

Later that day, having offered my supplications, I visited the many battle sites where Muhammad had fought against his enemies. I came back rather disappointed. There was so much more that I wanted to know, but so little that I could find. Above all, I wanted to see the *khandak,* the trench or the moat; the Tôrres Vedras of Islamic history. Had the Prophet, I wanted to know, really authorized the slaughter of hundreds of apparently neutral Jews – the same Prophet who forgave his sworn enemies, the Meccan pagans, on their surrender – or was this an exaggerated myth? Something didn't sound right about this story, and I was determined to get to the bottom of it. My search would begin at the trench.

By my reading of the history and geography of the city, every historic site in Medina should have been within an eight-kilometre radius. I saw the mountain of Ohud, the site of the first Muslim defeat in history. Later, Pasha took me to what was supposed to be the site of the Battle of the Trench, but the trench itself had disappeared. The moat that saved the Prophet and Islam had been filled in by time. "Where is it?" I asked.

"Gone, my friend," Pasha said with a shrug. "It was just a trench, not a mosque, so why save it?"

"And where," I asked with some trepidation, "were the Jews of Banu Qurayza slaughtered and buried?"

He reacted as if I had struck him. "Are you crazy? What Jews are you talking about?" He looked over his shoulder to ensure no one had heard my blasphemous question.

"Never mind," I replied, recognizing that asking questions about Jews was likely to land us in trouble.

I returned to Medina the following year, in the spring, this time alone. I had history on my mind, not religion or piety. Notwithstanding the obligatory visit to the Prophet's Mosque to pay respects to the apostle and say my early-morning prayers, I was focused on evidence-based truth, not blind faith.

I joined a group of pilgrims headed for Mount Ohud, and when the group moved on, I hung back to reflect on all I had read about the ferocity of the fight that day fourteen hundred years ago; the Prophet had been wounded in the battle and almost lost his life. I loitered on the rocky surface, trying to visualize the scene, until I was rudely interrupted by a Saudi security guard in jungle greens with his bootlaces untied. "Keep moving," he yelled, adding a racist slur, "ya Rafeek," a derisive term for Indians, Pakistanis, and Bangladeshis.

(This wasn't the first time I had heard such a slur in the city of my Prophet. The same people who take ownership of the Prophet as their birthright, and act as if his legacy is a franchise they have inherited, appear to find it completely acceptable to insult blacks, Indo-Pakistanis, East Asians, and, of course, the hated Persians – not seeming to realize that had it not been for a Persian, who suggested to the Prophet that he dig a defensive trench to stop the enemy, Islamic history would have been very different. I would like to think that the racist attitude of the Saudi towards the poor and the darker-skinned stems from Arabia's recently acquired oil wealth. However, in his classic account of his pilgrimage to Mecca and Medina in 1852, the English adventurer Richard Burton wrote: "Whenever an Ajemi [non-Arab] stood in the way of an Arab or a Turk, he was rudely thrust aside, with abuse muttered loud enough to be heard by all around." More than a century later, I was cautioned by friends to swallow such abuse, lest I run afoul of the law and disappear in the kingdom's prison system.)

The historical texts suggested the trench would have been dug to the north of the city, running east–west, beginning at Mount Sala and ending in the area known as Hara Sharqia (Eastern Lava Field), a distance of some two to four kilometres. However, try as I might, I could not find any trace of the trench, nor anyone willing to help me locate it. Could the trench have been a fiction, the figment of some scribe's imagination? This did not seem possible, since, unlike some other historical events in early Islam, the Battle of the Trench is specifically mentioned in the Quran. On asking around, I aroused more suspicion than I should have. "Why do you want to know?" a Saudi asked me. "Do you have a permit?" he enquired before starting an inquisition that I escaped thanks to the muezzin's call to prayer.

This lack of interest in the trench is also reflected in Burton's *A Secret Pilgrimage to Mecca and Medina*, in which it receives only one passing mention: "The principal places of pious visitation in the vicinity of El-Madinah are the Mosques of Kuba, the Cemetery of El-Bakia. . . . Shortly after leaving the suburb [outside Medina], an Indian, who joined our party upon the road, pointed out on the left of the way what he declared was the place of the celebrated Khandak, or Moat."[2]

After the death of Prophet Muhammad and the first four caliphs, the early Muslims abandoned Medina as the seat of their growing domain and moved to the luxurious abodes of captured Byzantine palaces in Damascus. The two holiest cities of Islam were literally cast away by the Arabs, who were tantalized by the advanced civilizations of Persia and Byzantium. Over the centuries, while Islamic civilization would blossom in the newly conquered territories of Persia, Egypt, Syria, Spain, and India, little attention would be paid to the birthplace of Islam – Arabia. The seventh-century Umayyads of Damascus, the ninth-century Abbasids of Baghdad, the tenth-century Fatimids of Cairo, the sixteenth-century Ottomans of Turkey, the seventeenth-century Mughals of India – all of them built monuments, libraries, tombs, and mosques, but little in the city where their Prophet lies buried.

It seems that once Medina had been abandoned, preserving the trench that saved Islam and the Prophet was the last thing on any caliph's mind. The Saudi scholar Ali Hafiz, in his book *Chapters from the History of Madina*, states, "There are no remains or ruins left at the trench to help define its exact location." In 2005, the renowned Saudi architect Sami Angawi lamented the destruction of historic sites in Arabia. He told *The Independent*, "The house where the Prophet received the word of God is gone and nobody cares. . . . This is the end of the history of Mecca and Medina and the end of their future." A people who could not care less for the house of the Prophet would certainly not bother to save the trench that saved his life.

In the absence of any physical evidence of the trench, I had to rely on the map used by the Indian diplomat and scholar Barakat Ahmad in his book *Muhammad and the Jews.* (The map matches the detailed description provided by Ali Hafiz in his book.) Ahmad, who earned a doctorate in Arab history from the American University of Beirut and another doctorate in literature from the University of Tehran, has challenged the Muslim understanding of the events of that time as they have been passed on to us through the biography of Ibn Ishaq.

The earliest detailed reference to the massacre of Medina's Jews is in Ibn Ishaq's *Sira,* part of which I have reproduced in the previous chapter. Given that Ibn Ishaq's account was written more than a hundred years after the event in question, it is surprising that hardly anyone has questioned the authenticity of his narrative. Later Muslim historians simply take his version of the story, at times creatively embellish it with their own fantasies, and almost always overlook Ibn Ishaq's uncertain list of authorities.

However, Ibn Hajar, the fourteenth century Egyptian scholar, denounces this story and related ones as "odd tales," while another contemporary of Ibn Ishaq, the jurist Malik ibn Anas, referred to him as an outright "liar" and "an impostor" who belonged to the charlatans.[3] But these were exceptions. Most historians from medieval times onward have blindly swallowed the legend of the slaughter of the Jews of Banu Qurayza. Even the great Muslim historian Tabari, who always drew on multiple sources in his rendering of history, does not rely on versions of the legend other than Ibn Ishaq's.

Ibn Ishaq himself relied on the stories that were told by Jewish children taken from their parents and raised as Muslims, or sons of Jewish women who were concubines of Muslim warriors. Converts to a religion are usually hostile to the faith they have left behind, and it is quite possible that the stories these former Jews told were the basis of the tales about the alleged Jewish conspiracies. Indeed, Ibn Hajar rejects the stories in question in the strongest terms, referring to them as "such odd tales."

While the Quran makes many references to the siege and the actual Battle of the Trench, the only reference to the supposed massacre is to a clash between the combatants of the Banu Qurayza and the Muslim army. In Sura 33:26 the Quran says: "He [God] caused those of the People of the Book [Jews] who helped them [the Meccan pagans] to come out of their forts. Some you killed, some you took prisoner."

But here God talks about a battle, not a mass killing. It concerns those who he says fought and, as in any battle, some of those were killed while others were taken prisoner. There is no mention whatsoever in the Quran of the massacre of Jews.

Is it possible Ibn Ishaq got it all wrong? And why is it that when making a choice between the words of Ibn Ishaq and the words of the Quran, Islamic scholars opt for the words of a man instead of Allah?

Over the course of many visits to Medina, searching for the truth, and many years reading Jewish and Muslim authors who have written about this epic event that frames the Muslim view of the Jew, I have come to believe that the massacre of the Jews never took place. My conclusion is based on my analysis of physical factors as well as the historical and religious incongruities in how we Muslims are told the story, but above all, on the absence of any mention of this monumental massacre in Jewish texts.

Jews have been persecuted all through history, expelled from dozens of countries, hated by people who have never been exposed to them or their faith, but what makes them unique is that they have survived centuries of pogroms, culminating in the Holocaust, and have had the ability to document their suffering faithfully and in great detail.

The account of the Jewish rebellion against the Romans, which ended in the destruction of the Second Temple in AD 70, has a close similarity to the Medina massacre. After the Romans destroyed Jerusalem, some of the radical Jews known as the Sicarii took over the nearby rock fortress of Masada for their last stand – an event that ended in the mass suicide of the besieged Jews. With the crushing of the Jewish revolt in Jerusalem, tens of thousands of Jews were enslaved while others fled to the Mediterranean and some to Arabia. Alfred Guillaume, who translated Ibn Ishaq, suggests that some of the Jews fleeing the Romans were the ones who settled in the oasis of Medina.

The author who detailed the Jewish rebellion against Rome is Flavius Josephus, a Jew who held office under the Romans. It is through his writings that we read of the tragedies that befell the Jews of Jerusalem and Masada between the years 66 and 73. In a strange coincidence, the number of Jews who died at Masada was around nine hundred, the same number reportedly slaughtered in Medina six centuries later. In another parallel to Medina, Josephus tells us that when the Jews reached the point of despair, they were addressed by their leader, Eleazar, who suggested they kill their women and children and fight to the last man. Later, he suggested a mass suicide; if suicide was considered a sinful practice, they should kill each other. In Medina too, the besieged Jews of Banu Qurayza are reported by Ibn Ishaq to have received similar advice from Ka'b bin Asad. These parallel stories, recorded six centuries apart, have led the scholar W.N. Arafat to conclude that the stories passed on to Muslim scribes about Medina came from Jews who had converted to Islam and who applied the earlier stories of Masada to what had happened at Medina. Arafat writes,

Clearly the similarity of details is most striking. Not only are the suggestions of mass suicide similar but even the numbers are almost the same. Even the same names occur in both accounts. There is Phineas, and Azar b. Azar, just as Eleazar addressed the Jews besieged in Masada. There is, indeed, more than a mere similarity. Here we have the prototype – indeed, I would suggest, the origin of the story of Banu Qurayza, preserved by descendants of the Jews who fled south to Arabia after the Jewish Wars. . . . A later generation of these descendants superimposed details of the siege of Masada on the story of the siege of Banu Qurayza, perhaps by confusing a tradition of their distant past with one from their less remote history. The mixture provided Ibn Ishaq's story. When Muslim historians ignored it or transmitted it without comment or with cold lack of interest, they only expressed lack of enthusiasm for a strange tale, as Ibn Hajar called it.[4]

It is inconceivable that a people with such a deep sense of their history, who would document the story of the nine hundred dead Jews of Masada in the year 73, would have no record of a slaughter of nine hundred Jews six hundred years later. However, this is the reality of the Medina massacre: there are no Jewish records, not even fables or stories, about such an incident in the Jewish chronicles of medieval times.

Among contemporary Jewish scholars who have written about the contentious Jewish-Muslim relationship, historian Shlomo Dov Goitein's work stands out as a model of scholarly argument devoid of the subjective passion that is often the hallmark of his Muslim contemporaries. Goitein, the German-born son of a Hungarian rabbi, studied Arabic and Islam at the University of Frankfurt at the time the Ottoman caliphate was crumbling after the First World War and Palestine came under the British Mandate. His landmark work, *Jews and Arabs: A Concise*

History of Their Social and Cultural Relations (1955), reflects little rancour against the Arabs, even though he was one of the early European Jews who moved to Palestine in 1923, when the arrival of the Jews was met with suspicion if not outright hostility, and even though he wrote in the aftermath of Israel's 1948 war with its Arab neighbours.

In tracing the history of the interaction between Jews and Arabs, Goitein makes no mention of the supposed massacre of the Jews of Medina. In a passing reference, he writes: "It is very unfortunate that the struggle, which very specific historical circumstances forced the Jews and Muhammad, has left its mark on the Holy Book of Islam."[5]

As the first professor of Islamic studies at Jerusalem's Hebrew University, Goitein would of course have been familiar with the biography of Prophet Muhammad by Ibn Ishaq and the subsequent Hadith literature that corroborated the Jewish massacre at Medina as an act of retribution carried out with the Prophet's approval. However, not only does he refuse to acknowledge that this seminal event took place, he states explicitly that there is no record of such a massacre in Jewish history. Goitein writes: "Concerning the fateful events and developments which took place at the time, during the three most decisive decades of oriental history (about 615 and 645 AD), not a single contemporary account has come down to us from Jewish sources."[6]

It is possible, although highly unlikely, that an event of such magnitude as the extermination of nine hundred Jews escaped the attention of all Jewish historians, poets, writers, traders, and travellers, either at the time or in the coming centuries, especially when they held influential positions in various Islamic caliphates during the era Jews call the Golden Period. At the time Ibn Ishaq was putting together the *Sira* and writing in detail about the massacre, it was the second and third century of Islamic caliphates, governed first from Damascus and later Baghdad, and Jews were a part of Muslim society. It is improbable that the Jewish community and their rabbis would not have been able to line up Jewish sources corroborating the said massacre if it had actually taken place.

Scholar Barakat Ahmad writes, "It is not normal with the Jews not to record their misfortunes." According to him, the descendants of the Jews of Khaybar who had been expelled by the second caliph a few years after the supposed massacre apparently had no memory of the tragedy that had befallen their grandfathers and great-grandfathers.

Abraham Geiger, a nineteenth-century German rabbi who spearheaded the founding of Reform Judaism, published an essay in Bonn in 1833 titled "Was hat Mohammed aus dem Judentum aufgenommen?" (What Did Muhammad Receive from Judaism?); it was later translated into English in India in 1896 as "Judaism and Islam." Geiger was the first to make a passing reference to the expulsion of Jews from Medina, but made no mention of the massacre of the Banu Qurayza. Rabbi Geiger had access to Islamic texts that allowed him to dwell on the Jewish roots of Islam, but the story of the massacre seems to have struck him as too outlandish, and he passed over it.

Another Jewish resource is a sixteenth-century book by the Portuguese Samuel Usque, *Consolation for the Tribulations of Israel*. Barakat Ahmad refers to Usque as "this deft painter of Jewish suffering who caused the long procession of Jewish history to file past the tearful eyes of his contemporaries in all its sublime glory and abysmal tragedy." Yet in his compilation of Jewish travails in history, Usque makes no reference to the massacre of the Banu Qurayza Jews. He does, though, write about an incident in Medina in 1163, when a group of Jews were accused of robbing the grave of Prophet Muhammad. "This report spread through all of Islam and the reaction was violent; merely on the basis of this rumor and supposition, the Moors killed many Jews and destroyed forty of their synagogues."[7]

In his prologue, Usque quotes Socrates, saying, "When people found themselves in trouble they should compare their misfortunes they had survived in the past with the present ones, and they would easily find consolation: for no past misfortune would prove to have been so small that it would not turn out to be much greater than the present one." If this was Usque's objective, why would he have omitted the Banu Qurayza massacre of 630, but include the less significant event that occurred in Medina in 1163?

Of course, there are contemporary Jewish authors and academics who do mention the massacre of the Banu Qurayza Jews and maintain that Prophet Muhammad was instrumental in that slaughter, but they rely on Islamic sources, not Jewish. Among them is Rabbi Reuven Firestone, a professor of medieval Jewish studies and Islam at Hebrew Union College and the author of *An Introduction to Islam for Jews*. That book depicts Islam's Prophet as the destroyer of Medina's Jews, but surprisingly has won praise from two of America's leading Islamists: Ingrid Mattson of the Islamic Society of North America and Muzammil Siddiqi of the Fiqh Council of North America.

Firestone writes about how Prophet Muhammad "successfully divided the Jewish community of Medina and destroyed it." About the actual killing, he writes, "According to the sources, the Jews of Qurayza surrendered. Trenches were dug in the marketplace of Medina, and Muhammad had the men's heads struck off in those trenches as they were brought out in batches. Sources put the number of people killed that day between 600 and 900."[8]

What Rabbi Firestone fails to mention is that the "sources" he cites are all Muslim, not Jewish, and that these Muslim sources surfaced a hundred years after the reported incident. It is interesting that both Mattson and Siddiqi ignore this depiction of Muhammad as a mass murderer. Mattson says, "Firestone's book shines as a beacon of scholarship and humanity," while Siddiqi calls the book "a valuable contribution toward making Islam understood and appreciated by the Jewish people."

Another excellent book on Islamic history from a Jewish perspective is Norman Stillman's *The Jews of Arab Lands: A History and Source Book*. Drawing on a treasure trove of medieval Muslim documents, Stillman provides his readers with a breathtaking view of Jewish life in the Arab world spanning several centuries. Unlike Firestone, Stillman goes into details about the fateful encounter between the Jews of Banu Qurayza and the Muslims of Medina, but he too relies almost entirely on Muslim sources and does not dwell on the absence of any Jewish version of the events. He does, however, speculate why the Prophet would have agreed to a mass slaughter of Jews when, earlier, he had simply expelled other Jewish tribes from the city. Stillman, a student of Shlomo Goitein, writes, "The slaughter of so many men was an extremely impressive act that enhanced Muhammad's prestige throughout Arabia. Here was a man to be reckoned with. He was now absolute master in Madina."[9] Stillman acknowledges that even after the massacre of the Banu Qurayza Jews and the expulsion of other tribes, Medina was still home to many Jews. He does not explain why none of these Jews, the survivors or the travellers, ever mentioned the incident in any oral or written communication.

It wasn't until the mid-nineteenth century that a book written by a Jew made a passing reference to the Medina massacre. Perhaps it is merely a coincidence, but Jewish authors began reproducing Islamic texts that showed Arabs identifying their own Prophet as a mass murderer just after the First Zionist Congress, held in Basel in 1897, and as the quest for a Jewish homeland in Palestine was meeting resistance from the Arab world and the Ottoman caliphate. Until then, it was as if world Jewry did not take the Muslim bravado seriously. Perhaps they recognized the tale as nothing more than one example of exaggeration among many. Of course, in the modern era of propaganda warfare, if the Muslims were willing to depict their own leader as a mass murderer, why wouldn't their Jewish adversaries oblige? Where else but in the Muslim world would one run into a situation where the case for the prosecution is made by the defence?

The absence of the Medina massacre in medieval Jewish texts strongly suggests that the Jews had no record of this incident because it was merely a myth created by Muslims. That the Quran itself is silent on the subject should give Muslims pause.

As we have seen, Ibn Ishaq in his biography of Muhammad claims that God sent a message to the Prophet through the Archangel Gabriel commanding Muhammad to besiege the Jews of Banu Qurayza. Many verses in chapter 33 of the Quran relate to the Battle of the Trench, some asking Muslims to eradicate their fear of the enemy, others addressing the role of hypocrites among the Muslims, but nowhere does Allah command Muhammad to besiege or massacre the Jews of Banu Qurayza. Later, Ibn Ishaq's story would be incorporated into the Hadith literature and sharia law. It would then make a back-door entry into Quranic studies when, in the fourteenth century, Ibn Kathir would write the multivolume commentary on the Quran that has become standard reading across the Arab world. This was followed by the twentieth-century exegesis by Syed Maududi, firmly embedding the massacre in the collective psyche of hundreds of millions of Muslims.

But let us look at some incongruities.

The Quran explicitly rejects the notion of collective punishment. Abdullah Yusuf Ali, the Indian scholar whose translation of the Quran into English is the world standard, says this about the Quranic doctrine of "personal responsibility": "We are fully responsible for our acts ourselves, we cannot transfer the consequences to someone else. Nor can anyone vicariously atone for our sins."[10]

Sura 6:164 of the Quran says:

Every soul earns [what it earns] for itself,
And no man shall bear another's burden.

For the Prophet to have inflicted a collective punishment on a people, even if it were proven that their leaders had conspired to attack the Muslims, would have been against the injunction of the Quran. It is unlikely that the Prophet would have violated the very book he said God had revealed to him. The above verse had been revealed to Muhammad long before he migrated to Medina, and if God had wanted his apostle to act in violation of his earlier commands, surely this would have been made clear in the Quran.

N.W. Arafat in his 1976 essay explores another gaping hole in Ibn Ishaq's story. He says, "Had this slaughter actually happened, jurists would have adopted it as a precedent. In fact, exactly the opposite has been the case. The attitude of jurists, and their rulings, has been more according to the Quranic rule in the verse, 'No soul shall bear another's burden.'" Arafat quotes from the ninth-century jurist Abu Ubayd bin Sallam, who relates a significant incident in his book *Kitab al-Amwal,* which Arafat reminds us was a book of jurisprudence, not a biography.

Sallam tells of an incident in the ninth century in which a group of Christians in Lebanon rebelled against the authority of the caliphate. One Abdullab bin 'All was the regional governor, and after putting down the revolt, he ordered the rebels and the entire community to be moved elsewhere. However, the leading jurist at the time, Imam al-Awza'i, immediately objected to the verdict. His argument was that the revolt against the caliphate was not the result of the community's unanimous agreement to rebel, and therefore collective punishment was not right. "As far as I know it is not a rule of God that God should punish the many for the fault of the few, but punish the few for the fault of the many."[11]

Arafat argues that if the story of the slaughter of Banu Qurayza were true and had been accepted as a historical fact, then Imam al-Awza'i would have had to treat it as a precedent and not intervene to stop the collective deportation of the Christian Lebanese.

Other Jewish-Muslim conflicts took place after the Battle of the Trench during the Prophet's lifetime. In all these confrontations, the Muslims prevailed; yet the defeated tribes did not meet the fate of the Banu Qurayza. Does this mean the Prophet himself was not following his own precedent and was defying the "command" sent by God through the agency of Gabriel?

What's more, could God or his Prophet inflict a punishment of mass murder on a people who had committed no crime other than being neutral? This is contrary to the rules of warfare in Islam and in the Quran and has no precedent. If such a punishment was imposed on the Jews of Banu Qurayza, certainly there is no evidence in the Quran that such a thing ever happened again during Muhammad's lifetime. (Of course, after his death, this episode was invoked as a Sunnah to give religious justification to countless massacres and ethnic cleansings in the name of Islam.)

There are two more examples of the Prophet's army inflicting comprehensive defeat on groups that, unlike the Banu Qurayza, had openly declared hostility and enmity towards Muhammad. One involved the Jewish town of Khaybar, where many of the Jews expelled from Medina had taken refuge, and the other the Meccan pagans led by the Quraysh tribe.

Despite the fact that the men who surrendered unconditionally at Khaybar had taken up arms against the Prophet and had built the confederacy that had almost wiped out the Muslims a year before, Muhammad did not inflict a collective punishment. Here is the account of the Khaybar surrender in the words of Ibn Ishaq: "The apostle besieged the people of Khaybar in their two forts al-Watih and al-Sulalim until they could hold out no longer. They asked him to let them go, and spare their lives, and he did so. . . . When the people of Khaybar surrendered on these conditions, they asked the apostle to employ them on the property with half the share in the produce, saying 'We know more about it than you and we are better farmers.' The apostle agreed to this arrangement on the condition that 'if we wish to expel you, we will expel you.'"[12]

Years later, when Muhammad's army conquered Mecca, the city he had fled ten years earlier, he "instructed his commanders when they entered Mecca only to fight those who resisted them."[13] These were men who had harassed and chased Muhammad into exile; they had conspired to kill him and had launched many raids in an attempt to wipe out Islam. Yet the Prophet decreed a general amnesty for all of them, barring a few, including the leader of the Meccan pagans, Abu Sufyan. Had the massacre of Jews in Medina been a precedent, Mecca would have turned into a slaughterhouse that would have dwarfed the supposed massacre in Medina.

According to Ibn Ishaq and the Hadith literature of Sahih Bukhari and Sahih Muslim, the death sentence passed on the Banu Qurayza was handed down by Saad bin Mu'adh after both parties agreed upon him as an arbiter. However, Saad was a Muslim who had recently railed against the Jews in an argument over their treaty with the Prophet, vowing to avenge their supposed treachery. Why would the Jews agree to appoint as judge of their fate a man who had vilified them just a few days earlier? Why would they sign their own death sentence? Yet this is the answer most Muslims give when asked why the Prophet approved such a horrendous punishment. Invariably, a cleric will say, "The Jews chose their own fate . . . it was their own choice."

The legend would have us believe that after the judgment, all the Jews were enclosed in the home of a woman named Bint al-Harith. If the massacred men totalled nine hundred, then it is safe to assume that, including women and children, the combined population of the Jews who surrendered was close to five thousand people. Notwithstanding the impossibility of accommodating so many people in one home, Ibn Ishaq and the Hadith literature would have us believe that no one among the five thousand attempted to flee; no one resisted as they heard the sound of their men succumbing to the sword; and that all this happened while the Muslims dug trenches in the Medina market.

Which raises another question. Why did the Prophet dig trenches for the massacred Jews when the Muslims already had a massive trench north of the city? That trench was deep and wide enough to stop an army of ten thousand Meccan soldiers; surely it would have sufficed as a place to dump the decapitated Jews of the Banu Qurayza. Digging fresh graves in the middle of Medina just does not make sense.

Moreover, if all the graves were dug in the vicinity of the Prophet's Mosque and the main marketplace, how much space was required to bury nine hundred souls? Ibn Ishaq says it was not one mass grave but that "trenches" were dug. By a conservative estimate, an area of ten thousand square feet would be needed to accommodate nine hundred graves.

During my stay in Medina, I searched endlessly for any evidence of these graves, but found none. While it is conceivable that the moat dug in the Battle of the Trench could have disappeared over time, skeletons do not vanish. If the Prophet of Islam killed nine hundred Jews and buried them near the Medina market, then surely the bones would have emerged during the twentieth-century excavations and expansion of the market. But there is no record of any bone fragments or other human remains being found when the market was expanded or the Prophet's Mosque was rebuilt to accommodate the millions like me who pray there.

To understand why the legend of the Banu Qurayza massacre was created, we need to consider the geopolitical conditions in which Ibn Ishaq compiled his biography of Prophet Muhammad.

While Ibn Ishaq was still living in Medina in the early 700s, the Umayyad caliphate was firmly in power in Damascus, controlling a realm that spread from the banks of the River Indus in India to the northern border of Spain with France. The challenges to the caliphs' rule came not from the Hindu east or the Christian north, but from disaffected Muslims, primarily the descendants of the Prophet who considered the caliphs' regime illegitimate and corrupt. However, amidst the turmoil and bloodshed of the time, there were two Jewish uprisings led by men who claimed they were the Messiah, the first in Isfahan, Persia, and the second in Damascus itself.

During the reign of Caliph Abd al-Malik ibn Marwan, a Persian Jew, Ishaq ibn Yakub Abu Isa al-Isfahani, maintained that the coming of the Messiah was to be preceded by five messengers, of whom he himself was the last – the Messiah's herald and the summoner. He claimed he had come to deliver the Jews from the rule of the Muslims and to take them back to Jerusalem and restore Palestine. Abu Isa al-Isfahani asserted that no miracle would rescue the Jews from their plight and urged them to use force. It is said he was able to raise an army of ten thousand Jews in Persia, who hailed him as the Messiah. The caliph's army met the rebels near the city of Ray (ancient Rhagae), where they crushed the revolt and killed the so-called Messiah.

(Abu Isa al-Isfahani introduced several changes to Judaism. He "regarded Jesus and Muhammad as genuine prophets, who were sent to pagans, and urged his followers to read not only the Old Testament, but also the Gospels and the Koran.")[14]

The other Jew who laid claim to prophethood, not just of the Jews but also of Muslims, was a Syrian by the name of Zonarius (or Serenus) during the reign of Caliph Yazid II. Zonarius had escaped the tyranny of Emperor Lev Isavrianin in Byzantine Constantinople and along with many Jews had sought refuge in the Muslim caliphate that was at war with that city. In Damascus, Zonarius declared himself the Messiah and challenged the existing Jewish order. He established religious observances that were contrary to rabbinical law, abolished prayer and certain incest laws formulated by the scribes, and allowed marriage without a contract. His fame was such that Jews from as far away as Spain and Persia rallied to his call against the caliph and the Jewish authorities.

As Simon Dubonov writes in his *History of the Jews:* "This turmoil went on for several years until the new prophet was taken into custody and brought before Caliph Yazid ɪɪ. The Caliph had interrogated Zonarius, became convinced that his teaching harboured no political motives, and therefore turned him over to the Jewish authorities, so they could punish him for his religious heresy."[15] The court ordered him beheaded.

It was in this climate of Jewish rebellion and the subsequent slaughter of the Umayyads by the Abbasids that Ibn Ishaq penned his biography of Prophet Muhammad. Taking this into consideration, Barakat Ahmad concludes that the legend of the Medina massacre was created to warn the Jews of the Abbasid Empire of the consequence of armed uprising as sanctioned by the practice of the Prophet himself. As Ahmad puts it: "One more Ibn Isa [revolt] and you will be exterminated like the B. [Banu] Qurayzah."[16]

Montgomery Watt, professor of Islamic studies at the University of Edinburgh, is considered one of the foremost non-Muslim interpreters of Islam in the West. In his book *Muhammad at Medina,* Watt speculates on "what would have happened had the Jews come to terms with Muhammad instead of opposing him." The thought is enticing to those of us who are deeply troubled by the institutional nature of anti-Semitism that drives twentieth-century Islamists. According to Watt, the Jews of Medina "could have secured very favourable terms from him [Muhammad], including religious autonomy, and on that basis, the Jews might have become partners in an Arab empire and Islam a sect of Jewry. How different the face of the world would be now, had it happened."[17]

Of course, Watt writes about Muslim-Jewish relations as seen through the prism of Ibn Ishaq's biography that accentuated the frictions between the "nation of Ishamel" – as many medieval Jews referred to Muslims – and Jews. Contemporary Islamist writers too paint a grim picture, as it confirms their view of Jews as a conniving enemy of Islam. If we depended only on the texts of contemporary Islamists, their apologists, and Ibn Ishaq, it may appear that Muslim-Jewish relations in the era following the death of Muhammad were governed by a mutual suspicion, if not hatred or resentment. However, a reading of history demonstrates otherwise.

Jewish-Muslim relations during the time of the eighth-century Umayyad dynasty, and their ninth- and tenth-century Abbasid successors, were fairly amicable. Jews were integrated into Muslim society and had considerable religious autonomy. True, they were accorded a second-class status as dhimmis, but Jewish texts of the time do not reflect an atmosphere of hostility between the two peoples. And true, the Sunni Arab caliphs ruled with a sense of entitlement, but compared to how they treated other Muslim sects and groups who challenged the authenticity of the caliph, they did not see the small Jewish community as a threat. Compared to Medina during the Prophet's time, when Jews were almost equal in number to Muslims and thus a possible threat to them both militarily and theologically, in Damascus or Baghdad, the Muslim empire was so huge that the Jews had no illusions about overcoming the caliphate and had reconciled themselves to living under the "protection" of the caliph.

The nineteenth-century German scholar Heinrich Graetz – the first historian to write a comprehensive history of the Jewish people from a Jewish perspective – paints a vivid picture of Jewish life in the eighth-century Abbasid caliphate that suggests that the autonomy Jews had under the pre-Islamic Persians was respected by the Arab caliphs. Graetz writes:

"The Jewish community . . . had the appearance of a state. . . . The Exilarch (leader of the Jewish Diaspora community) and the Gaon (spiritual leader and scholar who headed Talmudic academies) were of equal rank. The Exilarch's office was political. He represented Babylonian-Persian Judaism under the Caliphs. He collected the taxes from various communities, and paid them to the treasury. The Exilarchs, both in bearing and mode of life, were princes. They drove about in a state carriage; they had outriders and a kind of a bodyguard, and received princely homage."[18]

This would have been around the time Ibn Ishaq moved to Baghdad from Medina and was still compiling material for his biography of the Prophet. While he collected the tales of the Jewish massacre, he could not have missed the amicable environment within which Jews and Muslims lived alongside each other in Baghdad, though he makes no mention of this in his work.

Graetz's depiction of Jewish life under the Baghdad caliphs corresponds with Shlomo Goitein's description of Jewish life under Abbasid rule in the eighth and ninth centuries. In his history of Jews and Arabs, Goitein writes that the Exilarch "occupied a very honoured position as the general representative of the Jewish community. According to a Christian source, he had precedence over Christian dignitaries at the caliph's court, but as a rule, he had no administrative function within the Muslim state. He was addressed as 'Our Lord, the son of David,' and as David is described as one of the greatest prophets, naturally his office was surrounded by the halo of sanctity."[19]

Goitein does point out that despite the splendour of the Exilarch's court, he had little executive authority, he had no jurisdiction over criminal matters, and his income was restricted to the proceeds from his own lands and contributions from the community. Nevertheless, this is far from the picture of death and exile that was painted by Ibn Ishaq.

Before Ibn Ishaq wrote his biography, and before it was incorporated into the Hadith literature, Muslim clerics did not have the texts available to them to depict the killing of Jews as an example of following in the steps of the Prophet. The relative tolerance of Jews under Arab rule in the eighth century, as reflected in the writings of Graetz and Goitein, would have been impossible if Ibn Ishaq's claim that, barely a century earlier, Muslims had massacred nine hundred Jews in Medina was true.

The lack of evidence to substantiate the legend of the Medina massacre leaves us Muslims with two options:

We can continue to believe in the story about the massacre of the Banu Qurayza Jews, as written in the man-made texts of Ibn Ishaq and the Hadith literature. If we do, then we will have to live with the fact that we endorse collective punishment, mass murder, and ethnic cleansing as the Sunnah of our own Prophet.

Or, given the lack of physical and textual evidence, we can reject this legend as nothing more than a myth that has tarnished the name of our Prophet and has sullied Muslim-Jewish relations for centuries.

However, if we come to the second conclusion – that Ibn Ishaq and subsequent Islamic writers right up to our own time have indulged in promoting an unsubstantiated legend that goes against the teachings of the Quran – then we must face an even bigger dilemma: What else in the Hadith literature is untrue? Are there more legends in the Hadith that are mere myths but have been imparted as the gospel truth to Muslim children for centuries?

We Muslims may find ourselves in an arabesque quandary. We may have to choose between believing a made-up legend that promotes hatred against Jews and questioning the validity of texts that, though written by ordinary men, have over the centuries acquired the status of divine truth.

CHAPTER EIGHT

Towards a New Jerusalem

If there is a place on earth today where identifying oneself as a Jew means inviting serious danger to life and liberty, then the historic Pakistani city of Peshawar would easily win that honour.

The city that has its roots in Hindu Vedic mythology and the epic Ramyana and that was a major centre of Buddhist learning until the tenth century has undergone many transformations in its two-thousand-year history. From Alexander the Great to Babur the Mughal, from the Sikh emperor Ranjit Singh to Rudyard Kipling, Peshawar has witnessed the rise and fall of many empires. In modern times, it is also the city Nikita Khrushchev threatened to obliterate after the Soviets shot down, in 1960, an American spy plane that had taken off from a nearby secret CIA airbase. Decades later, the CIA would return to Peshawar, from where it would wage its jihad against the Soviet Union in Afghanistan, just across the nearby border. By the time the Red Army was defeated, Peshawar had lost much of its accommodating character, indigenous to Pashtun culture. The city was transformed into a hotbed of Islamic jihadism introduced in the area by Osama bin Laden and the thousands of "Arab Afghans" who arrived to fight a jihad for the CIA. Today, it is a place where men are willing to slit the throat of a kuffar and confess to the crime with pride. Lately these jihadis have extended their killing spree to target Muslims who promote secular democracy as an antidote to Islam.

It is in this environment that Simcha Jacobovici, a Jewish-Canadian film producer, shot his documentary *The Lost Tribes* in 2004. He told me of the anxiety he felt while filming. "The fear was palpable. I had been advised to not disclose my Jewishness under any circumstances; the murder of Daniel Pearl still resonated in my mind." The Jew, after all, was the ultimate enemy in the minds of the jihadis, the epitome of evil that needed to be crushed.

Yet this was not always the case. Until the early 1950s, Peshawar was home to a prosperous and thriving Jewish community with a synagogue that was open to the city's Muslim majority. Col. Anwar Ahmed of Toronto, a former officer in the Pakistan army who hails from Peshawar, remembers as a boy seeing the arrival of Jews in the city. "It was in the late 1930s when we first noticed them. They said they feared persecution in the U.S.S.R. after Hitler and Stalin had signed a pact and decided to . . . escape before it was too late." Like countless persecuted people before them, ranging from the family of the Prophet Muhammad to the Zoroastrians of Iran, the Jews of central Asian Soviet republics would choose to take refuge in India. Ironically, they would settle among the Muslim Pashtuns of India's northwest, today the heartland of Taliban country where not a single Jew lives. "By the time I finished high school . . . , these central Asian Jews had become a common sight in Peshawar," Colonel Anwar told me. Asked if there was any animosity towards the Jews of Peshawar at the time, he bristles. "Not even the slightest," he says.

And what about now? I ask. "Today, the word 'Jew' is a slur not just in the city of Peshawar but perhaps the entire Muslim world," sighs the doyen of the Pakistani-Canadian community in Toronto. "Times have changed. Today the deluge of petrodollars and the so-called jihad by bin Laden has destroyed the inherent decency and hospitality of the people of Peshawar and filled it with hate and suspicion of all non-Muslims."

The Jews of Peshawar numbered no more than a few hundred in the 1940s. They were prominent in the textile trade and dominated the cloth market of the city. Interaction between Muslim and Jew was remarkably pleasant. "They bought a huge house in one of the nicer districts of the city and converted it into a synagogue," says Colonel Anwar. "No one objected, not even the mullahs, and trust me, they were aplenty. This was also my first visit to a Jewish temple and I visited it frequently, always welcomed by the rabbi. . . . There was not even a hint that Muslims would have an issue with Jews. Today, people deny that Jews ever lived in Peshawar," he adds.

Ten years later, Israel emerged as a Jewish state after the partition of British Palestine. The same year, Pakistan came into being as an Islamic state after the partition of British India. One partition was mourned by Muslims, the other celebrated. How could Muslims, enjoying their new state, then tell Jews they could not have one of their own?

In the early 1950s, Peshawar's Jews and those domiciled in the capital, Karachi, started leaving for their new home in the Middle East, never to return. Pakistan lost a thread from its fabric that would be missed by no more than a handful. I asked Colonel Anwar if there was ever a backlash against the Jews considering the troubled events that were unfolding in British Palestine with the wars of 1936–39 and 1948. "None whatsoever," he said. "Of course, we were on the side of the Arabs, but it did not cross our minds to target the Jews of Peshawar."

Colonel Anwar reminds me that the chief instructor at the Pakistan Army Infantry School in Quetta in 1948 was a Jewish lieutenant-colonel. Being Jewish in Pakistan, officially called the world's first Islamic republic, was not then an issue. "In 1966, my first son was born in Rawalpindi, and guess who was the gynecologist? A Jewish physician from Poland who had been seconded as an officer in the Pakistan army."

Even the actions of the founder of Pakistan, Mohammed Ali Jinnah, showed there was no anti-Semitism among the Muslims of

Pakistan or even India. After the creation of Pakistan in August 1947, Jinnah invited a leading Jewish artist in Bombay to move to Pakistan and awarded him citizenship of the Islamic Republic of Pakistan. His name was Samuel Fyzee-Rahamin, and he became one of the country's leading figures in the arts. Even though an art gallery bearing his name still thrives in Karachi, the tolerance of Jews in the Pakistan of 1947 is a far cry from the visceral hatred directed towards them sixty years later.

Today, with the last Jewish Pakistanis having fled to Israel, where their children and grandchildren play cricket for the Israeli team, their Karachi cemetery remains, abandoned in one of the older neighbourhoods, on the banks of the Lyari River. A nondescript steel door bearing the Star of David marks the entrance to the last resting place of Jews who once lived in this city of my birth among Muslims, Catholics, Hindus, and Zoroastrians.

Through the tombstones one can learn about Karachi's once organized Jewish community. One tombstone reads: "In loving memory of Sheelo, beloved wife of Mr. Solomon David, late municipal surveyor and president of the Jewish Community Karachi, who departed this life on April 27, 1903, aged 56 years." Then there is the grave of the president of the Magain Shalome synagogue in Karachi, Gershone Solomon Oomerdaker (1861–1930).

Karachi's Jewish cemetery is neglected, but considering that no Jews live in the city any more, its condition could be worse. That none of the graves has been vandalized gave me hope as I said an Islamic prayer for the departed and abandoned Jews of Karachi. As I left the cemetery, I wondered if Daniel Pearl knew about this place during his short stay in my native city.

It is not only in Pakistan where today's Muslims believe their ill will towards Jews is deeply rooted and centuries old. Compared with the Arab world, the people of Pakistan could be considered moderate.

A 2010 report by the Pew Research Center on attitudes in the Muslim world makes for some disturbing reading.

The report is based on a survey carried out by the Washington-based think tank in 2009. Among other issues, the survey gauged the attitude of Muslims towards other religious groups, including Jews. The results confirm the anecdotal evidence. Ninety-five percent of Egyptians, 97 percent of Jordanians, 98 percent of Lebanese, and 97 percent of Palestinians had an unfavourable view of Jews. Among non-Arab Muslims, the rates were only slightly lower. The report said, "Negative views of Jews are also widespread in the predominantly Muslim countries surveyed in Asia: More than seven-in-ten in Pakistan (78 percent) and Indonesia (74 percent) express unfavourable opinions. A majority in Turkey (73 percent) also hold a critical view."[1]

However, lost in the gloomy statistics was a single ray of hope. Bucking the trend of the entire Muslim world were the Muslims who know the Jews best; whose lives are intertwined with those of Jews on a daily basis; who work with and travel with and at times serve in the same armed forces as Jews: Muslim Israelis. If the Jews were the monsters they have been made out to be in Muslim narrative, then conventional wisdom would dictate that Muslim Israelis, living under the banner of the Star of David in cities like Nazareth, Haifa, Beersheba, and Tel Aviv, would have the most negative opinion about the Jews. Instead, the Pew survey found that the majority of Muslims living in Israel hold a favourable view of Jews. The report says, "Only 35 percent of Israeli Arabs express a negative opinion of Jews, while 56 percent voice a favorable opinion."

How could Muslims who have no interaction with Jews – those living across the border in the West Bank, Jordan, Lebanon, or Egypt – hate them while Muslims who live among Jews have a favourable view? I asked the same question myself when I met with Israel's Arab community during my visit there in 2008.

While dining in an Arab restaurant in Haifa, I asked the former Arab deputy mayor of the city, Elias Mtanes, the question I had asked every Arab Israeli I met on the trip: "Do you believe Israel is an apartheid state?" Mtanes shook his head in bewilderment. "What sort of a question is that!" he said. "Do you think I could be deputy mayor of Haifa if Israel was an apartheid state? I am not saying relations between Arabs and Jews inside Israel are perfect or even cordial, but our lives are intertwined by destiny and there is no escape . . . so we make the best of what we have." He then talked about the 2006 Hezbollah-Israel conflict, during which Hezbollah fired missiles that killed Arab and Jew without discrimination. "Nasrallah gave fiery speeches asking the Arabs of Haifa and other towns in the Galilee to vacate the cities because his missiles were on the way. . . . My father reminded me of similar calls by Arab leaders in the 1948 war who asked us to leave our homes because the Arab armies were coming. Look what happened. We Israeli Arabs are Israelis, not the fifth column of some Arab leader who knows little about us nor cares for his own Arab population."

Similar sentiments were expressed by a waiter at a wayside restaurant in Tel Aviv. I asked Muhammad if he would like his village to become part of a future Palestinian state. "*Ya Khee* [brother], I am Arab – that does not make me stupid," he joked. "If my village is given over to the Palestinians, all of us will protest. I do not wish to live under the dictatorship of Hamas or Fatah." Muhammad found it curious that a Pakistani Canadian was probing him so. He threw back a question at me. "Would you want to give up your Canadian citizenship and live under your General Musharraf in Pakistan?" There. He stumped me.

Back in Canada, I discussed my conversations with fellow Muslims, only to be told that the men I met must have been Mossad agents or that I had been set up and given a false image about an oppressive regime that kills and starves Arabs. "Ask Jews like Naomi Klein and Judy Rebick and they will tell you how Israel oppresses its Arab population,"

I was chided. When I explained that the people I met were people on the street whom I chose at random, they doubted me. When I showed them pictures of the sign reading *"Allahu Akbar"* at the gateway of a northern Israeli town, or the Circassian Muslim wedding in the Israeli city of Kfar Kama, or the imam in Haifa, I was met with a unanimous dismissal of the facts. I had been brainwashed by the Jews, they said.

To the same friends, I sent the Pew report showing the contrasting attitude towards Jews held by, say, Egyptians on the one hand and Arab Israelis on the other. Some said bluntly that the Israelis must have manipulated the survey, while others confided that they were shocked by the variance. One Muslim couple admitted that they had visited Jerusalem and had found Arab-Jewish relations far more amiable than they had been conditioned to believe by media reports. "Why hide the fact you visited Israel?" I asked. "You know why," said the wife. "We have to live in our community and cannot be seen as not being anti-Israel."

Many pundits argue that this dislike of Jews was triggered by the creation of the state of Israel. However, fifteen years later, in 1963, Jew-hatred had not yet entered the collective consciousness of Pakistan's hundred million Muslims. That was the year cinemas across the country were showing the film *Yahudi ki Larki,* or The Jew's Daughter, to packed houses.

Cynics may scoff at the relevance of this movie's popularity. Such melodramatic entertainment, they would argue, should not be seen as a reflection of people's political or religious attitudes. To them I say, try showing *Yahudi ki Larki* in the Pakistan of today. Cinemas would be burned to the ground, such is the animosity towards Jews, fuelled by thirty years of anti-Semitism and financed by petrodollars. The fact that the original run of The Jew's Daughter ended without incident, and that the Jew in the film was the victim, not the villain, is significant. It shows that irrespective of how Muslims in India and Pakistan felt about the Israel-Arab dispute, hatred towards the Jew had not yet entered the consciousness of the man on the street, who still viewed the Jew in positive terms.

If, in the early twentieth century, Jews and Muslims lived as neighbours and friends in the Karachi of India and later in Pakistan, there is rich documentation of similar amity between the two peoples half a world away, in Algeria. Joëlle Bahloul, in her book *The Architecture of Memory*, documents the Jewish-Muslim neighbourhood of her grandparents in eastern Algeria between 1937 and 1962.

Bahloul's study centres on Dar-Refayil, a multi-family house in the historical city of Setif, where her maternal grandfather Moushi Sennousi's Jewish family had lived with Muslims not as separate families, but as one extended group. In the city itself, Bahloul writes, there were no Jewish or Muslim quarters. Both Jews and Muslims lived in mixed neighbourhoods, based on their social status, not religion.

However, the Algerian city was not free of anti-Semitism. Bahloul writes that Setif was a walled city before the French arrived in the nineteenth century. With the breaking of the walls came the Christian negative attitude towards Jews: "Virulent anti-Semitism produced a profound separation between Jews and their Christian compatriots and forced the Jews back to their native origins alongside the Muslim population. . . . In the Jewish memories of Dar-Refayil, Christian anti-Semitism in Algeria of the time contrasts with the cordiality of their relationships with local Muslims."[2]

This is not to say that there were no tensions between the two communities, especially during the long and bitter struggle of the Algerian nationalists against France's occupation, in which the Jewish community was viewed with suspicion because of its neutrality. Bahloul mentions a pogrom that broke out in the city of Constantine in the summer of 1934 in which twenty-five Jews died. Setif was again affected in early 1935, when rumours circulated that the policeman who had shot dead a local insurgent was Jewish. She writes of anti-Jewish slogans being heard for the first time and of the distribution of an Arabic leaflet that told the Jews, "You were once our subjects. . . . We are asking you not to get involved in the current dispute between us and the colonial rulers."

In the 1950s, Israel had already been born, but the Jewish community of Setif still considered itself Algerian, not Israeli. Bahloul writes about one of the local boys, Guy, joining Dror, a Zionist group with socialist leanings. When he informs his father about his membership, his father slaps him. In Guy's words, "For my father, Israel did not exist." The Jews of Setif were not too gung-ho about Israel. For them, going to Israel meant never coming back, and this was the reaction of most Jews of the Arab world at the time.

The turning point, when Jews and Muslims began to part company, evidently came after the 1956 Arab-Israel war, when Algeria's struggle for independence gained momentum. Within years, the Jews of Setif moved to Algiers; following independence in 1962, they and most of the country's 140,000 Jews, who had been granted French citizenship in 1870, left for France. They had little choice: the Algerian Nationality Code of 1963 excluded non-Muslims from acquiring citizenship.

Still, about ten thousand Jews stayed back and lived in the cities until the 1990s, when the civil war and threats by jihadi militants finally forced them to emigrate. In 1994, the Algerian synagogue was abandoned when the last of the Jews fled the area after a nearly 2,600-year presence in the Maghreb.

The question that remains unanswered is this: What happened that changed the city of Peshawar from being home to Jews in a city of a million Muslims to a place where no Jew can be found today? How did Dar-Refayil, where Jew and Muslim had lived in the same household, become a place where no Jews can survive? The knee-jerk answer in contemporary Muslim narrative is to point the finger at the state of Israel. That may partly be true, but I believe the innate hatred towards Jews in the Muslim world has a lot to do with the year 1973, when two events unfolded that changed the attitudes of many Muslims and shifted the balance of power in the Muslim world.

Up until 1973, the price of Saudi light crude oil stayed under five dollars per barrel. Although this gave the desert kingdom enough liquidity that the king and his five-thousand-strong royal family could have a fabulously lavish lifestyle and maintain an iron grip on the country, Saudi Arabia had neither the resources nor the inclination to export any commodity other than the oil it produced in surplus – jihadi Islam and the harsh doctrine of Wahhabism stayed at home. Saudi oil wealth was sufficient to place its royalty in lavish yachts and casinos, but not enough to buy them the credibility and respect of the Muslim masses. An ayatollah from Qom, a sheikh in Al-Azhar, and a mufti at a seminary in Pakistan had more of a following than their Saudi cousins. Most of the Muslim world looked up to the likes of Sukarno, Bhutto, Nasser, Boumedienne, Ismet Inonu, or their nationalist and left-wing opposition. The bearded clergy was good enough for supervising the rites of circumcision, performing wedding ceremonies, leading the Friday prayers, and being the butt of jokes, but little else.

Pakistan's pre-eminent intellectual and one of South Asia's leading nuclear physicists, Pervez Hoodbhoy put it best when he was asked to comment on the role played by Islamic clerics in shaping Muslim society. He told the *Middle East Quarterly:*

> In my childhood, the traditional ulema [clerics] – who are so powerful today – were regarded as rather quaint objects and often ridiculed in private. Centuries ago the greatest poets of Persia, like Hafiz and Rumi, stripped away the mullahs'

religious pretensions and exposed their stupidity. Today, however, those same mullahs have taken control of the Iranian republic. The answer lies just as much in the domain of world politics as in theology. Khomeini developed the doctrine known as "guardianship of the clergy," which gives the mullahs much wider powers than they generally exercised in the past. Instead of being simple religious leaders, they now became political leaders as well. This echoes the broader Islamic fusion of the spiritual and the temporal. . . . The traditional ulema are indeed a problem, but they are not the biggest one; the biggest problem is Islamism, a radical and often militant interpretation of Islam that spills over from the theological domain into national and international politics. Whenever and wherever religious fundamentalism dominates, blind faith clouds objective and rational thinking. If such forces take hold in a society, they create a mindset unfavourable for critical inquiry, including scientific inquiry, with its need to question received wisdom.[3]

If the mullahs were on the periphery of Muslim society and were "ridiculed in private," all of this was about to change in 1973. The Yom Kippur War would result in the metamorphosis of Saudi Arabia from a dusty desert kingdom named after a bandit to a power that could finance worldwide jihad.

On October 6, 1973, as Israelis observed Yom Kippur and the Muslim world fasted for the month of Ramadan, Syria and Egypt launched an attack on the Jewish state in an effort to recapture territories they had lost after the Six Day War of 1967. The Egyptians shocked the world as they began an amphibious assault and crossed the Suez Canal. The Israelis were taken by surprise and were forced to fall back. Muslims rejoiced as Egypt's tanks smashed through Israeli defence lines on all fronts. Not since the thirteenth century had an Arab army seen success on the battlefield.

In 1973, I was the producer of the English news bulletin at Pakistan's state-owned PTV network. I vividly remember getting the breaking story on the Reuters teleprinter in the newsroom. It was just a single line: "Egyptian armour crosses Suez. Breaks through Israeli defence lines." I tore the paper off the printer and raced to the studio, where the evening English bulletin was on-air. In a move unprecedented at the time, I walked into the studio and placed the raw copy smack in front of the newscaster. He froze for a second, startled by my presence, peered at the piece of paper, and then beamed at the camera. "I have good news. Egyptian tanks have crossed the Suez Canal and defeated the Israelis." Then improvising, he added, "Our tanks are heading towards Tel Aviv." There was a joyous roar in the control room, and in countless newsrooms, cafés, schools, and homes around the world, Muslims viewed the Egyptian-Syrian attack on Israel as victory itself.

Our jubilation was short lived. The pundits who were predicting the celebration of the festival of Eid al-Fitr at the end of Ramadan in "liberated" Jerusalem would on that day cry more tears of humiliation. By the time the guns fell silent, not only were the Arab armies comprehensively defeated but both Cairo and Damascus stood in the gunsights of Israeli tanks.

In the first week of the war, as fighting raged in the Sinai and the Golan Heights, two superpowers entered the fray on opposite sides. The U.S.S.R. started airlifting arms to both Syria and Egypt, while President Richard Nixon authorized an airlift to deliver weapons and supplies to Israel, reportedly right into the battle zone, as the Jewish state struggled to survive. Within a week, however, the Israelis managed to halt the Egyptian advance, which had lost momentum as Egyptian generals dithered, not knowing how to press home their advantage.

The tide soon turned in what had started as a war aimed at the swift destruction of Israel. Israeli paratroopers and armour launched a daring counteroffensive at a single section of the Suez Canal, captured a crucial bridge, and had soon trapped the entire Egyptian Third Army in the Sinai, cutting it off from logistical support. Instead of Tel Aviv falling to the Egyptians, within two weeks of fighting, it was Cairo that was in the sight of Israeli tanks, while Egyptian soldiers languished, desperate for food and water.

In Karachi, the daily current affairs show *Rozanama* devoted much airtime to the war. Veteran journalist Muhammad Mian, a Marxist who spoke Arabic, Persian, and German as fluently as his native Urdu, described the Golan Heights as if it was his backyard. He had been there, and he was passionate about the Palestinian cause; in 1970, he had covered the Black September uprising of the PLO against King Hussein of Jordan. Using detailed maps, he explained the daily developments. One day after the show, he said to me that he did not want to come in the next day. "It is all over, Tarek – the Arabs have blown it one more time." He said his Arab sources had confessed that the Syrian assault had been blunted and the Israelis had destroyed the last of the tanks that had managed to cross the ceasefire line. (In 2008, I visited this site and saw the hulk of the burnt-out Syrian tank, which the Israelis have kept to show how far the Syrians had advanced inside Israel before being beaten back.)

The Arab world was in shock. What had started as a war to restore Arab pride had quickly turned into the familiar rout. The Organization of the Petroleum Exporting Countries now entered the fray to pressure the West not to back Israel. On October 16, OPEC increased the price of oil by 70 per cent, to $5.11 a barrel, in order to put pressure on the United States to not back Israel. When this had no effect, Arab oil-producing countries announced an embargo, starting with a 5 per cent cut in production, with further cuts threatened in 5 per cent increments.

If the Arab countries thought such blackmail would make the United States more partial to the Arab position, they were badly mistaken. Three days later, Nixon asked Congress to give $2.2 billion in emergency aid to Israel, including $1.5 billion in outright grants. The next day, Libya announced it would embargo all oil shipments to the United States; soon, the rest of the Arab oil-producing states announced curbs on their exports to various countries and a total embargo on oil to the United States.

The price of oil immediately shot up from three dollars a barrel to twelve dollars, triggering a recession and high inflation in the West that persisted until the early 1980s. While the economy of the West took ten years to recover from the oil shock, Saudi Arabia basked in the petrodollar bonanza that spilled from its coffers straight into the hands of the kingdom's theological custodians and radical jihadi clerics.

From the smouldering ashes of defeat in the Sinai, a new Arab force emerged in the east that would relegate Egypt to the backwaters. Saudi financial might that today flexes its muscle in Harvard University and Citibank has its roots in the aftermath of 1973. Equipped with billions, the Saudis would work to impede all intellectual progress in the Muslim world, financing the spread of repressive and reactionary fascist ideologies that would turn Muslims against their own cultures and hark back to a fictitious medieval era of Islamic supremacy. In the next decades the Saudi exercise in funding radical ideologues would produce the likes of Osama bin Laden and Mullah Omar.

The kingdom became the Comintern of the world Islamist movement; its clerics as well as leading members of the royal family were the commissars who spread out to expand their realm without crossing any borders. Islamism was born in Egypt in the 1930s, but its practical manifestation was facilitated by Saudi money that simultaneously funded jihadis and bought influence around the world, including the United States, Canada, Britain, and France.

The humiliation of another defeat at the hands of the kuffar was explained by the Saudi clerics as Allah's way of punishing Muslims who had supposedly wavered from the true path of Islam, which, according to them, was Wahhabi Salafism and submission to the doctrine of armed jihad. The sheiks argued, as they still do, that while the land ruled by the Wahhabis came out of the crisis as the world's wealthiest nation, with Allah rewarding its citizens with billions, those who did not follow the oath of radical jihadi Islam had been punished. The clerics maintained that Allah had spoken; Arab defeats were proof of Allah's will.

To the Islamists, it all made sense. If Muslims were to remodel their lives according to the teachings of the Saudi hardliners, if they forced their women to cover their faces and forced their sons to inculcate within themselves the spirit of armed jihad, they too would be rewarded by Allah with the oil wealth and riches of the kingdom. If not, they would live in poverty like the Bangladeshis and Chadians.

The middle-class Muslims of Egypt and Pakistan, Turkey and Lebanon, who until now had scoffed at the Saudis, using the derisive term "bedoos" of the Arab deserts, were now subservient to them. Allah had spoken. If the Muslim world wished to end its miserable lack of enterprise and education, literacy and liberty, all it had to do was emulate the Saudis, follow in the footsteps of those Wahhabi clerics, and inshallah, the heavens would rain down the bounty. And if this did not happen, that would be evidence that the Muslims had not yet emulated the Saudi example to its fullest.

Thus, 1973 marked a turning point in the Muslim narrative. The last quarter of the twentieth century would slowly undo the progress we Muslims had made in the preceding century. Our intellectual and cultural revival was stifled by the forces unleashed in Saudi Arabia and which are perhaps best captured by the late Saudi king Ibn Saud, who told an Anglo-American delegation: "The Jews are our enemies everywhere. Wherever they are found, they intrigue and work against us."[4]

So, what is to be done? In any conflict, it takes two to tango. When history is written, the twenty-first century will be remembered as the great struggle between the Muslim world on the one hand and the West on the other. My ummah will be reflected in the jihadi terrorism of al Qaeda, the tyranny of theocratic Iran, and the medieval monarchy of Saudi Arabia. Western civilization, meanwhile, will be epitomized by Israel and world Jewry with its ally, the United States of America.

During the first ten years of this century and the clash of civilizations, while anti-Semitism has flourished across the Muslim world and wherever Muslims live as minorities, it is equally true that a deep suspicion of Muslim intentions is giving rise to resentment against Muslims in Europe and North America. In this prophetically foretold struggle till the end of times, the two sides that need to end this conflict are the state of Israel and the Muslim intelligentsia, academia, clerical establishment, and politicians.

For Israel, the only action that matters is a specific and tangible step: end the occupation of the Palestinian territories and cooperate in creating a sovereign Palestinian state. Once this happens, the most powerful excuse used to whip up anti-Semitism and hatred against Western civilization will lose its potency and cease to be the rallying cry of despots eager to distract attention away from their own follies. Not that Islamist Judeophobia will disappear, but the oxygen that nourishes it will be cut off. Admittedly, the task for Israel isn't easy, but compared to what the Muslim world must do to get its act together, it is simple and doable.

Muslims today need to wake up from their hate-induced slumber of distrust, suspicion, superstition, misogyny, racism, homophobia, and tribalism and walk away from the lure of conspiracy theories that have made them such a laughingstock. If we don't change our attitude, we may waste another century waiting for Allah to intervene on our behalf.

As we start to pick up the pieces of the shattered hopes of Muslim society, we cannot be unmindful of the failure of its leadership to develop the social structures and institutions that have taken root in comparable non-Muslim developing countries. Take, for example, two former French colonies, Vietnam and Algeria. After decades of French occupation, followed by thirty long years of fighting the American occupation, Vietnam is today a wonderfully resilient country brimming with hope and good prospects in all sectors of development. Meanwhile, Muslim vs. Muslim violence has left Algeria mired in conflict and stunted progress.

Shlomo Avineri, the Israeli academic whose 1968 book, *The Social and Political Thought of Karl Marx,* was one of the first texts I read as I explored Marxism, has made some poignant remarks about the failures of Muslim society as reflected in the Palestinian struggle. Analyzing the failed 1970 Palestinian uprising against Jordan's King Hussein, he writes:

> There was a deeper cause for the total failure of Al Fatah and the Popular Front for the Liberation of Palestine (PFLP) in their test of strength with the Jordanian army, a cause which many observers, especially those favorable to the guerrilla movement, chose to overlook. When Al Fatah and the PFLP claimed to be as effective as the Algerian revolutionaries and the Viet Cong, there were few Israelis, even among those who favor an independent Arab Palestinian state on the West Bank, who took this claim seriously. The failure of the guerrilla movement. is related to the failure of Arab society in general to come to terms with its social structure and to combine its ideological nationalism with a praxis of social transformation. Even among the Palestinians who lingered in camps for 20 years, no

attempt has been made to create nuclei of social transformation; not one case is known of an attempt to organize, among
the refugees, the social infrastructure that would herald a new
Palestinian Arab society. . . . No experiments at new forms of
communal and social reconstruction, have ever been under-
taken. The dream of the Return was never accompanied by a
social vision, and no attempt has been made to create within
the womb of the old society the embryo of the new.

Palestinian nationalism remained, like other expressions
of Arab nationalism, purely political; it viewed military action
(and sheer terrorism) as its main embodiment. The guerrillas
were successful at arming teenagers, especially when western
television photographers were around, but they never became
a movement of social transformation, which the Viet Cong
accomplished so successfully very early in its career. . . . Thus
Yasser Arafat, George Habash and Naif Hawatmeh showed
no better judgement than previous Palestinian military leaders – Fauzi Kaukji in 1948 and Ahmed Shukeiry in 1967. For
those who still had illusions about the guerrillas, the events
of September 1970 were the final proof that all the left-wing
rhetoric of the guerrillas was just so much hot air. The social
praxis was totally lacking.[5]

Since 1971, when Professor Avineri penned his analysis, it seems
neither his views nor the inability of the Palestinians to rectify their
mistakes has changed. In 2008, Avineri wrote this for the left-wing
Israeli newspaper *Haaretz*: "While Palestinians may see themselves,
with much justification, as the victims of the Zionist movement's successful establishment of a Jewish state in the Land of Israel, the reasons
for their historical failure should be sought elsewhere: in the inability
of the Palestinian national movement to create the political and social

institutional framework that is the necessary foundation for nation-building. The history of national movements teaches us that national consciousness, strong as it may be, is not enough: Movements that could not create the institutional system vital for their success failed."

He was commenting after yet another round of Palestinian vs. Palestinian bloodletting in Gaza: "The de facto shattering of the Palestinian Authority following the Hamas coup in Gaza is the extension of this failure. Even now the Palestinians are inclined to blame Israel, the Americans, the international community; but the real, essential responsibility ultimately lies with the Palestinians themselves. Elections were held, Hamas won, Fatah lost – and both groups have been unable to sustain a framework whose legitimacy is accepted by both sides."[6]

It is not just outside observers of the Arab scene who have recognized this morass. The Arab poet Adonis has joined a new breed of intellectuals who are critical of the political discourse in the Arab world and Palestine. In an interview that aired on Dubai television in 2006, the Syrian poet made critical observations about Arab society and the mixing of religion and state.

When asked about his views on democracy in Palestine, which had brought Hamas to power, Adonis said, "I support it, but I oppose the establishment of any state on the basis of religion, even if it's done by Hamas." When asked by the interviewer if he would oppose the mixing of religion and politics "even if it liberates Palestine," Adonis remarked, "Yes, because in such a case, it would be my duty to fight this religious state." (This was long before Hamas's military takeover of Gaza in June 2007, when its militia committed war crimes by executing in cold blood wounded fighters belonging to the rival Fatah.)

Painting a bleak picture of the Arab world, Adonis told his audience, "If I look at the Arabs, with all their resources and great capacities, and I compare what they have achieved over the past century with what others have achieved in that period, I would have to say that we

Arabs are in a phase of extinction, in the sense that we have no creative presence in the world. We have become extinct. We have the quantity. We have the masses of people, but a people becomes extinct when it no longer has a creative capacity, and the capacity to change its world."

When the interviewer interjects, saying Adonis's views are "very dangerous," he makes an even harsher prognosis. "That is our real intellectual crisis. We are facing a new world with ideas that no longer exist, and in a context that is obsolete. We must sever ourselves completely from that context, on all levels, and think of a new Arab identity, a new culture, and a new Arab society. . . . Imagine that Arab societies had no Western influence. What would be left? Nothing. Nothing would be left except for the mosque, the church, and the commerce, of course. . . . The Muslims today – forgive me for saying this – with their accepted interpretation [of the religious text] are the first to destroy Islam, whereas those who criticize the Muslims – the non believers, the infidels, as they call them – are the ones who perceive in Islam the vitality that could adapt it to life. These infidels serve Islam better than the believers."[7]

Both the Arab poet Adonis and the Jewish professor Avineri point to fundamental problems that plague the Muslim world, which shows no sign of moving away from the lure of medieval battle cries to the reality of post-modern civic society. Muslims must seriously examine the chances that they have so successfully managed to miss. Caught between a tornado and shelter, how do we always choose to be in the tornado's path? How do we ensure we do not repeat the mistakes of the past?

Acknowledging defeat and accepting reality would only be the first step. The mistakes Muslims have made all through the Palestinian crisis are not specific to one isolated conflict. Hating the Jew has a lot to do with

how Muslims have incorporated racism and the doctrine of racial superiority within the Muslim community itself – a doctrine that propelled
the genocide in Darfur, the persecution of the Shia Muslims in the Arab
world and Pakistan, the carving up of Kurdistan among four Muslim
countries, and the genocide committed by Pakistan in Bangladesh.

At the root of this doctrine of racism, tribalism, and ethnic superiority is the opinion voiced by a man who is considered the patriar-
chal guru of world Wahhabism and the Islamist jihadi movement: the
fourteenth-century Damascus scholar Ibn Taymiyya. The man who is
also referred to as Sheikh ul Islam was of the opinion that Arabs are
superior (*afdal*) to non-Arabs, and he claimed this was the view held by
the majority of Islamic scholars of his time. Ibn Taymiyya put the fin-
ishing touch on a racist doctrine that ran counter to the teachings of the
Quran yet appeased the ego of the defeated Arabs after their caliphate in
Baghdad fell to the Mongols. Ibn Taymiyya not only declared the Arab
to be superior to the non-Arab, but declared the tribe of the Quraysh
and their descendants superior to other Arabs. Further, he narrowed
the hierarchy of racial superiority to mean that within the Quraysh
tribe of Arabs, the clan of the Bani Hashim were the most superior.
Of course, this doctrine has nothing to do with Islam or the teachings
of Muhammad, but it was used on the night of the Prophet's death to
delegitimize the claim of Medina Arabs, the majority, over those of the
Arabs of Mecca who would take over the caliphate for the next eight
hundred years as a matter of birthright.

It is this belief in tribalism and racism that makes our imams pray
to Allah to defeat non-Muslims at the start of every Friday prayer,
a ritual of hate that is not spared even in the Dome of the Rock in
Jerusalem, where once Jews congregated but cannot any more, or
the holy mosques of Mecca and Medina. This dangerous doctrine of
Arab superiority over non-Arab Muslims plays itself out from Dubai to
Darfur. It is one of the reasons bin Laden and his Arab-Afghan terror

network finds protection among the Pashtuns, some of whom have been brainwashed to believe the Arab is superior and that it is therefore their destiny to serve and protect Arab jihadis.

Not until Muslims shed this notion of some Muslims being better than others because of race and sect will we be able to eradicate from our hearts the hatred of the Jew, the Hindu, the Sikh, the Christian, or the atheist. Nor will we eradicate the innate ability to compound this racism by denying that it even exists.

One could argue that these theories of racial and tribal superiority are part of medieval history and that contemporary Muslims are free of such racist baggage. If only this were true. SunniPath: The Online Islamic Academy is one of the West's leading Islamic education centres, which conducts online courses in Islam for North American Muslims. In December 2006, a student asked the resident online scholar whether "Arabs [were] preferred over other nations." In his answer, the Palestinian Sheikh Amjad Rasheed replied from Jordan: "The fact that Allah Most High has chosen the Arabs over other nations is affirmed in rigorously authenticated hadiths of the Prophet, may Allah bless him and give him peace. . . . So this hadith is a primary text about the preference of Arabs over others and the preference of some Arabs over other Arabs. . . . Therefore the preference of Arabs over other nations, and the preference of some Arabs over other Arabs is affirmed in the Sacred Law. . . . It is obligatory on a Muslim to believe that Arabs are preferred over other nations because there is a proof for it. However, this is not one of the pillars of our religion such that if someone rejected this, they would be considered outside of Islam. But if one does reject this, one has sinned for not believing in it because it is an affirmed [tradition]."[8]

Another major disseminator of Islamic education among the Muslim youth of the English-speaking world is the IslamQ&A website, run out of Saudi Arabia. In a 2009 exchange, a questioner asked

Sheikh Muhammad al-Munajjid whether it is true that the Prophet said, "By hating the Arabs you would hate me." In his answer, the Saudi cleric said that although the said Hadith is weak, "the weakness of this hadeeth does not mean that there is no virtue in the Arabs." Quoting Ibn Taymiyya, the cleric said, "The Prophet (blessings and peace of Allah be upon him) described hating the Arabs as being a cause of leaving Islam, and he stated that hating them implies hating him."[9]

These are not isolated questions or the rants of crazy clerics; this doctrine of Arab supremacy and judging people by their race and religion is at the heart of Muslim malaise in the modern world. Societies where race and religion do not affect a citizen's rights and obligations are progressing socially, culturally, and economically, whereas the Islamic nations are mired in race- and religion-based citizenship. Today, India, Brazil, and South Africa have emerged as leaders of the developing world, while Saudi Arabia, Iran, Egypt, and Pakistan have little to show in the way of accomplishments in the last half century other than sabre rattling and the oppressing their own people while blaming the Jews for the plight they are in.

Once hatred against the Jew becomes acceptable – and it has – there is every likelihood that such hate will also engulf the self. With the absence of Jews among them, many Muslims can only turn on each other. Dozens die every week, not at the hands of some foreign enemy, but by our own so-called brothers in Islam. The violence is rooted in the hate speech that is permitted in the mosques of the ummah.

Take, for example, a Friday sermon given in January 2010 at a mosque in Riyadh by the imam assigned to the Saudi Armed Forces, Sheikh Mohammad al-Ureifi. Al-Ureifi lashed out against Iraqi Shia Muslims, accusing them of, among other things, being "*majousiya*" – Zoroastrian occultists – and called Ayatollah Ali al-Sistani an "atheist and debauched sinner." Ayatollah al-Sistani, it must be said, is one of those rare Islamic clerics today who refrains from inflaming passions and instead calls for restraint and peace, and he is respected by both Sunni and Shia Muslims as a voice of reason. On January 26, 2010, as outrage spread among Shia Muslims worldwide, forty-one Saudi Wahhabi clerics, instead of condemning al-Ureifi's hateful language, issued a strongly worded statement supporting him. On the Islamic website Almoslim.net, they described Shias as "rejectionists" and "infidels" and called on them to repent.

How long can we afford to sit silently by while men with hate-filled hearts govern our spiritual affairs?

In an era when information is just a few keystrokes away, words of hate and racism can seldom be hidden. What was once the private domain of the mosque pulpit, from where Jews, Hindus, and Christians would be derided as kuffar, is today accessible to the entire world. Yet our sheikhs continue to make hurtful comments about other races and religions with impunity.

On the popular Islamic website IslamOnLine, on March 22, 2004, a user named Heba asked about the status of Jews in the Quran: "Dear Sheikh! As-Salam Alaykum. Jews have played a considerable role throughout history, before and after the advent of Islam. The Qur'an referred to them in many places. What, according to the Qur'an, are the main characteristics and qualities of Jews?"

IslamOnLine referred Heba to a fatwa by Mufti Atiyyah Saqr, former head of the Fatwa Committee of Al-Azhar University, in which he states: "The Quran has specified a considerable deal of its verses to talking about Jews, their personal qualities and characteristics. The Quranic description of Jews is quite impartial; praising them in some occasions where they deserve praise and condemning them in other occasions where they practice blameworthy acts. Yet, the latter occasions outnumbered the former, due to their bad qualities and the heinous acts they used to commit."

Among the "bad qualities" of the Jews, the mufti lists the following:

- They feel pain to see others in happiness and are gleeful when others are afflicted with a calamity. This is clear in the verse that reads: "If a lucky chance befall you, it is evil unto them, and if disaster strike you they rejoice thereat." (Al-'Imran:120)
- They are known of their arrogance and haughtiness. They claimed to be the sons of Allah and His beloved ones. Allah tells us about this in the verse that reads: "The Jews and Christians say: We are sons of Allah and His loved ones." (Al-Ma'idah:18)
- Utilitarianism and opportunism are among their innate traits. This is clear in the verse that reads: "And of their taking usury when they were forbidden it, and of their devouring people's wealth by false pretences." (An-Nisa':161)
- It is easy for them to slay people and kill innocents. Nothing in the world is [more] dear to their hearts than shedding blood and murdering human beings. They never give up this trait even with the Messengers and the Prophets. Allah says: ". . . and slew the prophets wrongfully." (Al-Baqarah:61)
- They are merciless and heartless. In this meaning, the Qur'anic verse explains: "Then, even after that, your hearts were hardened and became as rocks, or worse than rocks, for hardness." (Al-Baqarah:74)
- They never keep their promises or fulfil their words. Almighty Allah says: "Is it ever so that when ye make a covenant a party of you set it aside? The truth is, most of them believe not." (Al-Baqarah:100)
- They rush hurriedly to sins and compete in transgression. Allah says: "They restrained not one another from the wickedness they did. Verily evil was that they used to do!" (Al-Ma'idah:79)
- Cowardice and their love for this worldly life are their indisputable traits. To this, the Qur'an refers when saying: "Ye

are more awful as a fear in their bosoms than Allah. That is because they are a folk who understand not. They will not fight against you in a body save in fortified villages or from behind walls. Their adversity among themselves is very great. Ye think of them as a whole whereas their hearts are diverse." (Al-Hashr:13–14) Allah Almighty also says: "And thou wilt find them greediest of mankind for life and (greedier) than the idolaters." (Al-Baqarah:96)

• Miserliness runs deep in their hearts. Describing this, the Qur'an states: "Or have they even a share in the Sovereignty? Then in that case, they would not give mankind even the speck on a date stone." (An-Nisa':53) [10]

As I read this fatwa from the Al-Azhar scholar, what struck me was that in not one of the verses he quotes from the Quran does the word *Jew* appear. How, then, can this mufti and his coterie of clerics claim that these passages of the Quran are aimed at Jews? Have they considered the possibility that these texts refer to us Muslims, not Jews?

The mufti goes further. In his response to Ileba he blames Jews for the pogroms they suffered and then predicts "the coming victory of Muslims over them":

> After this clear explanation, we would like to note that these are but some of the most famous traits of the Jews as described in the Qur'an. They have revolted against the Divine ordinances, distorted what has been revealed to them and invented new teachings which, they claimed, were much more better than what has been recorded in the Torah. It was for these traits that they found no warm reception in all countries where they tried to reside. Rather, they would either be driven out or live in isolation. It was Almighty Allah who placed on them His

Wrath and made them den of humiliation due to their transgression. Almighty Allah told us that He'd send to them people who'd pour on them rain of severe punishment that would last till the Day of Resurrection. All this gives us glad tidings of the coming victory of Muslims over them once Muslims stick to strong faith and belief in Allah and adopt the modern means of technology.

In case his prophecy of impending Muslim victory doesn't come true, he ends by saying, "Almighty Allah knows best."

It is incredible that Islamist clerics today would be so oblivious to Muslim history. If Islam had such a harsh view of Jews, then why was it that in 657, Ali ibn Abu Talib, the Prophet's closest companion, the son-in-law who became the fourth caliph of Islam, embraced the Jewish community with open arms when he extended the Muslim conquest into Iraq? Ezra Chwat, of the Hebrew University of Jerusalem, writes that Ali "was greeted wholeheartedly by the Jews there [Iraq], then the most important of the world's Jewish communities. Ali saw the Jews of Iraq as a natural ally and granted them autonomy. This was the dawn of a new era of Jewish cultural creativity, one that lasted almost 600 years and was central in the development of Judaism."[11]

Today, Muslims need to educate their clerics and inform them that the days of caliphates and kingdoms are long gone. Never again will any Jew be willing to live as "dhimmis" under Muslim protection. In medieval times, this arrangement may have worked and was much more progressive than the harsh treatment the Jews received in Christendom, but the world has evolved into a place where neither race nor religion, gender nor sexual orientation, can be invoked to legislate a hierarchy of citizenship rights, be it in Saudi Arabia today or South Africa under apartheid.

We Muslims need to reflect on our predicament. We need to understand that our hatred of the Jew or the West is an admission of our own sense of failure. We need to recognize that blaming the other for our dismal contribution to contemporary civilization is a sedative, not the cure for the disease that afflicts us all. To join the nations and peoples of this world, as brothers and sisters of a common humanity, we need to wean ourselves from our addiction to victimhood and hate. Without rejecting our heritage, we need to recognize that in the modern nation state as it exists in the United States, Europe, and the West; in countries like India, Brazil, and South Africa, the doctrines of jihad and sharia law cannot apply, will not be accepted, and should not be preached. We need to stand up to members of our community who spread hate against the Jew, the atheist, the apostate, the Hindu, and the Christian and then hide behind the Quran. We should not hesitate to say they are hate-mongers and cowards.

Muslim history and heritage allow us to enter the modern era without the baggage of anti-Semitism. Many Muslims and Jews in the past have worked together and befriended each other. If Averroes and Maimonides could do it in the twelfth century, surely we can do it in the twenty-first. Together, we can build a New Jerusalem. But to arrive there, we Muslims will have to remember that the Jew is not the enemy. It is us.

The author with Holocaust survivor Max Eisen, at Auschwitz in March 2010

EPILOGUE

The infamous Nazi slogan *Arbeit macht frei* ("work makes you free") stared at me as I stood at the entrance of Auschwitz. Beyond the arched iron gate was the camp where sixty years ago, hate had triumphed over humanity during Hitler's Third Reich.

The slight chill of the Polish morning air in March 2010 was not the reason I felt a shiver run up my spine. The prospect of walking through the corridors of a death camp, where more than a million people had been brought to die, left an uneasy feeling. A strange sense of fear touched me, a fear of the unknown. Would I feel the spirits of those who were gassed to death as part of Hitler's Final Solution? As a Muslim, I also felt the burden of guilt knowing how the moral crime of Holocaust denial was today the almost exclusive preserve of my community.

In 2006, my daughter Natasha Fatah had come to Auschwitz to pay her respects to the victims of the Holocaust; she was so shaken by her experience that it was two years before she penned her thoughts. In an article for CBC News, she talked of the "conflicting emotions" that overcame her as she walked towards Auschwitz. She wrote:

"Was I coming to pay tribute to the millions killed by the Nazis or was I a tourist coming to check off one more world historic site? I decided this was to be a private sojourn and I would not talk or write about it. And so I didn't, until now — when I've begun to realize that Holocaust deniers continue to insist that the event never happened; that it is a Jewish conspiracy. In denying the Holocaust, we fall prey to the same evil that almost wiped out one of humanity's most ancient people."[1]

Her words echoed in my mind as I prepared to enter Auschwitz in the company of a Holocaust survivor who had lived in the camp. Standing next to eighty-five-year-old Max Eisen made the moment a bit surreal, as if the present and the past had merged. As a young man, Max had survived not just Auschwitz, but also the death march that followed. As the Red Army advanced towards the camp in 1945, Nazi guards would take him and a large number of starving prisoners on a march towards German-controlled areas to the south.

I wanted a photograph with Max, standing in front of the iron gates of Auschwitz, but felt terrible guilt. Would I be desecrating the sacredness of the place? I wondered. After all, a concentration camp where more than a million people were put to death deserved not to be treated as a run-of-the mill tourist spot. Max noticed my hesitation as I fidgeted with the camera. Recognizing my trepidation, he said, "Come, Tarek, let me have a picture with you." As he gave my camera to a mutual friend to take a snap, he chuckled:

"How often does a Jew get a chance to get photographed with a Muslim at Auschwitz?"

Today, the picture of Max and me, with the "work makes you free" iron sign in the background, graces the wall in my office, a constant reminder that yes, a Jew and a Muslim can come together, even in Auschwitz.

Max Eisen and I were part of a group of academics, parliamentarians, authors, educators, and police chiefs, all guests on this visit of the Friends of the Simon Wiesenthal Center for Holocaust Studies. As the only Muslim in the group, I was conscious of the fact that some Muslim leaders not only deny the Holocaust, but also consider the tragedy just another example of Jews manipulating history. This made me a brother of such anti-Semites as Ayman Zawaheri, Hassan Nasrallah, and Osama bin Laden. However, I also knew that there were countless Muslims who had died fighting the Nazis. Unfortunately, while the world knew a lot about the Jew-hating Muslim Holocaust deniers, they knew next to nothing about the Muslims who too had died in the Nazi death camps of Poland.

When Max Eisen joked about the odds of a Jew and a Muslim being together in Auschwitz, I asked him if he knew of any Muslims among the many non-Jews – the Poles, the gypsies, the communists – while he was interned at the camp. He said he was unaware that there were any, but was intrigued by my suggestion. I felt too embarrassed to share with Max the fact that among the Nazi troops that crushed the Warsaw Uprising in 1944 was a Muslim division of the Wehrmacht, the East Turkestan Armed Formation. Muslims may have died fighting the Nazis, but many of my co-religionists had also aided Hitler's war machine.

A day earlier, while visiting the death camp known as Majdanek near the city of Lublin, I had come across a memorial for the many non-Jewish national groups who had died alongside the millions of Jews who were systematically gassed to death. In a large room next to the crematorium and the gas chambers, I saw black tombstones in memory of the many non-Jewish victims of the Nazis. The tombstones were marked, "Turk," "Tadjik," "Uzbek," "Albanian," "Bashkir," "Kirghiz," "Turcoman," and other Muslim peoples. Sadly, today neither Muslim nor Jew is aware that Muslims also died alongside the six million Jews killed by the Nazis. Overwhelmed, I felt the need to read a silent Muslim prayer – the verse of the Quran known as Surah al-Fatiha, primarily for the six million Jews who died in the Holocaust, but also for the thousands of Muslims who gave their lives too.

Majdanek was unique among the German Nazi concentration camps in many ways. Unlike other camps it was built near a large city, not in a rural area. In addition, because it was in eastern Poland, there was not enough time for the Nazis to destroy the evidence before the Red Army arrived, and so it is the best preserved of all the Nazi concentration camps.

However, for me as a Muslim, Majdanek had another uniqueness that is rarely discussed or even mentioned. The camp was known as Majdanek because it was built near a Muslim district of Lublin known as Majdan Tatarski or the "Tatar Maidan." (The word Maidan is rooted in the Persian language, introduced in Poland by the Tatars.)* While walking through the camp, I thought of the irony in Iranian president Mahmoud Ahmedinejad casting doubt on the Holocaust, not realizing that the best-preserved Nazi concentration camp has a name with Persian roots.

There is almost nothing written about the Muslims of Auschwitz. In a rare mention of this subject, Prof. Gil Anidjar of Columbia University wrote a poignant column for the left-wing Israeli newspaper *Ha'aretz*.

---

* "Maidan," pronounced as Maida'an, is a Persian word that has entered the languages of many Muslim people. From Bangladesh's famous "Paltan Maidan" in Dhaka to the "Tartar Maidan" in Poland, the word means living quarters or an open space or, as in South Asia, a public meeting place or playground.

"We reside in this moment, and the 'image of our time,' which Primo Levi placed before our eyes as recapitulating the course of our history, is that of Muslims in Auschwitz. . . . And in this moment of danger, the image that flashes still is the image Primo Levi figured as the 'image of our time.' It is the name of our collective blindness enduring. There were Muslims in Auschwitz."[2]

Muslim presence in Auschwitz is also mentioned by the late Egyptian scholar Abdel-Wahab Elmessiri (d. 2008). In his book, *Arabs, Muslims and the Nazi Genocide of Jews, Judaism and Zionism*, I was surprised how frequently the word "Muselmann" (Muslim) appeared in the Auschwitz concentration camp lists.[3] However, he adds a new twist. According to Elmessiri, the word "Muselmann" was also used by the Nazis as a slur to describe Jews who were close to death by starvation. If the Nazis hated Jews, their choice of language shows they had no less contempt for the Muslim.

Muslims and Jews are locked in a unique animosity, with few parallels in history. While Islamist Muslims show disdain for Jews, not Judaism, extremist Jews show contempt for Islam and the Quran, not necessarily Muslims. While the former hates a people, the latter mocks a religion and its holy book.

This makes the mistrust difficult to understand, let alone resolve. When one side hates a faith and the other the faith's followers, the path to peace is seriously complicated.

What is required by good men and women on both sides is for

• Jews to show some respect to Islam, and

• Muslims to show some respect for Jews.

There is, however, a significant difference. If one tried hard enough, one can always find the odd Jew who insults Islam and the Prophet Muhammad. One can even run into a rabbi who mocks Arabs. When the former Sephardi chief rabbi of Israel, Ovadia Yosef, says, "God regrets creating the Arabs," his acerbic and hateful comment is the exception to the rule. On the other hand, to find an Islamic cleric or politician spouting hatred towards Jews, one wouldn't have to look too far. From Jakarta to Jerusalem one only needs to attend a Friday congregation at any mosque to hear the imam berating the Yahood while praying for the victory of Islam and the defeat of the Jews.

It is no wonder that well-meaning people who have indulged in "interfaith" exercises among Jews and Muslims have met with little or no success. The reason, I believe, is that they have not grasped the significance of what Professor Ronald Nettler of Oxford calls the "emotional hatred which [is] uniquely modern as part of Muslim thinking on the Jews."[4]

Nettler blames this modern Muslim hatred of the Jew on the politicization of Islam by such figures as the Islamist Sayyid Qutb.

In taking the first step to show my respect for the Jewish people, I salute their enormous contribution to human civilization that far outstrips their tiny population. They deserve our admiration, not our envy.

In exchange, I hope my Jewish counterpart – if there is one – would show respect for my faith, Islam, and recognize the enormous contributions Islam has made to human civilization. We need to be given credit where credit is due. Muslims are a people who are a billion and a half strong and who are spread from the Philippines to Peru, bound by their love for their Prophet and their belief in the Quran. In addition, Muslims who recognize the Jewish national aspirations manifested in the State of Israel, who criticize Israel any time the Jewish State errs, or who ask it to vacate the occupied Palestinian Territories, should not be labelled anti-Semitic.

While I was in Poland I learned of the planned Museum of the History of Polish Jews that will be dedicated to the famous Jewish traveller, diplomat, and merchant, Ibrahim ibn Yakub. Ibn Yakub is considered to be the first Jew in Poland; he authored the first extensive account of Poland. While visiting Poland in AD965 or 966, Ibn Yakub made mention of the city of Krakow in his travelogues. Here too emerges a Muslim-Jewish connection. Ibn Yakub was in the diplomatic service of the Caliph in Spain. In the tenth century, Muslim power in Iberia was at its pinnacle, where Jews and Muslims together created what author Erna Paris describes as "a remarkable era of science, philosophy, philology, biblical commentary and literature."[5]

In addition to his Arabised name, Ibn Yakub wrote his memoirs in the Arabic language, evidence of a time Muslims demonstrated little of the hatred they do towards Jews today.

As I left Poland to return to Canada, my thoughts wandered from Ibrahim Ibn Yakub in medieval times to that early morning in 1944 in the Dachau concentration camp when a Muslim princess, Noor Inayat Khan from India, faced a Nazi firing squad. She did not have to die, but she did, as did countless other Muslims in the fight to destroy Hitler and his Third Reich. Both Jew and Muslim must recognize these unsung heroes, for they provide us some solace on the lonely path towards peace among the Israelite and the Ishmaelite. This is why this book is dedicated to the memory of Princess Noor Inayat Khan.

NOTES

Unless otherwise noted, all translations are my own.

PREFACE

1. http://filthyjewishterrorists.com/the-attempted-false-flagging-in-toronto-canada-on-9-11-2006/.
2. "A Case Study in Hate," editorial, *National Post*, March 6, 2010, http://www.nationalpost.com/opinion/story.html?id=2648640.
3. Tun Mahathir, "If U.S. Could Create 'Avatar,' It Could Fake 9/11 Attacks," *Jakarta Globe*, January 21, 2010.
4. "Özdemir Worried by Muslim Anti-Semitism," The Local: Germany's News in English, February 23, 2009, http://www.thelocal.de/society/20090223-17609.html.
5. Alex Sorin, "The Shape of the Holy," *Jerusalem Post*, July 14, 2009.

CHAPTER ONE

1. "New York Terror Plot Foiled," *New York Post*, May 20, 2009, http://www.nypost.com/seven/05202009/news/regionalnews/bronx/ny_terror_plot_foiled_170221.htm.
2. Charles Lewis, "Address on niqab not meant to be offensive: Imam," *National Post*, October 23, 2009. http://network.nationalpost.com/NP/blogs/holy-post/archive/2009/10/23/address-on-hijab-not-meant-to-be-offensive-imam.aspx#ixzz0riVLKPPc.
3. "Are we allowed to call a Christian person kafir?" Muhammad Al-Mukhtar Al-Shinqiti, director of the Islamic Center of South Plains, Lubbock, Texas,

http://www.islamonline.net/livefatwa/english/Browse.asp?hGuestID=8zOFOr.

4. "Saudi Cleric Says Don't Pray for 'Infidel' Downfall," September 6, 2009, http://in.reuters.com/article/worldNews/idININdia-42256820090906.

CHAPTER TWO

1. Susan Sachs, "Anti-Semitism Is Deepening among Muslims," *New York Times*, April 27, 2002.

2. Rick Westhead, "Public Schools Not Always Tolerant in Pakistan," *Toronto Star,* February 21, 2010, http://www.thestar.com/news/world/pakistan/article/768976 – public-schools-not-always-tolerant-in-pakistan.

3. Bernard Lewis, "Muslim Anti-Semitism," *Middle East Quarterly,* 1998; "The New Anti-Semitism," *American Scholar* 75, no. 1 (Winter 2006), pp. 25–36, http://hnn.us/blogs/entries/21832.html.

4. Bernard Lewis, *Semites and Anti-Semites: An Inquiry into Conflict and Prejudice* (New York: W.W. Norton, 1999), p. 132.

5. Ibid.

6. Ibid., pp. 136–37.

7. David Von Drehle, "A Lesson in Hate," *Smithsonian Magazine,* February 2006.

8. "Unnoticed Clues Haunt Fort Hood: Nidal Hasan Left a Trail of Suspicious Actions," NBC News, December 31, 2009, http://www.nbcphiladelphia.com/news/breaking/Unnoticed_clues_haunt_Fort_Hood-80401817.html.

9. Sayyid Qutb, *Milestones*, Dar al-Ilm, Damascus, Syria p. 62.

10. Sayyid Qutb, "Ma'rakatuna ma'a al-Yahud" [Our Fight against the Jews] (Cairo: Dar al-Shuruq, 1989), English translation by Ronald L. Nettler in *The Legacy of Islamic AntiSemitism,* edited by Andrew G. Bostom (New York: Prometheus Books, 2008), p. 361.

11. Ibid., p. 357.

12. Ibid., p. 357.

13. Ibid., p. 360.

14. Lawrence Wright, *Looming Tower: Al-Qaeda and the Road to 9/11* (New York: Knopf, 2006), p. 79.

CHAPTER THREE

1. Norman H. Gershman, *Besa: Muslims Who Saved Jews in World War II* (Syracuse, NY: Syracuse University Press, 2008), p. 2. Besa is a code of honour deeply rooted among Albanian Muslims. It dictates that one take responsibility

for the lives of others in their time of need. A similar code is found among Pashtun Muslims, which they call Pukhtoonwali.

2. Ian Johnson, *A Mosque in Munich: Nazis, the CIA, and the Risk of the Muslim Brotherhood in the West* (New York: Houghton Mifflin Harcourt, 2010), pp. 9–11.

3. Mathias Küntzel, *Jihad and Jew-Hatred* (New York: Telos Press, 2007), p. 45.

4. Walter Laqueur and Barry Rubin, eds., *The Israel-Arab Reader* (New York: Penguin Books, 2001), pp. 51–55.

5. Küntzel, *Jihad and Jew-Hatred*, p. 35.

6. Ibid.

7. Sahar Huneidi, *A Broken Trust: Herbert Samuel, Zionism and the Palestinians.* (New York: St. Martin's Press, 2001), p. 35.

8. Lewis, *Semites and Anti-Semites*, p. 136.

9. Said K. Aburish, *A Brutal Friendship: The West and the Arab Elite* (New York: St. Martin's Press, 1997), p. 153.

10. Rashid Khalidi, *The Iron Cage: The Story of the Palestinian Struggle for Statehood* (Boston: Beacon Press, 2006), p. 41.

11. Kuntzel, *Jihad and Jew-Hatred*, p. 28.

12. Klaus Gensicke, *Der Mufti von Jerusalem Amin el-Husseini und die Nationalsozialisten* (Frankfurt, 1988), p. 234, quoted in Küntzel, *Jihad and Jew-Hatred*, p. 28.

13. Micha Odenheimer, "The Islamization of Anti-Semitism," YNet News, November 9, 2009, http://www.ynetnews.com/articles/0,7340,L-3775495,00.html.

14. Ibid.

15. Yehoshua Porath, *From Riots to Rebellion, 1929–1939*, vol. 2, *Palestinian Arab National Movement* (London: Frank Cass, 1977), p. 250.

16. Kurt Fischer-Weth, *Amin al-Husseini, Grofsmufti von Palestine* (Berlin: Walter Tietz, 1943), p. 82, quoted in Küntzel, *Jihad and Jew-Hatred*, p. 42

17. Khalidi, *The Iron Cage*, p. 116.

18. Quoted in Jeffrey Herf, "What Does Coming to Terms with the Past Mean in the 'Berlin Republic' in 2007," Telos Press, February 4, 2008, http://www.telospress.com/main/index.php?main_page=news_article&article_id=216.

19. Neil Caplan, "Faisal Ibn Husain and the Zionists: A Re-examination with Documents," *International History Review*, vol. 5, no. 4 (November 1983), p. 561, http://www.jstor.org/stable/40105338.

20. Benny Morris, *1948: A History of the First Arab-Israeli War* (New Haven and London: Yale University Press, 2008), p. 33.

21. Quoted in ibid., p. 45.

CHAPTER FOUR

1. Andrew Bostom, "Silencing the Jews," Pajamas Media, March 18, 2010, http://pajamasmedia.com/blog/silencing-the-jews/.

2. Former Muslims United, March 13, 2010, http://formermuslimsunited.americancommunityexchange.org/2010/03/13/exposing-the-myth-of-moderate-islam/.

3. Licia Corbella, "Attacks against Tarek Fatah Are Unfair and Wrong," *Calgary Herald*, March 19, 2010, http://communities.canada.com/CALGARYHERALD/blogs/corbellareport/archive/2010/03/19/attacks-against-tarek-fatah-are-unfair-and-wrong.aspx.

4. Victor Ostrovsky, *The Other Side of Deception: A Rogue Agent Exposes the Mossad's Secret Agenda* (New York: HarperCollins, 1994), p. 196.

5. Ziad Abu Amr, *Islamic Fundamentalism in the West Bank and Gaza: Muslim Brotherhood and Islamic Jihad* (Bloomington: Indiana University Press, March 1994), p. 49.

6. Robert Dreyfuss, *Devil's Game: How the United States Helped Unleash Fundamentalist Islam* (New York: Metropolitan Books, 2008), p. 208.

7. *Corriere della Sera*, December 11, 2001, quoted in ibid., p. 209.

8. Matthew Wagner, "Book Advocating Killing Gentiles Who Endanger Jews Is Hard to Come By," *Jerusalem Post*, November 11, 2009.

9. Patrick Martin, "For Israel, Every Traveller Is an Ambassador," *Globe and Mail*, February 24, 2010.

10. Barak Ravid, "Think Tank: Israel Faces Global Delegitimization Campaign," *Haaretz*, February 12, 2010, http://haaretz.com/hasen/spages/1149274.html.

11. Moshe Davis, ed., *The Yom Kippur War: Israel and the Jewish People* (New York: Arno Press, 1974), pp. 104–5.

12. Jimmy Carter, "Precedents for Mideast Peace," *New York Times*, December 23, 2001.

13. Rory McCarthy Herzliya, "Barak: Make Peace with Palestinians or Face Apartheid," *The Guardian*, February 3, 2010, http://www.guardian.co.uk/world/2010/feb/03/barak-apartheid-palestine-peace.

14. "Question from the Studio," Kol Israel Radio, December 28, 1968, in Shlomo Avineri, ed., *Israel and the Palestinians* (New York: St. Martin's Press, 1971), pp. 67–68.

15. Moshe Dayan, "The Challenge of Conscience," in ibid., pp. 71–72.

16. Ibid.

17. Lewis, *Semites and Anti-Semites*, p. 240.

18. Ibid., p. 242.

CHAPTER FIVE

1. "Muslim Speaker Denounced: U.S. Scholar Tells Montreal Conference Theologians Teach Anti-Semitism," Montreal *Gazette*, March 16, 2004, http://www.canada.com/montreal/montrealgazette/story.asp?id=311ECF1A-9651-4165-A37A-D00EC24952F6.

2. Ibid.

3. Ibn Kathir, *Tafsir Ibn Kathir* (abridged), vol. 1 (Riyadh: Darussalam Publishers, 2003), p. 87.

4. Nizam al-Din al-Hasan al-Nisaburi, *Ghara'ib al-Qur'an wa Ragha'ib al-Furqan* (Cairo: Mustafa al-Babi al-Halabi, 1962–1964), 1:113.

5. "Saudi Textbooks Preach Intolerance, Hate," NBC, July 11, 2006, http://www.msnbc.msn.com/id/13804825/.

6. Simon Rocker, "What the Koran Says about the Land of Israel," *Jewish Chronicle*, March 19, 2009.

7. Khaleel Muhammad, "For Whom the Holy Land? A Qur'anic Answer," Jerusalem Summit, November 27–30, 2004 http://www.jerusalemsummit.org/eng/fullft.php?topic=0&speaker=238.

8. Yoav Stern, "Misfit at the Mosque," *Haaretz*, December 3, 2004, http://www.haaretz.com/hasen/spages/507226.html.

9. Muhammad, "For Whom the Holy Land? A Qu'ranic Answer."

10. Ali Akbar, *Israel and the Prophecies of the Holy Quran* (Cardiff: Seraj Publications, 1971), p. 38.

11. Robert Spencer, "The Qur'an: Israel Is Not for the Jews. Claims to the Holy Land," *Middle East Quarterly* (Fall 2009), pp. 3–8.

12. Andrew Bostom, interview by Alan Johnson, December 16, 2008, http://www.jewcy.com/post/inteview_andrew_bostom.

13. Khaleel Mohammed and Kadir Baksh, "Demonizing the Jews: Examining the Antichrist Tradition in the Sahihayn," *Journal of Religion and Culture*, no. 12 (1998), pp. 151–66.

14. Fazlur Rahman, *Islam* (Chicago: University of Chicago Press, 1979), p. 41.

15. Muslim Students Association, University of Southern California, Center for Jewish-Muslim Engagement, http://www.usc.edu/dept/MSA/fundamentals/hadithsunnah/.

16. "Islam and Reform," Cairo, October 5–6, 2004. http://www.mengos.net/events/04newsevents/egypt/october/ibnkhaldun-English.htm.

17. Dale F. Eickelman, "The Coming Transformation in the Muslim World," August 1999, http://www.drsoroush.com/PDF/E-CMO-20000100-Eickelman.pdf.

18. Ghulam Ahmed Pervez, "The Fundamental Principles of the Islamic System," http://www.tolueislam.com/Parwez/skn/SK_05.htm.

19. Ibid.

CHAPTER SIX

1. There are many English translations of this work, the most prominent among them by Alfred Guillaume of Oxford University. There is an abridged version by Michael Edwardes, better known for his books on British India. I have quoted from both in the text. Norman Stillman of Oklahoma University, who specializes in the intersection of Jewish and Islamic culture and history, has also translated and annotated this crucial text in his classic, *Jews of Arab Lands*.

2. Ibn Ishaq/Ibn Hisham, "The Extermination of Banu Quraiza," AH 5/627, in *The Legacy of Islamic Anti-Semitism*, ed. Andrew Bostom (New York: Prometheus Press, 2008), pp. 275–81.

3. All Amr Khaled quotes are from AmrKhaled.nethttp://amrkhaled.net/articles/articles1138.html.

4. Tariq Ramadan, *In the Footsteps of the Prophet* (New York: Oxford University Press, 2007), p. 146.

5. Ibn Kathir, *Tafsir Ibn Kathir* (abridged), vol. 7 (Jeddah: Maktab Darusalam, 2003), pp. 667–68.

CHAPTER SEVEN

1. Ali Hafiz, *Chapters from the History of Madina* (Jeddah: Al Madina Printing and Publication), pp. 4–6.

2. Richard Burton, *A Secret Pilgrimage to Mecca and Medina* (London: Folio Society, 2004), pp. 260–61.

3. Ibn Hajar, Tahdhib al-Tahdhib, IX, 45, quoted in W.N. Arafat, "New Light on the Story of Banu Qurayza and the Jews of Medina," *Journal of the Royal Asiatic Society of Great Britain and Ireland* (1976), p. 107; Malik Ibn Anas, Mujam al-Udaba Yaqut, quoted in Barakat Ahmad, *Muhammad and the Jews* (New Delhi: Vikas Publishing, 1979), p. 11.

4. Arafat, "New Light on the Story of Banu Qurayza and the Jews of Medina," p. 102

5. S.D. Goitein, *Jews and Arabs: A Concise History of Their Social and Cultural Relations* (Mineola, NY: Dover Publications, 2005), p. 64.

6. Ibid., p. 6.

7. Samuel Usque, *Consolation for the Tribulations of Israel* (1550), trans. Martin Cohen (Philadelphia: Jewish Publication Society of America, 1977), pp. 170–71.

8. Reuven Firestone, *An Introduction to Islam for Jews* (Philadelphia: Jewish Publication Society of America, 2008), p. 38.

9. Norman A. Stillman, *The Jews of Arab Lands: A History and Source Book* (Philadelphia: Jewish Publication Society of America, 1979), p. 16.

10. Abdullah Yusuf Ali, *The Meaning of the Holy Quran* (New York: Amana Publications, 1983), p. 343.

11. W.N. Arafat, "New Light on the Story of Banu Qurayza and the Jews of Medina," from *Journal of the Royal Asiatic Society of Great Britain and Ireland*, (1976), pp. 100–107.

12. Alfred Guillaume, *The Life of Muhammad: A Translation of Ibn Ishaq's Sirat Rasul Allah* (Karachi: Oxford University Press, 2006), p. 535.

13. Ibid., p. 550.

14. Simon Dubonov, *History of the Jews,* vol. 2 (South Brunswick, NJ: A.S. Barnes, 1968), p. 335.

15. Ibid., p. 336.

16. Barakat Ahmad, *Muhammad and the Jews,* p. 10.

17. Montgomery Watt, *Muhammad at Medina* (London: Oxford University Press, 1981), p. 219.

18. H. Graetz, *History of the Jews,* vol. 3 (Philadelphia. The Jewish Publication Society of America, 1897), pp. 93–94.

19. Goitein, *Jews and Arabs,* p. 120.

CHAPTER EIGHT

1. *Little Enthusiasm for Many Muslim Leaders* (New York: The Pew Global Attitudes Project, 2010), http://pewglobal.org/reports/pdf/268.pdf.

2. Joëlle Bahloul, *The Architecture of Memory* (New York: Cambridge University Press, 1992), p. 47.

3. Pervez Amirali Hoodbhoy, "Islam and Science Have Parted Ways," *Middle East Quarterly* (Winter 2010), pp. 69–70, http://www.meforum.org/2593/pervez-amirali-hoodbhoy-islam-science.

4. Morris, *1948*, p. 43.

5. Shlomo Avineri, *Israel and the Palestinians* (New York: St. Martin's Press, 1971), pp. xxi–xxii.

6. Shlomo Avineri, "The Real Nakba," *Haaretz*, May 9, 2008, http://www.haaretz.com/hasen/spages/981931.html.

7. Adonis, interview on Dubai TV, March 11, 2006.

8. SunniPath http://qa.sunnipath.com/issue_view.asp?HD=7&ID=9427&CATE=1.

9. IslamQ&A http://islamqa.com/en/ref/117609.

10. IslamOnLine http://www.islamonline.net/servlet/Satellite?pagename=IslamOnline-English-Ask_Scholar%2FFatwaE%2FFatwaEAskTheScholar&cid=1119503545136.

11. Ezra Chwat, Great Rabbis of the Muslim Empire, Jewish Virtual Library, http://www.jewishvirtuallibrary.org/jsource/Judaism/muslim_rabbis.html.

EPILOGUE

1. Natasha Fatah, "Holocaust deniers should spend a day at Auschwitz." CBC News, April 29, 2008. http://www.cbc.ca/News/viewpoint/vp_Fatah/20080429.html.

2. "Muslims in Auschwitz," by Gil Anidjar, *Ha'aretz*, Jerusalem. November 10, 2006. http://www.haaretz.com/news/Muslims-in-auschwitz-1.204868.

3. Abdel-Wahab Elmessiri, *Zionism, Nazism and the End of History*, Dar al-Sharouk, Cairo, 1997. http://www.arabphilosophers.com/Arabic/aphilosophers/acontemporary/acontemporary-names/Abdl-Wahab%20Elmessiri/Material/Al-Ahram_Weekly_%20Arabs_%20Muslims_and_the_Nazi_genocide_of_the_Jews.htm.

4. Ronald L. Nettler, *Past Trials and Present Tribulations: A Muslim Fundamentalist's View of the Jews* (Published for the Vidal Sassoon International Center for the Study of Antisemitism, New York: The Hebrew University of Jerusalem by Pergamon Press, 1987), p. 51.

5. Erna Paris, *The End of Days: A Story of Tolerance, Tyranny, and the Expulsion of the Jews from Spain.* New York: Prometheus Books, 1995. pp. 46–47.

BIBLIOGRAPHY

Abu-Amr, Ziad. Islamic *Fundamentalism in the West Bank and Gaza: Muslim Brotherhood and Islamic Jihad.* Bloomington and Indiana: Indiana University Press, 1994.

Aburish, Said K. *A Brutal Friendship. The West and the Arab Elite.* New York: St. Martin's Press, 1997.

Abu-Sahlieh, Sami A. Aldeeb. *Muslims in the West: Redefining the Separation of Church and State.* Trans. by Sheldon Lee Gosline. Warren Center, PA: Shangri-La Publications, 2002.

Achcar, Gilbert. *The Arabs and the Holocaust: The Arab-Israeli War of Narratives.* Translated by G. M. Goshgarian. New York: Metropolitan Books, 2009.

Adang, Camilla, Sabine Scmidtkc, and David Sklare, ed. *A Common Rationality: Mu'tazilism in Islam and Judaism.* Istanbul: Orient Institute, 2007.

Ahmad, Barakat. *Muhammad and the Jews. A Re examination.* New Delhi: Vikas Publishing, 1979.

Ahmad, Sayed Riaz. *Maulana Maududi and Islamic State.* Lahore: People's Publishing House, 1976.

Ahmed, Shabbir. *Who Wrote the Quran?* Lauderhill, FL: Our Beacon, 2007.

Akbar, Ali. *Israel and the Prophecies of the Holy Quran.* Cardiff: Seraj Publications, 1971.

Akhtar, Shabbir. *A Faith for All Seasons: Islam and the Challenge of the Modern World.* Chicago: Ivan R. Dee Publisher, 1990.

Alangari, Haifa. *The Struggle for Power in Arabia: Ibn Saud, Hussein and Great Britain, 1914–1924.* Reading: Ithaca Press, 1998.

Al-Baladhuri, Abu-l Abbas Ahmad ibn Jabir. *The Origins of the Islamic State.* Trans. by Philip Khuri Hitti. New Jersey: Gorgias Press, 2002.

Albright, William Foxwell. *Archaeology and the Religion of Israel*. Baltimore: The John Hopkins Press, 1942.

Ali, Ahmed. *Al-Qur'an*. Princeton, NJ: Princeton University Press, 1984.

Al-Ghazali. *The Incoherence of the Philosophers*. Trans. by Michael E. Marmura. Provo, UT: Brigham Young University Press, 2000.

Al-Hanbali, Ibn Rajab. *The Heirs of the Prophets*. Introduction and Trans. by Zaid Shakir. Chicago: The Starlatch Press, 2001.

Ali, Abdullah Yusuf. *The Meaning of The Holy Qur'an*. Beltsville, MD: Amana Publications, 2004.

Allen, Charles. *God's Terrorists: The Wahhabi Cult and the Hidden Roots of Modern Islam*. London, UK: Abacus, 2007.

Al-Maqdisi, Elias, and Sam Soloman. *Al-Yahud: Eternal Islamic Enmity and the Jews*. Charlottesville, VA: ANM Publishers, 2010.

al-Misri, Ahmad ibn Naqib. *Reliance of the Traveller: A Classic Manual of Islamic Sacred Law*. Beltsville, MD: Amana Publications, 1994.

al-Mubarakpuri, Safi-ur-Rahman. *Ar-Raheeq Al-Makhtum* (The Sealed Nectar): Biography of the Noble Prophet. Saudi Arabia, UK, USA, Pakistan: Maktaba Dar-us-Salam, 1979.

al-Razik, Ali 'Abd. *Islam and the Fundamentalism of Authority: A Study of Caliphate and Government in Islam*. 1925.

Al-Qayrawani, Ibn Abi Zayd. *A Madinan View on the Sunnah, Courtesy, Wisdom, Battles and History*. London: Ta-Ha Publishers, 1999.

Al-Suhrawardy, Allama Sir Abdullah and Al-Mamun. *The Wisdom of Muhammad*. New York: Citadel Press, 2001.

Al-Yaqubi. *Tareekh Al-Yaqubi* (The History of Al-Yaqubi). 2 vols. Beirut: Dar Sader..

Amir-Ali, Hashim. *The Message of the Quran Presented in Perspective*. Rutland / Tokyo: Charles E. Tuttle Company, 1974.

Armstrong, Karen. *The Battle for God*. New York: Ballantine Books, 2001.

Armstrong, Karen. *Jerusalem: One City, Three Faiths*. New York: Alfred A. Knopf, 1996.

———. *Muhammad: A Biography of the Prophet*. San Francisco: HarperSanFrancisco, 1992.

Asad, Muhammad. *The Road to Mecca*. Gibraltar: Dar Al-Andalus Limited, 1980.

———. *The Message of the Quran*. London: The Book Foundation, 2003.

Averroes. *Decisive Treatise and Epistle Dedicatory*. Introduction and Trans. by Charles E. Butterworth. Provo, UT: Brigham Young University Press, 2001.

———. *Faith and Reason in Islam: Averroes' Exposition of Religious Arguments*. Oxford, England: Oneworld Publications, 2005.

Avineri, Shlomo. *Israel and the Palestinians. Reflections on the Clash of Two National Movements.* New York: St. Martin's Press, 1971.

Ayoub, Mahmoud M. *The Qur'an and Its Interpreters.* Albany, NY: State University of New York Press, 1984.

Ayubi, Nazih. *Political Islam: Religion and Politics in the Arab World.* London: Routledge, 1991.

Bahloul, Joelle. *The Architecture of Memory. A Jewish-Muslim Household in Colonial Algeria 1937–1962.* New York / Cambridge: Cambridge University Press, 1996.

Baker, Raymond William. *Islam Without Fear: Egypt and the New Islamists.* Cambridge, MA, and London, UK: Harvard University Press, 2003.

Bakhtiar, Laleh. *Encyclopedia of Islamic Law: A Compendium of the Major Schools.* Chicago: ABC International Group, Inc., 1996.

———. *Shariati on Shariati and the Muslim Woman.* Chicago, IL: ABC International Group, Inc., 1996.

Baksh, Kaiyume. *Islam and the Other Major World Religions.* Victoria, BC: Trafford Publishing, 2007.

Balagha, Nahjul. *Peak of Eloquence: Sermons, Letters and Sayings of Imam Ali ibn Abu Talib.* Trans. by Sayed Ali Reza. Elmhurst, NY: Tahrike Tarsile Qur'an, Inc., 1996.

Bamyeh, Mohammed A. *The Social Origins of Islam: Mind, Economy, Discourse.* Minneapolis: University of Minnesota Press, 1999.

Basu, Shrabani. *Spy Princess: The Life of Noor Inayat Khan.* New York: Omega Publications, 2007.

Bawer, Bruce. *While Europe Slept: How Radical Islam is Destroying the West from Within.* New York, London, Toronto and Sydney: Doubleday, 2006.

Black, Antony. *The History of Islamic Political Thought: From the Prophet to the Present.* New York: Routledge, 2001.

Blankinship, Khalid Yahya. *The End of the Jihad State: The Reign of Hisham Ibn 'Abd al-Malik and the Collapse of the Umayyads.* Albany, NY: State University of New York Press, 1994.

Bostom, Andrew G., ed. *The Legacy of Islamic Antisemitism. From Sacred Texts to Solemn History.* Amherst, NY: Prometheus Books, 2008.

———, ed. *The Legacy of Jihad: Islamic Holy War and the Fate of Non-Muslims.* Amherst, NY: Prometheus Books, 2005.

Bosworth, C.E., and Joseph Schacht, ed. *The Legacy of Islam* (Second Edition). Oxford / New York / Toronto / Melbourne: Oxford University Press, 1979.

———. *The History of al-Tabari, Volume V: The Sasanids, the Byzantines, the Lakhmids, and the Yemen.* Albany, NY: State University of New York Press, 1999.

————. *The History of al-Tabari, Volume XXXII: The Reunification of the 'Abbasid Caliphate*. Albany, NY: State University of New York Press, 1987.

Bowen, John R. *Religions in Practice: An Approach to the Anthropology of Religion*. Boston/London/Toronto/Sydney/Tokyo/Singapore: Allyn and Bacon, 1998.

Brooks, Geraldine. *People of the Book*. New York: Viking, 2008.

Brown, Daniel. *Rethinking Tradition in Modern Islamic Thought*. Cambridge: Cambridge University Press, 1996.

Burton, Richard F. *Personal Narrative of a Pilgrimage to Al-Madinah and Meccah: Volume 1*. New York: Dover Publications Inc., 1964.

Charfi, Mohamed. *Islam and Liberty: The Historical Misunderstanding*. London and New York: Zed Books, 2005.

Chejne, Anwar. *Succession to the Rule in Islam*. Lahore, Pakistan: SH. Muhammad Ashraf, 1979.

Chomsky, Noam. *Middle East Illusions*. Lanham / New York / Oxford / Boulder: Rowan & Littlefield Publishers, Inc., 2003.

Cohen, Mark R., and Abraham L. Udovitch, ed. *Jews Among Arabs*. Princeton, NJ: Darwin Press, 1989.

Cook, David. *Contemporary Muslim Apocalyptic Literature*. Syracuse, NY: Syracuse University Press, 2005.

————. *Understanding Jihad*. Berkeley, Los Angeles and London: University of California Press, 2005.

Crone, Patricia. *God's Rule: Government and Islam*. New York: Columbia University Press, 2004.

Crosson, John Dominic. *The Birth of Christianity*. New York: HarperSanFrancisco, 1998.

Dalin, David G., and John F. Rothman. *Icon of Evil: Hitler's Mufti and the Rise of Radical Islam*. New York: Random House, 2008.

Davis, Gregory M. *Religion of Peace?: Islam's War Against the World*. Los Angeles, CA: World Ahead Publishing, 2006.

Davis, Natalie Zemon. *Trickster Travels: A Sixteenth Century Muslim Between Worlds*. New York: Hill and Wang, 2006.

Dayan, Moshe. *Story of My Life: An Autobiography*. New York: William Morrow and Company, 1976.

Davis, Moshe, ed. *The Yom Kippur War: Israel and the Jewish People*. Jerusalem: Arno Press, 1974.

DeLong-Bas, Natana. *Notable Muslims: Muslim Builders of World Civilization and Culture*. Oxford, England: Oneworld Publications, 2006.

Dirk, Jerald F. Abraham. *The Friend of God*. New York: Amana Publications, 2002.

Dubonov, Simon. *History of the Jews*. New York / London: A. S. Barnes & Company, 1976.

El Fadl, Khaled Abou. *The Great Theft: Wrestling Islam from the Extremists*. San Francisco: HarperSanFrancisco, 2005.

————. *Rebellion and Violence in Islamic Law*. Cambridge / New York: Cambridge University Press, 2001.

————. *Speaking in God's Name: Islamic Law, Authority and Women*. Oxford: Oneworld Publications, 2001.

Enayat, Hamid. *Modern Islamic Political Thought*. Austin, TX: University Of Texas Press, 1982.

Engineer, Asghar Ali. *The Origins and Development of Islam*. Kuala Lumpur, Malaysia: Ikraq, 1990.

Fakhry, Majid. *Averroes (Ibn Rushd): His Life, Works and Influence*. Oxford, England: Oneworld Publications, 2001.

————. *A History of Islamic Philosophy*. New York: Columbia University Press, 1983.

Fatah, Tarek. *Chasing a Mirage. The Tragic Illusion of an Islamic State*. Toronto: John Wiley & Sons, 2008.

Fatoohi, Dr. Louay. *Jihad in the Qur'an: The Truth from the Source*. Kuala Lumpur, Malaysia: A.S. Noordeen, 2002.

Firestone, Reuven. *An Introduction to Islam for Jews*. Philadelphia: The Jewish Publication Society, 2008.

Friedman, Yohann. *Tolerance and Coercion in Islam: Intefiath Relations in the Muslim Tradition*. Cambridge: Cambridge University Press, 2003.

Fromkin, David. *A Peace to End all Peace: The Fall of the Ottoman Empire and the Creation of the Modern Middle East*. New York: Henry Holt, 1989.

Fuller, Jean Overton. *Noor-un-Nisa Inayat Khan*. London / The Hague: East-West Publications, 1988.

Fyzee, Asaf A.A. *Outlines of Muhammadan Law*. Various Publishers. New Delhi: Oxford University Press, 1964.

Gerber, Jane S. *The Jews of Spain*. New York: The Free Press, 1994.

Gershman, Norman H. *Besa: Muslims Who Saved Jews in World War II*. New York: Syracuse University Press, 2008.

Gilsenan, Michael. *Recognizing Islam: Religion and Society in the Modern Arab World*. New York: Pantheon Books, 1982.

Glubb, John Bagot. *The Course of Empire: The Arabs and Their Successors*. London: Hodder and Stoughton, 1965.

————. *The Lost Centuries: From the Muslim Empires to the Renaissance of Europe 1145–1453*. London: Hodder and Stoughton, 1967.

————. *The Life and Times of Muhammad*. Lanham / New York / Oxford: Madison Books, 1998.

Goitein, S.D. *Jews and Arabs: A Concise History of Their Social and Cultural Relations*. Mineola, NY: Dover Publications, 2005.

————. *A Mediterranean Society. The Jewish Communities of the World as Portrayed in the Documents of the Cairo Geniza*. Berkeley / Los Angeles / London: University of California Press, 1999.

Guillaume, Alfred. *The Life of Muhammad: A Translation of Ibn Ishaq's Sirat Rasul Allah*. Karachi: Oxford University Press, 2006.

Habeck, Mary. *Knowing the Enemy: Jihadist Ideology and the War on Terror*. New Haven and London: Yale University Press, 2006.

Hafiz, Ali. *Chapters from the History of Madina*. Jeddah, Saudi Arabia: Al Madina Printing and Publication Co., 1987.

Halevi, Yossi Klein. *Memoirs of a Jewish Extremist: An American Story*. Boston: Little, Brown and Company, 1995.

Hamidullah, Muhammad. *The First Written Constitution in the World: An Important Document of the Time of the Holy Prophet*. Lahore: SH. Muhammad Ashraf, 1994.

————. *The Prophet's Establishing a State and His Succession*. New Delhi: Adam Publishers & Distributors, 2006.

Haykal, Muhammad Husayn. *The Life of Muhammad*. Trans. Isma'il Rāgī A.al Fārūqī. United States: North American Trust Publication, 1976.

Hellman, Peter. *When Courage Was Stronger Than Fear: Remarkable Stories of Christians and Jews Who Saved Jews from the Holocaust*. New York: Marlowe & Company, 2004.

Herf, Jeffery. *Nazi Propaganda for the Arab World*. Ann Arbour, MI: Sheridan Books, 2009.

Herzog, Chaim (Maj. Gen). *The War of Atonement*. Tel Aviv: Steimatzky's Agency, 1975.

Hinds, Martin, and Patricia Crone. *God's Caliph: Religious Authority in the First Centuries of Islam*. Cambridge: Cambridge University Press, 2003.

Hitti, Philip K. *History of the Arabs: From the Earliest Times to the Present*. London and Basingstoke: The MacMillan Press Ltd., 1970.

Hodgson, Marshall G.S. *The Venture of Islam: Conscience and History in a World Civilization*. Chicago and London: The University of Chicago Press, 1974.

Hoelzl, Michael, and Graham Ward, ed. *Religion and Political Thought*. London / New York: Continuum, 2006.

Hoodbhoy, Pervez. *Islam and Science: Religious Orthodoxy and the Battle for Rationality.* London and New Jersey: Zed Books Ltd, 1991.

Hourani, Albert. *A History of the Arab Peoples.* New York: Warner Books, 1992.

———. *Islam in European Thought.* Cambridge: Cambridge University Press, 1996.

Hussein, King of Jordan. *My "War" with Israel.* London: Peter Owen, 1968.

Iqbal, Allama Muhammad. *The Reconstruction of Religious Thought in Islam.* Lahore, Pakistan: Institute of Islamic Culture, 1989.

Ishaq, Ibn. *The Life of Muhammad.* Edited by Michael Edwardes. London: The Folio Society, 2003.

———. *The Life of Muhammad.* Notes by A. Guillaume. Oxford: Oxford University Press, 2006.

Issawi, Charles. *The Fertile Crescent 1800–1914.* New York / Oxford: Oxford University Press, 1988.

Izetbegovic, Alija 'Ali. *Islam Between East and West.* Plainfield, IN: American Trust Publications, 1994.

Johnson, Ian. *A Mosque in Munich: Nazis, the CIA, and the Rise of the Muslim Brotherhood in the West.* New York: Houghton, Mifflin Harcourt, 2010.

Kaegi, Walter E. *Byzantium and the Early Islamic Conquests.* Cambridge: Cambridge University Press, 1992.

Kamil, Abd-al-'Aziz 'Abd-al-Qadir. *Islam and the Race Question.* Place de Fontenoy: Unesco, 1970.

Karsh, Efraim. *Palestine Betrayed.* Cornwall, UK: Yale University Press, 2010.

Kathir, Ibn. *Tafsir Ibn Kathir.* Trans by Muhammad Junagarhwi, 5 vols. Maktab Qudoosia, Lahore, 2003.

Kedourie, Elie. *Afghani and Abduh.* London: Frank Cass & Co., 1966.

Kennedy, Hugh. *The Court of the Caliphs: The Rise and Fall of Islam's Greatest Dynasty.* London: Weidenfeld & Nicolson, 2004.

Kepel, Gilles. *The War for Muslim Minds: Islam and the West.* Trans. by Pascale Ghazaleh. Cambridge, MA and London, UK: The Belknap Press of Harvard University Press, 2004.

Khaldûn, Ibn. *The Muqaddimah: An Introduction to History.* Trans. by Franz Rosenthal. Princeton, NJ: Bollingen Series, Princeton University Press, 1989.

Khalidi, Rashid. *The Iron Cage: The Story of the Palestinian Struggle for Statehood.* Boston: Beacon Press, 2006.

Khalifa, Rashad. Quran, *Hadith and Islam.* Fremont, CA: Universal Unity, 2001.

Khan, Maulana Wahiduddin. *The True Jihad: The Concepts of Peace, Tolerance and Non-Violence in Islam.* New Delhi: Goodword Books, 2002.

Khan, Muhammad Muhsin. *Summarized Sahih Al-Bukhâri*. Riyadh, Saudi Arabia: Maktaba Dar-us-Salam, 1994.

———. *The Translation of the Meanings of Sahih al-Bukhari*, 9 vols. Riyadh, Saudi Arabia: Maktaba Daru-us-Salam, 1997.

Kinross, Lord. *The Ottoman Centuries: The Rise and Fall of the Turkish Empire*. New York: Morrow Quill Paperbacks, 1977.

———. *The Ottoman Empire*. London: The Folio Society, 2003.

Kraemer, Joel L. *Maimonides*. New York: Doubleday, 2008.

Kramer, Gudrun. *A History of Palestine*. Princeton, NJ: Princeton University Press, 2008.

Kuntzel, Matthias. *Jihad and Jew-Hatred: Islamism, Nazism and the Roots of 9/11*. New York: Telos Press, 2007.

Lacoste, Yves. *Ibn Khaldun: The Birth of History and the Past of the Third World*. Trans. by David Macey. London: Verso, 1984.

La Guardia, Anton. *War Without End: Israelis, Palestinians, and the Struggle for a Promised Land*. New York: Thomas Dunne Books, 2003.

Lakhani, M. Ali, Reza Shah-Kazemi, and Leonard Lewisohn. *The Sacred Foundations of Justice in Islam: The Teachings of 'Ali ibn Abi Talib*. North Vancouver: World Wisdom Inc and Sacred Web, 2006.

Lalani, Arzina R. *Early Shi' i Thought: The Teachings of Imam Muhammad al-Baqir*. NewYork: I.B. Tauris & Co Ltd., 2004.

Landau, Jacob. *Jews, Arabs, Turks: Selected Essays*. Jerusalem: The Magnes Press, 1993.

Lane-Poole, Stanley. *The Muslims in Spain*. New Delhi: Goodword Books, 2006.

Lapidus, Ira M. *A History of Islamic Societies*. Cambridge, UK: Cambridge University Press, 2002.

Laquer, Walter, and Barry Rubin, ed. *The Israel-Arab Reader. A Documentary History of the Middle East Conflict*. New York: Penguin Books, 2001.

Lawrence, Bruce. *The Qur'an: A Biography*. London,UK: Atlantic Books, 2006.

Lewis, Bernard. *The Arabs in History*. New York: Oxford University Press, 1993.

———. *The Crisis of Islam: Holy War and Unholy Terror*. New York: Random House Trade Paperbacks, 2004.

———. *From Babel to Dragomans: Interpreting the Middle East*, New York: Oxford University Press, 2004.

———. *The Jews of Islam*. Princeton, NJ: Princeton University Press, 1997.

———. *The Muslim Discovery of Europe*. New York / London: W.W. Norton & Company, 1982.

———. *The Political Language of Islam*. Chicago and London: The University of Chicago Press, 1988.

———. *Semites and Anti-Semites.* New York / London: W. W. Norton & Company, 1999.

———. *What Went Wrong?: Western Impact and Middle Eastern Response.* Oxford / New York: Oxford University Press, 2002.

Lia, Brynjar. *The Society of the Muslim Brothers in Egypt: The Rise of an Islamic Mass Movement 1928–1942.* Reading, UK: Ithaca Press, 1998.

Lings, Martin. *Mecca: From Before Genesis Until Now.* Cambridge, UK: Archetype, 2004.

———. *Muhammad: His Life Based on the Earliest Sources.* Rochester, VT: Inner Traditions International, 1983.

Maalouf, Amin. *The Crusades Through Arab Eyes.* New York: Schocken Books, 1984.

Madelung, Wilfred. *The Succession to Muhammad: A Study of the Early Caliphate.* Cambridge: Cambridge University Press, 1997.

Maghen, Ze'ev. *After Hardship Cometh Ease: The Jews as a Backdrop for Muslim Moderation.* Berlin / New York: Walter de Gruyter, 2006.

Margalit, Avishai, and Ian Buruma. *Occidentalism: The West in the Eyes of Its Enemies.* New York: Penguin Books, 2004.

Matar, Nabil. *Turks, Moors and Englishmen: In the Age of Discovery.* New York: Columbia University Press, 1999.

Maudoodi, Sayyed Abul ala. *The Process of Islamic Revolution.* Lahore, Pakistan: Markazi Maktaba-e-Jama'at-e-Islami Pakistan, 1955.

Maudoodi, Syed Abul 'Ala. *Islamic Law and Constitution.* Karachi, Pakistan: Jamaat-e Islami Publications, 1955.

———. *Tafhimaat.* 3 vols. Lahore, Islamic Publications Limited, 2004.

———. *Call to Jihad.* Trans. and Edited by Misbahul Islam Faruqi. Lahore, Pakistan: Islamic Publications (Pvt.) Limited, 1980.

———. *Fundamentals of Islam.* Lahore, Pakistan: Islamic Publications (Pvt.) Limited, 1975.

———. *Jihad in Islam.* Lahore, Pakistan: Islamic Publications (Pvt.) Limited, 1991.

———. *The Meaning of The Quran* (Tafhimul Quran). Trans by Muhammad Akbar, 6 vols: Islamic Publications, Lahore, 2005.

———. *Political Theory of Islam.* Edited and Trans. by Khurshid Ahmad. Lahore, Pakistan: Islamic Publications (Pvt.) Limited, 1985.

———. *A Short History of the Revivalist Movement in Islam.* Lahore, Pakistan: Islamic Publications Limited, 1986.

———. *The Sick Nations of the Modern Age.* Edited and Trans. by Khurshid Ahmad. Lahore, Pakistan: Islamic Publications (Pvt.) Limited, 1979.

————. *Unity of the Muslim World*. Edited and Trans. by Khurshid Ahmad. Lahore, Pakistan: Islamic Publications (Pvt.) Limited, 1982.

Mauwdudi, Abul A'la. *Human Rights in Islam*. Edited and Trans. by Khurshid Ahmad. Leicestershire, England: The Islamic Foundation, 1990.

Mawdudi, Sayyid Abul A'La. *The Islamic Movement: Dynamics of Values, Power and Change*. Edited by Khurram Murad. Leicester, UK: The Islamic Foundation, 1991.

Mauwdudi, Abul A'la. *Toward Understanding Islam*. Edited and Trans. by Khurshid Ahmad. Leicestershire, England: The Islamic Foundation, 2000.

McAuliffe, Jane Dammen, ed. *The Cambridge Companion to The Qur'an*. Cambridge, UK: Cambridge University Press, 2006.

Meddeb, Abdelwahab. *The Malady of Islam*. Trans. by Pierre Joris and Ann Reid. New York: Basic Books, Inc., Publishers, 2003.

Menocal, Maria Rosa. *The Ornament of the World: How Muslims, Jews and Christians Created a Culture of Tolerance in Medieval Spain*. New York: Back Bay Books, 2002.

Merhav, Peretz. *The Israeli Left*. San Diego / New York: A. S. Barnes & Company, 1980.

Meyer, Beate, Hermann Simon, and Chana Schutz. *Jews in Nazi Berlin: From Kristallnacht to Liberation*. Chicago: University of Chicago Press, 2009.

Moaddel, Mansoor. *Islamic Modernism, Nationalism and Fundamentalism: Episode and Discourse*. Chicago and London: The University of Chicago Press, 2005.

Moaddel, Mansoor, and Kamran Talattof, ed. *Modernist and Fundamentalist Debates in Islam: A Reader*. New York: Palgrave MacMillan, 2000.

Morgan, Michael Hamilton. *Lost History: The Enduring Legacy of Muslim Scientists, Thinkers, and Artists*. Washington, DC: National Geographic Society, 2007.

Morris, Benny. *1948. The First Arab-Israeli War*. New Haven / London: Yale University Press, 2008.

Musa, Aisha Y. *Hadith as Scripture: Discussion on the Authority of Prophetic Traditions in Islam*. Houndsmill, England: Palgrave Macmillan, 2008.

Nasr, Seyyid Hossein. *Mecca the Blessed, Medina the Radiant: The Holiest Cities of Islam. Photographs by Ali Kazuyoshi Nomachi*. US and England: Aperture, 1997.

Nasr, Vali. *The Shia Revival: How Conflicts Within Islam Will Shape the Future*. New York and London: W.W. Norton & Company, 2006.

Nettler, Ronald L. *Past Trials and Present Tribulations: A Muslim Fundamentalist's View of the Jews*. Oxford and New York: Pergamon Press, 1987.

Nettler, Ronald L., and Suha Taji-Farouki. *Muslim-Jewish Encounters: Intellectual Traditions and Modern Politics*. Amsterdam: Harwood Academic Publishers, 1998.

Noorani, A.G. *Islam and Jihad: Prejudice Versus Reality*. London and New York: Zed Books, 2002.

Norris, Pippa, and Ronald Inglehart. *Sacred and Secular: Religion and Politics Worldwide*. Cambridge: Cambridge University Press, 2004.

O'Leary, De Lacy. *Islamic Thought and Its Place in History*. New Delhi: Goodword Books, 2001.

Omar, Abdul Mannân. *Dictionary of the Holy Qur'ân*. Hockessin, DE: Noor Foundation International Inc., 2006.

Oren, Michael B. *Power, Faith, and Fantasy: America in the Middle East 1776 to Present*. New York and London: W.W. Norton & Company, 2007.

Ostrovsky, Victor. *The Other Side of Deception: A Rogue Agent Exposes the Mossad's Secret Agenda*. New York: Harpercollins, 1995.

Paris, Erna. *The End of Days: A Story of Tolerance, Tyranny and the Expulsion of the Jews from Spain*. Amherst, NY: Prometheus Books, 1995.

Patai, Raphael. *The Seed of Abraham: Jews and Arabs in Contact and Conflict*. New York: Charles Scribner's Sons, 1987.

Payne, Robert. *A History of Islam*. New York: Dorset Press, 1990.

Pearl, Mariane. *A Mighty Heart: The Brave Life and Death of My Husband Danny Pearl*. New York /London/Toronto/Sydney/Singapore: Scribner, 2003.

Pearson, Michael N. *Pilgrimage to Mecca: The Indian Experience 1500–1800*. Princeton, NJ: Markus Wiener Publishers, 1996.

Pipes, Daniel. *In the Path of God: Islam and Political Power*. New York: Basic Books, Inc., Publishers, 1983.

Piscatori, James P., ed. *Islam in the Political Process*. Cambridge/New York/ Melbourne: Cambridge University Press, 1983.

Prescott, William H. *History of the Reign of Isabella, The Catholic*. Philadelphia: J.B. Lippincott & Co, 1863.

Qutb, Sayyid. *Basic Principles of the Islamic Worldview*. North Haledon, NJ: Islamic Publications International, 2006.

———. *Ma'rakatuna ma'a al-Yahud* (Our Battle Against the Jews). Jeddah, Saudi Arabia: The Government Printer, 1970.

Qutb, Seyyid. *Milestones*. Damascus, Syria: Dar Al-Ilm.

Qutb, Sayyid. *Social Justice in Islam*. Trans. by John B. Hardie (trans. revised by Hamid Algar). New York: Islamic Publications International, 2000.

Rahman, Fazlur. *Islam* (Second Edition). Chicago and London: University of Chicago Press, 1979.

Rahman, Syed Azizur. *The Story of Islamic Spain*. New Delhi: Goodword Books, 2001.

Ramadan, Tariq. *To Be a European Muslim*. Leicester, England: The Islamic Foundation, 2002.

Ramras-Rauch, Gila. *The Arab in Israeli Literature*. London: I. B. Tauris & Company, 1989.

Rashid, Ahmed. *Taliban: Militant Islam, Oil and Fundamentalism in Central Asia*. New Haven and London: Yale Nota Bene / Yale University Press, 2001.

Rees, Laurence. *Auschwitz: The Nazis and The Final Solution*. London: BBC Books, 2005.

Reilly, Robert R. *The Closing of the Muslim Mind: How Intellectual Suicide Created the Modern Islamist Crisis*. Wilmington, DE: ISI Books, 2010.

Robinson, E., E. Smith and Others. *Later Biblical Researches in Palestine, and in the Adjacent Regions: A Journal of Travels in the Year 1852*. Boston: Crocker and Brewster, 1857.

Robinson, Francis, ed. *Cambridge Illustrated History: Islamic World*. Cambridge, UK: Cambridge University Press, 1996.

Rodinson, Maxime. *Muhammad*. Trans. by Anne Carter. New York: The New Press, 2002.

Rogerson, Barnaby. *The Heirs of Muhammad: Islam's First Century and the Origins of the Sunni-Shia Split*. Woodstock & NewYork: The Overlook Press, 2007.

Roy, Olivier. *The Failure of Political Islam*. Trans. by Carol Volk. Cambridge, MA: Harvard University Press, 1996.

Roy, Olivier. *Globalised Islam: The Search for a New Ummah*. London: Hurst & Company, 2004.

Rubenstein, Richard E. *Aristotle's Children*. Orlando, FL: Hartcourt Books, 2003.

Russell, Bertrand. *History of Western Philosophy: And Its Connection with Political and Social Circumstances from the Earliest Times to the Present Day*. London: The Folio Society, 2004.

Ruthven, Malise. *Islam in the World*. New York: Penguin Books, 1984.

Sa'd, Ibn. *Kitab Al-Tabaqat Al-Kabir*. Trans. by S. Moinul Haq, 2 vols: Kitab Bhavan, New Delhi, 1944.

Safi, Omid. *Memories of Muhammad: Why the Prophet Matters*. New York: HarperCollins, 2009.

Safran, Janina M. *The Second Umayyad Caliphate: The Articulation of Caliphal Legitimacy in Al-Andalus*. Cambridge, MA: Harvard University Press, 2000.

Said, Edward. *The Question of Palestine*. New York: Vintage Books, 1992.

Said, Edward W. and Christopher Hitchens. *Blaming the Victims: Spurious Scholarship and the Palestinian Question*. New York: Verso, 2001.

Sakr, Ahmad H. *Muslims and Non-Muslims Face to Face*. Lombard, IL: Foundation for Islamic Knowledge, 1991.

Samir, Amin. *Political Islam*. Trans. by Gabi Christov. Washington, DC: Covert Action Publications, 2001.

Sartre, Jean-Paul. *Anti-Semite and Jew.* New York: Schocken Books, 1965.

Sells, Michael. *Approaching The Qur'an: The Early Revelations.* Introduced and Translated by Michael Sells, Ashland, OR: White Cloud Press, 1999.

Shadid, Anthony. *Legacy of the Prophet: Despots, Democrats, and the New Politics of Islam.* Boulder, CO, and Oxford, UK: Westview Press, 2001.

Shaheed, Hasan al Banna. *Selected Writings of Hasan al Banna Shaheed.* Trans. by S.A. Qureshi. New Delhi: Millat Book Centre, 1999.

Sharif, M. M. *A History of Muslim Philosophy,* 2 vols: Low Price Publications, Delhi, 2004.

Sifaoui, Mohamed. *Inside Al-Qaeda: How I Infiltrated the World's Deadliest Terrorist Organization.* Trans. by George Miller. London: Granta Books, 2003.

Smith, Wilfred Cantwell. *Islam in Modern History.* Princeton, NJ: Princeton University Press, 1957.

Solway, David. *The Big Lie: On Terror, Antisemitism, and Identity.* Toronto: Lester Mason & Begg, 2007.

Spencer, Robert. *The Truth About Muhammad: The Founder of the World's Most Intolerant Religion.* Washington, DC: Regency Publishing, Inc., 2006.

Stillman, Norman. *The Jews of Arab Lands.* Philadelphia: The Jewish Publication Society of America, 1979.

Sultan, Wafa. *A God Who Hates.* New York: St. Martin's Press, 2009.

Swarup, Ram. *Understanding the Hadith: The Sacred Traditions of Islam.* Amherst, NY: Prometheus Books, 2002.

Takim, Liyakat N. *The Heirs of the Prophet: Charisma and Religious Authority in Shi'ite Islam.* Albany, NY: State University of New York Press, 2006.

Timmerman, Kenneth R. *Preachers of Hate: Islam and the War on America.* New York: Crown Forum, 2003.

Thubron, Colin. *Mirror to Damascus.* London: Vintage Books, 2008.

The Holy Quran. Translated and Commented by S. Abdul A'La Maududi. Lahore, Pakistan: Islamic Publications (Pvt.) Limited, 6th ed. 1991.

Usque, Samuel. *Consolation for the Tribulations of Israel* (1553). Trans. from Portuguese by Martin Cohen. Philadelphia: The Jewish Publication Society of America, 1977.

Viorst, Milton. *In the Shadow of the Prophet: The Struggle for the Soul of Islam.* Boulder, CO and Oxford, UK: Westview Press, 2001.

Warraq, Ibn. *The Quest for the Historical Muhammad.* Amherst, NY: Prometheus Books, 2000.

————. *Why I Am Not a Muslim*. Amherst, NY: Prometheus Books, 2003.

Watt, W. Montgomery. *Muhammad: Prophet and Statesman*. London / Oxford / New York: Oxford University Press, 1961.

Willis, Michael. *The Islamist Challenge in Algeria: A Political History*. New York: New York University Press, 1996.

Wolfe, Michael. *The Hadj: An American's Pilgrimage to Mecca*. New York: Grove Press, 1993.

————, ed. *One Thousand Roads to Mecca: Ten Centuries of Travellers Writing about the Muslim Pilgrimage*. New York: Grove Press, 1997.

Wood, Simon A. *Christian Criticism, Islamic Proof: Rashid Rida's Modernist Defence of Islam*. Oxford: One World Publications, 2008.

Yeor, Bat. *The Dhimmi: Jews and Christians under Islam*. London / Toronto: Associated University Presses, 1985.

Yuksel, Edip. *Peacemakers' Guide to War Mongers*. New York: Brainbrow Press, 2010 .

Zakaria, Rafiq. *Muhammad and the Quran*. Various cities: Penguin Books, 1991.

INDEX

Abbas, Mahmoud, 92, 100
Abbasid caliphate, 169, 170-72
Abu Isa al-Isfani, Ishaq ibn Yakub, 168
Adonis, 192-93
Afghanistan, 33-34, 194-95
African-American Muslims, 12-13
Agha-Soltan, Neda, 118
Ahl al-Quran, 126
Ahmad, Barakat, 155, 160, 169
Ahmadinejad, Mahmoud, xx, 94
Ahmed, Anwar, 175
Akbar, M.J., 11
Al-'adala al-Ijtima'iyya fi-l-Islam, 27
Al-Aqsa Mosque, 58, 64
al-Assad, Bashar, 21
al-Awdah, Sheikh Salman, 15-16
Al-Azhar University, 197
al-Banna, Hasan, 56, 77, 146
Al Fatah. See Fatah
al-Husayni, Hajj: and the Arab
    Revolt, 64-67; background, 51-52;
    and Britain, 53-55, 57, 64; during
    World War II, 42-50, 67-68; in
    Egypt, 43, 45, 68; influence of,
    36-37; in Palestine, 56-58, 58, 60;
    post-World War II, 68, 73; rise to
    power, 55-57, 67; on the United
    States, 51

al-Husseini, Haj Amin. See al-Husayni,
    Hajj
al-Husseini, Sheikh Muhammad,
    112-13, 118, 119
al-Kaylani, Rashid Ali, 67
al-Malik, Abd, xxii
al-Munajjid, Sheikh Muhammad, 196
al-Nashashibi, Fakir, 64
al Qaeda, 27, 33-34, 36, 189
Al-Shinqati, Sheikh Muhammad, 16
al Sistani, Ayatollah Ali, 196-97
al Tabari, Abu Ja'far, 112, 113
al-Tabarsi, Abu Ali, 113
al-Ureifi, Sheikh Mohammad, 196-97
al-Zawahiri, Ayman, 27, 36
Albanians, 39-42, 211n1(Ch.3)
Algeria, 181-82, 190
Ali, Abdullah Yusuf, 163
Ali, Akbar, 117-18
Ali, Ayaan Hirsi, 119
Ali, Shawkat, 60
Alibhai-Brown, Yasmin, xv, 118
All-India Muslim League, 56
Almoslim.net, 197
Amara, Fadela, xx, 118
America. See United States
American Islamic Forum for
    Democracy, xx

American Task Force on Palestine, 81, 100
Amin, Samir, 53
Amr, Ziad Abu, 83-84
An-Na'im, Abdullah Amed, 118
Angawi, Sami, 154-55
Anidjar, Gil, 205-6
anti-Israelism, 99-100, 115
anti-Semitism: among various Muslim
    groups, 178-79; Christianity as
    source of, 21, 23, 24, 60; and the
    creation of Israel, 81, 180, 189;
    discerning, 100; in Muslim theol-
    ogy, 103, 106-8; myths behind,
    xx-xxi, 130, 142, 146, 172-73; and
    the Quran, 106-8, 110; in the United
    States, 12-13; versus anti-Zionism
    and Israelism, 99, 115
anti-Western ideology, 28-29
anti-Zionism, 61, 99-100
apes and pigs, xxi, 26, 35-36, 109, 127
Arab Afghans, 33-34
"Arab Club" of Damascus, 60
Arab High Command, 73
Arab High Executive, 73
Arab Higher Command, 73, 74
Arab Higher Committee, 63, 66
Arab Higher Front, 73
Arab-Israel war (1956), 182
Arab League, 45, 73
Arab Legion, 46
Arab Peace Corps, 64
Arab Revolt, 62-65, 72
Arab Secret Revolutionary Committee, 71
Arabia, 154. See also Saudi Arabia
Arabian peninsula, 28, 29
Arabic language, 108
Arafat, W.N., 157-58, 164-65, 166
Arafat, Yasser, 84, 92, 191
Archangel Gabriel, 135, 139, 145, 163

armed jihad: 28-29. See also jihadi
    Islamism
Asali, Ziad, 81, 100
Atatürk, Kemal, 25, 35, 56
Auschwitz, 202-4, 205-6
Avineri, Amos, 96
Avineri, Shlomo, 190-92, 193
Ayoub, Mahmoud, 108

Babylonians, 30-31
Baghdad, 22
Bahloul, Joëlle, 181-82
Baker, Nora, 38-39
Baldwin, Shauna Singh, 39
Balfour Declaration, 53-54, 62-63, 69-70, 111
Balkans, 40-41
Balla, Destan, 39-40
Balla, Lime, 39-440
Bangladesh, 153, 194
Bani Israelis, 3
Banu Qurayza Jews, 15, 133-35, 137, 144-45, 155-56, 160-61, 172. See also Medina
Barak, Ehud, 7, 92, 96-97
Barghouti, Marwan, 84
Battle of the Confederates, 130-33, 135-42, 143
Battle of the Trench, 130-33, 135-42, 143, 153-54, 156, 163
Begin, Menachem, 91
Beilin, Yossii, 93, 94
Beirut, 25
besa, 211n1(Ch.3)
Bhutto, Benazir, 118
bin Affan, Uthman, 32
bin Khattab, Umar, 129
bin Laden, Osama, xx, 19, 27, 36, 187, 194-95
bin Mohamad, Tun Mahathir, xv-xvi
bin Mu'adh, Saad, 166

bin Sallam, Abu Ubayd, 164
bird flu, 18
the "Black Letter", 59
blame, 77, 200-201
blood libel, 23-24
B'nai B'rith, 13
Bosnians, 40-41
Bostom, Andrew, 82, 119
BrassTacks, 11
Britain: and Iran, 49; and Iraq, 48, 49;
    Islamism in, xv, 187; and Israel, 89;
    Muslim opposition to Islamism
    in, xx; Muslim reformers in,
    118; Muslims in, 112-13, 117; in
    Palestine, 37, 44, 54, 58-59, 62-64,
    69-76; post-World War II, 44, 73-74;
    in World War I, 52, 57; in World
    War II, 46, 48, 49, 67; Zionists in, 54
British Mandate of Palestine *See*
    Mandate Palestine
British Muslims for Secular Democracy,
    xv, xx
Brunton, C.D., 53
Bunglawala, Inayat, xv
Burton, Richard, 153, 154

caliphs, secularism of, 22
Camp David Accords, 91-92
Canada: Islamism in, 12, 15-16, 109, 187;
    on Israel, 88, 90-91, 179; Muslim
    hate speech in, 16; Muslim reform-
    ers in, 118; Muslims in, 103, 179-80;
    opposition to Islamism in, xx
Canadian Islamic Congress, 104
Canadian Jewish Congress, 81
Carter, Jimmy, 91, 92
Center for Religious Freedom, 109
Chabad House (Mumbai), 1-2, 5-6, 10
Christianity: the Hadith on, 125,
    127; Muslim call to defeat, 103;
    Muslim-Christian associations, 60;

the Quran on, 115-16; as source of
    Muslim anti-Semitism, 21, 23, 24, 60
citizenship, 196, 200
clerics, Muslim, xxi, 15-16, 36, 103-5,
    143-44, 183-84, 187-88, 196-97, 200
Clinton, Bill, 92
collective punishment, 163-64, 172
colonialism, European, 22, 23, 126,
    146-47, 190
Compact of Medina, 132
conspiracies, Jewish, xv, 18-20, 25-26,
    32, 34, 188-90
converts to Islam, xvii, 23, 32
Cotler, Irwin, 90
critics of Arab-world politics, 192-93
curse of Allah, xxi

Dachau, 38-39
Damascus, 21, 24, 60, 145, 154, 168, 194
Dar-ul-Islam, 29
Darfur, xvii, 194
Darwish, Sheikh Abdullah Minr,
    111-12, 114-15
Dati, Rachida, 118
Dayan, Moshe, 97-99
Deligöz, Elkin, xx
democracy: xx, 126, 192. *See also*
    secular democracy
Denmark, xix-xx, 118
Deutsch, Julius, 79
dissent among Muslims, 104
Dome on the Rock, xxii, 58, 194

East Jerusalem, 87, 93
East Turkestan Armed Formation, 43,
    50, 204
Eban, Abba, 87
education: anti-Semitic, 108; basic
    texts, 172; in Egypt, 16-17; Islamic
    universities, 60; in Jerusalem,
    60; in Jordan, 21; of the middle

classes, 126; Muslim religious, 14-15, 195; in North America, 195-96; online, 195-96; in Pakistan, 21, 108; Saudi Arabia-funded, xxi; Zionist, 86
Edwards, Michael, 215n1(Ch.6)
Egypt: al-Husayni in, 43, 45, 68; attacks on Israel, 76, 90, 184-86; attitude to Jews, 35, 178; clerics in, xxi, 36, 143-44; decline of, 187, 188; and free speech, 126; Islamic jihad in, 36; leaders, 27; medieval, 22; modernism in, 126, 188; Muslim Brotherhood in, 56; Muslim education in, 16-17, 126; Muslim reformers in, 118; Nazi sympathy in, 44, 61-62; Soviet support for, 185; works published in, 26; in World War II, 61
Eichmann, Adolf, 60
eighteenth century, 126
eighth century, 34, 168-72
Eisen, Max, 202, 203-4
Elmasry, Mohamed, 104
Elmenyawi, Salam, 103
Elmessiri, Abdel-Wahab, 206
Eltahawy, Mona, xx
England See Britain
"Esplanade of the Mosques", 93
ethnic cleansing, 172
ethnic superiority, xxi, 194-95
Europe: 22, 23, 26. See also colonialism; particular countries by name

Facebook, xiv
Faisal, Emir, 70-72
Faisal-Weizmann Agreement, 70-72
Faris, Habib, 25
Farouk, King of Egypt, 45
fascism, 36
Fatah, 31, 97, 179, 190-91, 192

Fatah, Natasha, 203
fatwas, 197-200
Fayyad, Salam, 97, 100
Fi zilal al-Qu'ran, 27, 36
Filthy Jewish Terrorists, xiv
Fiqh Council of North America, 161
Firestone, Reuven, 161
First World War, 69-71
First Zionist Congress, 111
forced conversion to Islam, 23
former Muslims, 119-20
Fort Hood, Texas, 28
450th Infantry Battalion, 42-43
fourteenth century, 155, 163
France: and al-Husayni, 43-45, 67; in Algeria, 181-82, 190; colonies, 190; Islamism in, 187; Muslim opposition to Islamism in, xx; Muslim reformers in, 118; Vichy, 41-42
Freiman, Mark, 81
Friday prayers and sermons, 15-16, 103, 194, 196-97, 207
Friends of the Simon Wiesenthal Center for Holocaust Studies, 204
Fyzee-Rahamin, Samuel, 177

Gaza, 31, 87, 91-92, 192
Geiger, Abraham, 160
General Islamic Congress, 59-60
Geneva Accord, 92-94
Geneva peace talks, 87
Germany: xx, 42-50, 60-62, 67-68. See also Hitler; Naziism
Ghamidi, Javed Ahmad, 118
Goitein, Shlomo Dov, 158-59, 162, 171-72
Golan Heights, 185, 186
Graetz, Heinrich, 170-71
Grand Mufti of Palestine See al-Husayni, Hajj
Green Line, 93

"guardianship of the clergy", 184
Guillaume, Alfred, 157, 215n1(Ch.6)

Hadith literature: Arab superiority,
195, 196; on Christians, 125, 127;
contradicting the Quran, 123, 163;
influence of, 60; on Jews, xxiii, 104,
110, 111, 122, 123-25, 127; linked to
the Quran, 106, 108; on the Medina
slaughter, 145, 159, 163, 166-67,
172; most authentic books of, 124;
Muslims' relationships with, 122;
origins of, xxi, 104, 123, 127, 129;
and Prophet Muhammad, 128;
questioning validity of, 125-29,
172-73
Hafiz, Ali, 154, 155
haggadahs, 40-41
Haiti, 12-13
Hamas: Arab Israelis' attitudes to, 179;
in Gaza, 192; ideology of, 31, 63, 70,
73; Israel's encouragement of, 83,
84; Palestinians on, 100-101; use of
the Quran, 115
Hamid, Zaid, 11
Hasan, Nidal, 28
Hashmi, Taj, 112
Hassan, Farzana, 118
Headley, David, 12
heaven, 2, 4
Hejaz, Kingdom of, 70, 72
Hezbollah, 88, 179
history: ignorance of facts, 200; as
theology, xxi
Hitler, Adolf: and al-Husayni, 43, 45-50;
and the Holocaust, 202-3; and the
Middle East, 67; Muslim support
for, 40, 42-44, 50, 60-62, 68, 73, 204;
Muslim victims of the Holocaust,
38-39, 204-6, 209; Muslims opposed
to, 38-42, 204-6, 209; Qutb on, 30;

support for Arab Revolt, 65. *See also*
Germany; Naziism
Holland *See* Netherlands
Holocaust, 38-39, 73, 202-6
Holtzberg, Gavriel, 5
Holtzberg, Moshe, 6, 10
Holtzberg, Rivka, 5
Holy Land *See* Jewish homeland
Hoodbhoy, Pervez, 183-84
Hossain, Salman, xiv
Hudson Institute, 109
Husayni, *See* al-Husayni, Hajj
Hussein, Imam, 33
Hussein, King of Jordan, 190
Husseini family, 73, 75
Husseini, Jamal, 75

Ibish, Hussein, 81
ibn Abu Talib, Ali, 200
ibn Ali, Sharif Husein, 53
Ibn Hajar, 155
Ibn Hisham, 133, 144-45
Ibn Ishaq: biography of Prophet
Muhammad, 133-34, 137-38, 140,
159, 163-66; in the Hadith, 172;
historical context of, 167-69; incon
sistencies with other histories, 172;
influence of, 170, 172; sources used,
140, 155-56, 158; translators of, 157,
215n1(Ch.6)
Ibn Kathir, 106-7, 110, 113, 145-46, 163
Ibn Khaldun Center for Development
Studies, 118
Ibn Saad, 129
ibn Safa, Abdullah, 32-33
Ibn Saud, King of Saudi Arabia, 188-89
ibn Sulayman, Muqatil, 114
Ibn Taymiyya, 194, 196
Ibn Warraq, 119
ibn Yakub, Ibrahim, 208
Ibrahim, S'ad al-Din, 118, 125-26

Imran, Babar, 2, 3, 4, 6, 8-10
India: army in World War II, 41;
    home rule movement in, 57-58;
    Islamism in, 56-57; Jews in, 1-10,
    175, 181; modernism in, 56, 126;
    Muslim-Jewish relations in, 3, 10-11;
    Muslims in, 10-11; partition of,
    176; post-World War II, 44, 176;
    Shias and Sunnis in, 33; and the UN
    Special Committee on Palestine,
    74. See also Indians; Mumbai; South
    Asia
Indians: converted to Islam, xvii;
    opposed to Hitler, 39, 42, 50; Saudi
    attitudes to, 153. See also India
Indonesia, 18, 118
"interfaith" exercises, 207
International Islamic Conference, 59-60
Internet: xiv, 195-96. See also websites
intifada, 101
Iqbal, Muhammad, 56, 60
Iran: modernism in, 56; Muslim
    reformers in, 118; Palestinian
    freedom from, 101; policies of, 70,
    73; theocracy in, 189; and the UN
    Special Committee on Palestine, 74;
    view of in the Middle East, 94; in
    World War II, 49, 50
Iraq, 48, 67, 76, 200
Islam: basics of, 35; compared with
    Judaism xxi-xxii; homeland of, 28,
    29
Islam Today, 16
Islamic Center of South Plains, 16
Islamic classical literature, 26
Islamic law, 22, 126-27. See also sharia law
Islamic Movement, 111
Islamic Society of North America, 161
Islamische Zentral-Institut, 43
Islamism: attitude to dissent, 104; in
    Britain, xv; defined, 184; dislikes

of, 1; influences on, 144-46; and
    Medina slaughter story, 131, 143-44;
    origins of, 56-57, 187; in Pakistan,
    11, 19; in Palestine, 83-84; Saudi
    funding for, 57, 183-84, 186-88;
    in the United States, 161. See also
    jihadi Islamism
IslamOnLine, 197
IslamQ&A, 195-96
Israel: accommodation of Palestine,
    97-98; American support for, 185,
    187, 189; as anti-Islamist, 86; and
    anti-Semitism, 81; Arab citizens of,
    96, 178-80; Arab non-recognition of,
    xvii, 68; Arab-world Jews' attitudes
    to, 182; borders of, 68-69, 76; cen-
    trality to Judaism, xxii; Hadith on,
    111; international reputation of, 80,
    87-90, 99-100; Muslim blame of, 77;
    1948 war, 26-27, 30, 76; occupation
    of Palestine, xvi-xvii, xx-xxi, xxiii,
    21, 78, 80, 86-87, 89-92, 96, 115, 189;
    origins of, 79-80; and Palestinian
    leadership, 83-84; peace opportuni-
    ties, 94-95, 96-97, 101-2, 189-90;
    responsibility for peace, 79, 84-85;
    right to exist, 79-80; values of, 88;
    Yom Kippur War, 184-86. See also
    anti-Israelism; Jewish homeland;
    West Bank
Israel and the Prophecies of the Holy
    Quran, 117-18
Israel Right, 83
Israeli flag, 20

Jacobovici, Simcha, 101, 175
Jaha, Lamija, 41
Jamaat-e-Islami, 56-57, 145-46
Jasser, Zuhdi, 118
Jerusalem, 26, 58, 69, 93, 111. See also
    East Jerusalem

Jewish Agency, 75
Jewish conspiracies. *See* conspiracies
Jewish homeland: and anti-Semitism,
    180, 189; Arab fears regarding,
    53; Arab non-recognition of, xvii;
    Balfour Declaration on, 53, 63,
    69; boundaries of, 63; British on,
    59; Germany on in World War
    II, 47-48; origin of, 71, 79-80, 111;
    Palestinian acceptance of, 100-101;
    the Quran on, 110, 111-13; site of,
    112-14; support for, 73, 79-80, 112;
    United States on, 73. *See also* Israel
Jewish Internet Defense Force, 82
Jews: as apes and pigs, xxi, 26, 35-36,
    109, 127; call to defeat, 103; carica-
    tures of, 20-21; central Asian, 175;
    early uprisings, 168-69; as ethno-
    religious group, 80; histories of,
    160, 161-62, 170-71; killing, 3, 104;
    Muslim attitudes to, 21, 29, 117-18,
    147, 177-80, 188-89, 197-200, 206-9;
    persecution of, 156-57, 175, 206;
    Persian, 168; prophecies of Muslim
    victory over, 199-200; the Quran on,
    xxiv, 22, 30, 104, 108, 110, 115-16,
    120, 122, 123, 197-200; relationship
    with Muslims, 22, 158-60, 170-72,
    181-82, 189, 206-9. *See also* Banu
    Qurayza Jews; conspiracies
"The Jew's Daughter", 180
jihadi Islamism: centres of, 174, 183,
    187; defined, 28-29; and educa-
    tion, 108-9; influences on, 36, 77,
    183, 194; internationalization of,
    77; leaders of, 145-46, 189; Muslim
    opposition to, xix-xx; reward for,
    188; as true Islam, 188; and war
    defeats, 188; in the West, 201;
    widespread nature of, 103; works
    supporting, 28-29. *See also* Islamism

Jinnah, Mohammed Ali, 56, 176-77
Jordan, 21, 76, 178, 190. *See also*
    Transjordan
"Judaism and Islam", 160
Judaism and Islam compared, xxi-xxii
Judeophobia *See* anti-Semitism
jurists, 164

Ka'b, 137-38, 141
kafir *See* kuffar
Karachi, 18-20, 181
Kasab, 12
kataba, 113-14
Katzir, Ephraim, 90
Khaled, Amr, 143-44
Khaled, Leila, 78
Khalidi, Hazim, 41
Khalidi, Rashid, 66, 81, 100
Khalifa, Rashad, 126-27
Khan, Ismail, 2, 4
Khan, Noor Inayat, 38-39, 209
Khan, Sultan Mohamed Aga, 56
Khan, Veli Kayum, 42-43
Khaybar, 165-66
Khedar, Naser, xix-xx, 118
Khilafat Movement, 60
Khomeini, 184
killing: collective punishment, 163-64,
    172; of Jews, 3, 104; of non-Jews
    and children, 85-86
The King's Torah, 85-86
Koran *See* Quran
Korkut, Dervis, 40-41
Korkut, Servet, 41
Kosovo, 41
kuffar, 15-16
Kurdish people, xvii, xx
Kurdistan, 194

League of Nations, 59, 70
Lebanon, 64, 76, 178, 188

Lewis, Bernard, 23, 99-100
Libya, 61, 187
Liebowitz, Yeshayahu, 101
The Lost Tribes, 175
Lubaba, Abu, 139-40

"Maalim fil-Tareeq", 28-29
MacDonald, Ramsay, 58-59
madrassahs, xxi, 15, 60, 108
Maimonides, xii, 22, 23, 86
Majdanek, 204-5
Malaysia, xv
man-made texts. See Hadith literature
Mandate Palestine, 63, 70, 72, 75, 76
Manji, Irshad, 79
"Ma'rakatuna ma'a al-Yahud", 29, 34, 68
Masada, 157-58
Mattson, Ingrid, 161
Maududi, Syed, 56-57, 145-46, 163
"The Meaning of the Quran", 146
Mecca, xvii, 53, 130, 194
medieval Islamdom: attitude to Jews,
    22-23; biography of Prophet
    Muhammad, 133; break from, 56;
    development of, 154; documents
    from, 162; Hadith commentaries,
    125, 129; Muslims as world power,
    146; myths of, 142, 145-46, 155,
    172; Quran commentaries, 112-15,
    145-46; return to, 64-65, 187, 189,
    193, 195, 200
Medina: abandonment of, 154-55;
    about, 148-51; Arabs of, 194; battle
    details, 132-41, 144, 145, 166-67;
    battle site, 151-52, 154-55, 167;
    debate at, 34; effects of story of,
    xxiii, 30, 130, 143-44, 147; Hadith
    on, 166-67, 172; Ibn Ishaq on,
    166-67; interpretation of story of,
    172-73; "Islamic State" in, 32; Jewish
    records regarding, 158, 159-62, 163;

Jews as responsible for slaughter,
    146; Meccan Arabs overtaking, 194;
    mosques at, 194; Muhammad at,
    132-33, 151, 169-70; Muslims in,
    149; occupation of by the Saudi
    royal family, xvii; origins of slaugh-
    ter story, 155-56, 157-58, 167-69;
    other possible outcomes, 169-70;
    story of as myth, 147, 164-65,
    172-73; works on, 169-70
Mercaz Harav Yeshiva, 86
Mernissi, Fatema, 118
Meshaal, Khaled, 31
Mian, Muhammad, 186
Middle East. See particular countries by
    name
Midrashes, xxii
Milestones, 28-29
miracles, 135
modernism, 56-57, 118-19, 192-93, 201
Mohammad V, King of Morocco, 41-42
Mohammed, Khaleel, 103-5, 108,
    111-12, 113-14, 118
Mohn, Paul, 75
Montreal, 103
Morocco, 41-42, 118
mosques, 194. See also Friday prayers
    and sermons
Mossad, 11, 83
the mufti. See al-Husayni, Hajj
Mufti in Jerusalem, 26
Muhammad, Prophet See Prophet
    Muhammad
mullahs, 183-84
Mumbai, xix, 1-10
Muslim Brotherhood, 37, 44, 45, 56, 65,
    68, 77, 84
Muslim Canadian Congress, xx
Muslim Council of Montreal, 103
Muslim intelligentsia (20th century), 34
Muslim-versus-Muslim violence, 33,

64-66, 190, 192, 196-97

Na'at poetry, 150-51
Nakba, 76
Nariman House, 4-5, 8, 10
Nasir, 2, 3, 4, 6, 9
Nasser, Gamal Abdel, 27, 94
nationalism, Arab, 61
Nawroz, 33
Naziism, 50-51, 60-62. *See also*
    Germany; Hitler
Netanyahu, Benjamin, 96
Netherlands, xx
new Arab society, 192-93
New Democratic Party, 88
New York, 12-13, 14-15
Newburgh, New York, 12-13
9/11, 19
1948 war, 26-27, 30, 76
1920s, 56
1956 Arab-Israel war, 182
1973, 183-86, 187, 188
nineteenth century, 22, 23
ninth century, 170-72
Nistarot Rabbi Shimon Bar Yohai, xxii
North American Muslims, 195. *See also*
    Canada; United States

oil wealth, 183, 186-87, 188
Omar, Mullah, 187
OPEC, 186
Operation Tiger B, 42-43
Oriental Service, 50
Orpaz, Yoheved, 6, 9-10
Oslo Accords, 79, 84
Ostrovsky, Victor, 83
Ottoman caliphate, 23-24, 51-54, 59-61,
    69-71, 111
"Our Fight Against the Jews". *See*
    "Ma'rakatuna ma'a al-Yahud"
Oz, Amos, 96

Özdemir, Cem, xx

Pahlavi, Reza Shah, 56
Pakistan: anti-Semitism in, xviii, 130;
    and Bangladesh, 194; creation of,
    75, 176; education in, 21, 108; Islam
    in, xvii; Islamists in, 11, 19, 57, 128;
    on Israel, 185, 186; Jewish conspira-
    cies in, 18-20; on Jews, 33, 174-77,
    180-81, 182-83; Jews in, 175-76,
    177; madrassahs, 15; modernism
    in, 128; and Mumbai attack, 1, 6,
    11; Muslim reformers in, 118, 127;
    Muslim-versus-Muslim violence in,
    33; Pakistanis in North America,
    12; pseudo Anti-Americanism in,
    19; and Saudi Arabia, 153, 188; Shia
    Muslims in, 194. *See also* South Asia
Pakistani intelligence service, 11
Palestine: al-Husayni in, 56-58, 63; "all
    or nothing" policy, 70, 73, 91-92;
    Arab Revolt in, 62-67; Arabs in,
    69-70, 72; British, 37, 44, 54, 58-59,
    62-64, 69-76; capital for, 87, 93;
    failures in, 190-92; and Hitler, 46,
    50; intifada, 101; intra-Palestinian
    violence, 64-66, 192; Islamists in,
    83-84; Israeli accommodation of,
    97-98; leadership of, 68-69, 83-84,
    87, 91-92, 96, 99, 191-92; migration
    to post-World War II, 73; migra-
    tion to pre-World War II, 26, 48,
    57, 59, 66-67, 71; Muslim view of,
    68; nationalism, 191-92; occupation
    of, xvi-xvii, xx-xxi, xxiii, 21, 78, 80,
    86-87, 89-92, 96, 115, 189; Ottoman,
    51, 53, 59; partition of, 63, 65, 72-76;
    post-World War I, 53, 58-65, 69-72;
    post-World War II, 44, 52-53; the
    Quran on, 110; refugees, 76, 87, 93,
    99, 190-91; shortcomings of, 190-92;

sovereign rights, 80; state creation, 90-91, 93, 96, 101-2, 189; tribalism in, 55, 73; United Nations committee on, 74; United States on, 73. *See also* Palestinians

Palestine Liberation Organization, 83-84, 92

Palestine Question, 58-59

Palestine Regiment, 41

Palestinian Authority, 100, 192

Palestinians, 31, 41, 60, 96. *See also* Palestine

Paris Peace Conference, 71

Pashtuns, 175, 195, 212n1

Passfield, Lord, 58-59

peace, 79, 84-85, 92, 94-97, 189-90, 197, 207-9

Peace Now, 96

Pearl, Daniel, 146, 175

Peel Commission, 62-63, 65, 72-73, 76

Peel, Earl, 62-63, 72

Persians, 153, 168, 171

Pervez, Ghulam Ahmed, 127-28

Peshawar, 174-77, 182-83

petrodollars *See* oil wealth

Pew Research Center, 178, 180

PLFP, *See* Popular Front for the Liberation of Palestine, 31, 79, 190-191

poetry, 56, 97, 150-51, 183, 192-93

Poland, 204-5, 208

politicization of Islam, 207

Popular Front for the Liberation of Palestine, 31, 79, 190-91

Porath, Yehoshua, 65

post-modern civic society, 192-93

prayers, 15-16, 103, 194, 196-97, 207

Prophet Muhammad: battles, 130, 146, 166; biographies of, 133, 159, 163, 167-70; centrality to Islam, xxii; character of, 142-43; as conqueror, 141-43; debate at Medina, 34; defending, 82; effects of battle at Medina, xxiii, 170, 172-73; and the Hadith, 128, 129; and Jews, xxi, 124-25, 160; in Mecca, 166; miracles, 135; Muslims' relationships with, 151; power struggle after death of, 32; rape by, 81; as slaughterer of Jews, 146, 161, 172; songs and poems praising, 150-51; statements of in the Hadith, 104; on superiority of Arabs, 196; works on, 155

Prosor, Ron, 89

The Protocols of the Elders of Zion, 18, 20, 29, 34, 60

Punjab, xvii-xviii

Quran: and anti-Semitism, 106-8; authorities on, 107; and the Battle of the Trench, 153-54, 156, 163; on Christians, 115-16; on collective punishment, 163-64; commentaries on, 145, 163; current use of, 105-8, 117-18; divinity of, 129; explaining to children, 105, 106, 108; extremist Jews' attitude to, 206-7; and the Hadith, 106, 108; Hamas's use of, 115; "Jew" in, 199; on a Jewish homeland, 110, 111-14; on Jews, xxiv, 22, 30, 104, 108, 110, 115-16, 120, 122, 123, 197-200; medieval commentaries and myths, 112-15, 145-46; and the Medina battle, 131, 153-54, 163; and modernity, 118-19; Muslims' relationships with, 122; origins of, 129; racist doctrine contradicting, 194; translations of, 109-10, 127, 163; on women, 27; works on, 27, 106-7, 117-18, 145-46

Qu'ran. *See* Quran

Qutb, Sayyid: on Hitler, 68; influence of,

33-36, 146, 207; influences on, 36; on Jews, 29-30, 31-33, 34; rise of, 77; works of, 27-33, 36, 68
Qutub, Syed *See* Qutb, Sayyid

Rabbo, Yasser Abed, 92-93, 94
Rabin, Yitzhak, 84
Rabinovitch, Norma, 6, 7, 9-10
race and racism, xxii, 153, 194-95, 196
radical Islam. *See* Islamism
Rageah, Said, 15-16
Rahman, Fazlur, 123
Ramadan, Tariq, xxiii, 77, 144
Rana, Tahawwur Hussain, 12
Rasheed, Sheikh Amjad, 195
Raza, Raheel, 118
Red Army, 42
reformers, Muslim, 118-19, 125-28
refugees, 76, 87, 93, 99, 190-91
Resolution 181, 75-76
Reut Institute, 88-89
Rida, Rashid, 59-60
Russian Jews, 54

Sabuni, Nyamko, xx
Sadat, Anwar, 44, 91
Samuel, Herbert, 54-55, 57
Saqr, Mufti Atiyyah, 197-200
"Sarajevo Haggadah", 40-41
Saudi Arabia: and blood libel, 23; clerics educated in, 15-16, 196; education, xxi, 195-96; and the General Islamic Congress 1931, 60; intra-Muslim conflicts, 196-97; and Islamism, 57, 108-9, 183-84, 187-88; oil wealth, 183, 186-87; Palestinian freedom from, 101; Quran translation, 109-10; repressive ideologies, 187, 189; rise of, 184, 188; works published in, 29
Saudi royal family, xvii

Second World War *See* World War II
secular democracy, xv, xx, 174-75
secularism, 35, 56
Semitic family, 71
Serenus, 168-69
sermons, 15-16, 103, 194, 196-97, 207
Setif, 181-82
seventh century, 200
Shahzad, Sohail, 109
Shamir, Prime Minister, 84
sharia law, 29, 31, 57, 64, 163, 201. *See also* Islamic law
Sharon, Moshe, xxii
Shea, Nina, 109
Shia Muslims, 32, 33, 56, 194, 196-97
Shia-Sunni relations, 32, 33, 196-97
Shoaib, 2-3
Shuman, Hazem, 35-36
Siddiqi, Muzammil, 161
Sinai, 87, 99, 112, 185, 186
the *Sira*. *See Sirat Rasul Allah*
Sirat Rasul Allah, 133, 137-38, 140, 155-56
Six Day War, 76, 87, 90, 97
social networking, xiv
Solanki, Amar Singh, 2-3
songs and poems, 150-51
South Asia, 146. *See also* India; Pakistan
South Lebanon, 87
Soviet Union, 42, 54, 67
Spain, 22, 23
Spencer, Robert, 119
SS, 43, 50
Stillman, Norman, 162, 215n1(Ch.6)
Suez Canal, 184, 186
Sufi prayers, 33
Sultan, Wafa, 81, 83
Sunni: caliphs, 170; Islamists, 33-34
Sunni-Shia relations, 32, 33, 196-97
SunniPath: The Online Islamic Academy, 195

superiority, Arab, 194-96
Supreme Muslim Council, 55-56, 57, 65
Sura al-Fatiha, 105-6, 108, 110
swastikas, 20
Sweden, xx
Switzerland, 77, 111
Sykes-Picot Agreement, 70
synagogues, 12-13
Syria, 54, 61, 70, 71, 168-69, 184, 185, 192

Tabari, 155
Tafheem al Quran, 146
*Tafsir al-quran al-Azim See Tafsir Ibn
    Kathir*
Tafsir Ibn Kathir, 106, 145
Taj Hotel, 7
Taliban, 33-34
Talmud, 23, 25
The Talmudic Human Sacrifices, 25
televangelists, 143
Temple Mount, 93
tenth century, 170-72, 208
terrorism, 189, 194-95
textbooks, 21
theocracy, 189
13th Waffen SS Mountain Division, 50
Tirailleurs Senegalese, 42
Torah, xxi-xxii
Torat Hamelech, 85-86
Toronto, 15-16
Toukan, Fadwa, 97
Transjordan, 54, 63, 70
tribalism, 55, 73, 194-95
Turkey: attitude to Jews in, 22; and the
    General Islamic Congress 1931,
    60; and Hitler, 50; modernism in,
    56, 126; Muslim reformers in, 127;
    Ottoman, 24, 52; and Palestine, 71;
    post-World War I, 70; and Saudi
    Arabia, 188; status of Muslims in,
    24-25; in World War II, 67

Turkish-origin people, xx
twelfth century, 22
twentieth century, 34, 126, 163, 181,
    187-89
twenty-first century, 189
Twin Towers, 19

ul Islam, Sheik, 194
ulema, 183
Umayyad caliphate, 33, 134, 154, 168,
    169, 170
ummah, xvi, 31, 189
UN Security Resolution 242, 87
United Kingdom. *See* Britain
United Nations, 26, 27, 73-76, 79
United Nations Special Committee on
    Palestine, 74-75, 76
United States: African-American
    Muslims, 12-13; and al-Husayni, 44,
    51; anti-Semitism in, 12-13; Arab
    community in, 81; Islamists in, 109,
    161, 187; and Israel, 185, 187, 189;
    Jewish control of, 26; Jewish lobby
    in, xvi, xvii, xix; Jews in, xviii-xix;
    jihadists in, 12-14, 109; Muslim
    clerics in, 16, 103-5; Muslim opposi-
    tion to Islamism in, xx; Muslim
    reformers in, 118; Pakistani attitudes
    to, 19; and Palestine, 73, 81, 91-92
universities, 60, 197
Usque, Samuel, 160-61
U.S.S.R., 26, 54, 185

Vichy government, 41-42
victim mentality, xvi-xvii, 201
von Leers, Johann, 61-62

Wadud, Amina, 118
Wahhabism, 183, 188, 194, 197
Wahid, Abdurrahman, 118
Warsi, Sayeeda, 118

Washington, D.C., 13
Watt, Montgomery, 169-70
Webb, Sidney, 58-59
websites, xiv, xv, 15, 16, 195-97
Weizmann, Chaim, 59, 70-72
Wellesley, William Robert, 62-63
Wermacht, 42-43, 204
the West: anti-Western ideology, 28-29; Islamic education in, 195; jihad promoted in, 103; minority religious rights in, 15; Muslim criticism of, 143-44; Muslim relationships with, 29, 57, 189, 201; in the twenty-first century, 189, 201
West Bank: as capital of future Palestinian state, 87; Israeli occupation of, xvii, 21, 88, 96, 97; Israeli withdrawal from, 91-92; Muslims in, 31
Wilcox, Philip, 84
women, 27-28, 35
World Trade Center (1993), 14
World War I, 69-71
World War II, 73. *See also* Hitler; *particular countries by name*
World Zionist Organization, 59

Yaaqub, Muhammad Hussein, xxi
Yad Vashem, 39, 41
"Yahoodis", 18
"Yahudi", 3

Yahudi ki Larki, 180
Yaqub, Muhammad Hussein, 36
Yassin, Sheik, 31, 84
Yemen, 23
Yom Kippur War, 89-90, 183-86, 188
Yosef, Ovadia, 207
Yugoslavia, 40, 44, 45, 74
Yuksel, Edip, 127
Yusuf, Ramzi, 14

Zionism: and al-Husayni, 45, 73; Algerian, 182; anti-Zionism, 61, 99-100; and Arabs, 71; and attacks in Mumbai, 11-12; in Britain, 54; and creation of Israel, 68, 75; and criticism of moderate Palestinians, 101; early, 111; Hindu, 12; and Jewish immigration to Palestine, 59, 73; Orthodox, 86; and the UN Special Committee on Palestine, 74, 75; in the United States, 101. *See also* anti-Zionism
Zog, King of Albania, 41-42
Zonarius, 168-69